Revealing Minds

Revealing Minds

Assessing to Understand and Support Struggling Learners

Craig Pohlman

JOSSEY-BASS
A Wiley Imprint
www.josseybass.com

Published by Jossey-Bass
A Wiley Imprint
989 Market Street, San Francisco, CA 94103-1741   www.josseybass.com

Jossey-Bass books and products are available through most bookstores. To contact Jossey-Bass directly call our Customer Care Department within the U.S. at 800-956-7739, outside the U.S. at 317-572-3986, or fax 317-572-4002.

Jossey-Bass also publishes its books in a variety of electronic formats. Some content that appears in print may not be available in electronic books.

Library of Congress Cataloging-in-Publication Data

Pohlman, Craig.
    Revealing minds: assessing to understand and support struggling learners / Craig Pohlman; foreword by Mel Levine.
        p. cm.
    Includes bibliographical references and index.
    ISBN 978-0-7879-8790-9 (pbk.)
1. Learning, Psychology of. 2. Brain. I. Title.
    LB1060.P64 2007
    370.15'23–dc22

                                                                          2007017877

Printed in the United States of America
FIRST EDITION
PB Printing   10 9 8 7 6 5 4 3 2 1

For my sons, Josh and Gabe—watching you learn and grow is a joy and an inspiration.

Contents

Foreword:
Reassessing Assessing

"Everywhere I go, all day long, everyone's evaluating me. My mom and dad check me out in the morning to make sure my breath smells good and I'm wearing clean boxer shorts. My teachers give me quizzes all the time and can't stop threatening us about the horrible things that will happen to us if we fail end of grade testing. My soccer coach and my piano teacher are always evaluating whether I'm practicing and trying hard enough. The kids in my class and other dudes test me to decide if I'm cool or some kind of dork, and the girls are trying to evaluate whether or not I'm 'cute.' And when I get home, my parents spy on me to see if I'm messing up on my math homework. Next Monday I'm going for testing in school because I'm failing social studies, and I can't spell for beans, and my handwriting stinks, so they think I must have some kind of total brain damage. I wonder when they'll cool it and everyone will decide that Jeffrey is just plain Jeffrey, a very nice kid."

—*Jeffrey H., Age 13*

WE FEEL COMPELLED TO pass judgment on minds—especially young ones. Clinicians are expected to functionally dissect the minds of some children to identify obstructed pathways that underlie their academic and/or behavioral shortfalls. Educators are asked to observe and evaluate academic skills in various ways. There exists a population of kids who seem so bright yet have a terrible time succeeding in school. They are the innocent victims of their own "wiring." Many benefits can accrue from assessing the minds of such success-deprived students. Presumably, we can most effectively help a struggling child if we can fathom his or her plight with accuracy.

But assessment brings with it some serious risks. Ironically, whenever we evaluate a child, it is he, not we, who must assume those risks and do so without any informed consent. What then are the risks? First of all, our tests are far from infallible and so are we professionals. So what if we are just plain wrong in our conclusions? And what if an incorrect evaluation leads to improper management at home and in school? What if we have dangerously oversimplified and over-pigeon-holed a young mind? What if our assessment has a negative effect upon a child's self-image or a parent's respect for a son or daughter? What if the evaluation generates a label which causes a child to grow up feeling deviant, pathological, or hopelessly inferior to his peers and siblings? What if testing leads directly to medication that may be the wrong solution, perhaps a band-aid masking a child's significant issues? What if the testing is one-sided, reflecting the diagnostic biases, interests, or narrowly focused training of the examiner rather than the multifactorial problems and broad needs of the child? What if there is a conflict of interest and the testing harbors a hidden agenda, such as not having to offer services to too many students or else to recruit clients into some form of therapy conveniently provided by the tester? These "what if's. . . ?" are not hypothetical. They represent negative consequences of evaluation that take place every day. In part, we can prevent these harmful side effects by protecting children's rights when they undergo assessment. Here are some of those rights, which, if acknowledged, might provide some indemnity from testing damage.

A Bill of Rights for the To-Be-Assessed

1. *The right to be assessed through more than one source of information—* Ideally a child's history, samples of his work, his own interpretation of his problems and his parents' and teachers' views as well as diverse test scores should be integrated. Any one source of information is suspect unless and until it is corroborated by other sources of information.

2. *The right to have your strengths diagnosed and highlighted*—The centerpiece of any assessment ought to emphasize the "diagnosis" of strengths and content affinities and suggestions for their future cultivation.

3. *The right to be understood without being labeled*—Labels for kids are intrinsically pessimistic, and they oversimplify a child's attributes and life situation. Children should be described and not categorized.

4. *The right to be tested by someone who will not harbor disciplinary or commercial conflicts of interest and biases*—Children should be assessed by professionals who have no vested interest in the outcome and will not refer cases to themselves without offering parents viable alternatives.

5. *The right to be evaluated thoroughly rather than merely assessed to determine eligibility for services*—Parents sometimes mistakenly believe that testing for eligibility is the same as a complete evaluation. The examinations used may fail to pinpoint specific breakdown points in learning while overlooking discrete strengths.

6. *The right to a second opinion and to reevaluation*—No assessment is airtight. When parents or teachers question a result or when treatment isn't working, an outside opinion is necessary.

7. *The right to be assessed beyond what tests purport to test for*—Not everything is on a test. Many critical issues, such as organizational skill, expressive language fluency, graphomotor function, various parameters of attention, and critical and creative thinking cannot be found on commonly used psychometric tests. Yet these can be critical determinants of academic success or failure.

8. *The right to be provided with highly specific management suggestions stemming from an assessment*—An evaluation should lead to practical suggestions that can be implemented collaboratively by teachers, parents, and the child himself.

9. *The right to be evaluated by a professional with a strong knowledge of learning and education*—Knowing how to give tests is insufficient. An evaluator should have the background knowledge to know the kinds of breakdowns that can occur in math learning in 5th grade and the kinds of dysfunctions that can impede written output in middle

school. A child seeing such an individual should be receiving a consultation from a knowledgeable person rather than just "testing."

10. *The right to self-knowledge and an optimistic view of possibilities for the future*—An assessment should be a form of therapy. An assessed student should sense that he understands himself more clearly than ever before. Such a child should come from an assessment feeling good about himself, feeling accountable and motivated.

These rights can only be realized if we are willing and able to rethink the missions and methods of assessment, so that we can become increasingly helpful, while building in safeguards against evaluation damage. There is a dire need for such a reassessment of assessment.

Revealing Minds makes a compelling case for a phenomenological, non-labeling approach that is highly specific in its findings and solidly strength-based. It is a work that has the potential to orient and formulate assessment as a healing process. The book provides both a methodology and a conceptual framework for understanding and assisting a struggling child or adolescent.

Dr. Craig Pohlman, the author of *Revealing Minds,* is a gifted psychologist with whom I have worked for many years. He has collaborated and contributed richly as we have sought to establish assessment methods that are highly specific, accurate, helpful, and nonstigmatizing. They are based on the premise that the best prescription derives from the best description. Dr. Pohlman has devised and integrated assessment techniques that take us beyond the compulsion to label and an overreliance on test scores. He has played a leading role in developing software for clinical work and computerized guidelines for teachers, so that they can manage specific differences in learning. He has rendered it practical to offer training and provide the tools needed to implement more targeted and comprehensive evaluations of differences in learning across a range of clinical settings. In numerous ways, his work has supported young people's basic right to a fair and thorough assessment.

Dr. Mel Levine, February 2007

Preface

EDUCATION CAN and should extend beyond what takes place in a classroom. Case in point—one of the most important learning experiences I had in graduate school took place rolling along 301 North in Virginia. It was fall 1992, the first semester of my school psychology doctoral studies at the University of North Carolina at Chapel Hill (UNC-CH). I got a ride to New York City to visit my brother with Bill, a second-year student in my program. During the drive we got to sharing impressions of professors and courses and the topic eventually turned to psycho-educational testing. I commented that assessment was a real challenge because of all the administration and scoring procedures inherent in standardized intelligence and achievement batteries. Bill then posed an astonishingly simple question, one I had never considered: "What is assessment?" Understanding the point behind his question, I resisted my initial urge to rattle off all the tests I had been trained to administer. After a moment, he answered his own question in the negative, "Assessment is not the same as testing. Testing is just one part of assessment."

So maybe my professors had made that point during a lecture or I had come across it in a textbook. But until I heard it from a peer it never clicked with me, and I have never forgotten it. The notion that assessment *includes* testing complemented one of the reasons I left teaching for school psychology. I wanted to be able to diagnose learning problems—not just in terms of assigning kids to categories or labels, but to really understand why a student is struggling. Why is writing such a challenge for this eighth grader? What makes math so complicated for this fifth grader? I wanted this diagnostic ability, obviously, so that I could help struggling learners. It made perfect sense that understanding the root causes of an academic problem would guide the solutions.

Earlier that year I was still teaching in New York City and had already committed to the school psychology program at UNC-CH. Along with fellow faculty I attended a day-long lecture on memory by Dr. Mel Levine. The presentation fascinated me because it started to provide a framework for understanding what I observed in my students; it gave me initial tools for diagnosing, for understanding why a student might be struggling. I was thrilled to discover that, coincidentally, Dr. Levine was a professor of pediatrics at UNC-CH. I remember thinking that perhaps I would get the chance to learn more from him some day, or maybe even work with him. I got that chance during my third year of graduate school in an externship at the Center for Development and Learning, where Dr. Levine was the director. I got to see Dr. Levine in action assessing students with learning problems—how he avoided labels in favor of descriptive profiles, delved into specific breakdown points, relentlessly searched for assets, and demystified students by explaining their profiles and delivering messages of optimism. That year solidified my goal of being a psychologist who specializes in learning problems and who uses a descriptive, asset-driven approach. I also wanted to promote this approach with other professionals (e.g., pediatricians, educators, speech-language pathologists) and so reach as many students as possible.

Following the completion of my dissertation and internship, I earned a fellowship at the Center for Development and Learning and, later, at the All Kinds of Minds Institute, which Dr. Levine co-founded. For the past nine years I have worked at All Kinds of Minds with Dr. Levine and many other talented, devoted individuals. Building on the philosophical core of Dr. Levine's approach we have developed service-delivery models for clinicians and educators, professional development programs, and tools to help understand and support struggling learners. This book is a detailed description of a critical aspect of this approach—how to assess so you really understand a student's learning issues.

And because I have not forgotten what I learned over a decade ago on 301 North, the approach is not bound by tests.

Acknowledgments

THIS BOOK WOULD NOT HAVE BEEN possible without Dr. Mel Levine. I could not have asked for a better mentor—one who stimulated my thinking and inspired my work. I am proud to follow his trailblazing lead. I melded the superb training Dr. Steve Hooper provided me in his neuropsychology clinic with Dr. Levine's model to create the initial version of this assessment approach. I thank Dr. Paul Yellin for his leadership in the Student Success Program, and for illuminating the connections between this assessment approach and resiliency theory. Dr. Beth Briere has always been in my corner in our years of working together and I value her immensely as a friend and colleague.

The All Kinds of Minds Institute is in great hands with Mary-Dean Barringer, who has been tremendously supportive of this book; I also thank her for sharing with me the etymology of the word *assessment.* I have been fortunate to work with many talented, dedicated professionals at All Kinds of Minds. I am proud to have served thousands of families with my fellow clinicians, from whom I have also learned a great deal. Thank you to all the administrative staff who have worked so hard on behalf of families. I also thank my colleagues in information technology, especially Jeff Low, Lauren Mann, and Nancy Lockhart, with whom I have collaborated in creating digital tools to support clinical work. My work over the last eight years would not have been possible without the generous support and vision of the All Kinds of Minds Board of Trustees.

Thanks also to Margie McAneny and her colleagues at Jossey-Bass for their work in bringing this book to publication. Kathi Howard and Doug Bouman provided valuable feedback on this manuscript; as fellow "Profile Advisors" they also have been kindred spirits in this assessment approach and

I have learned much from them over the years. Carole Ellis often served as a one-person focus group on issues related to this book, and I thank her for her frequent reality checks. Patti Donnelly provided the digital photography in this book, and her daughters made terrific handwriting models!

My parents instilled in me the work ethic required to write this book. My mother, Peggy Conwell, has been a role model for the dogged pursuit of a completed project. My father, Dolphy Pohlman, has shown me the beauty of building something piece by piece over time (this book has been my line shack).

I have had the privilege of meeting hundreds of students and families over the years. They have been my teachers—how young minds learn, develop, and persevere.

Finally, I am profoundly grateful to have Dr. Jen Neitzel as my wife. She has been my sounding board, part-time research assistant, and best friend. Thank you, Jen, for putting up with the hundreds of hours of "free time" I devoted to this book.

The Author

CRAIG POHLMAN is a clinician and program developer at the nonprofit institute All Kinds of Minds, where he has worked since 1998. A licensed psychologist and nationally certified school psychologist, He began his career teaching science to elementary and middle school students in New York City. He later went on to earn his doctorate in school psychology at the University of North Carolina at Chapel Hill (UNC-CH), where he first worked with Dr. Mel Levine at The Clinical Center for the Study of Development and Learning, University of North Carolina School of Medicine (CDL). After completing an internship in the Dallas Public Schools, where he worked as a school psychologist in one of the largest and most diverse districts in the country, he returned to the CDL for a postdoctoral fellowship. He has since earned appointments at UNC-CH as a clinical assistant professor for the school psychology program and as a clinical scientist at the CDL.

Dr. Pohlman has conducted or supervised thousands of assessments of struggling learners, and has trained thousands of professionals on assessment techniques. He developed the Profile Advisor program for school-based clinicians and other professionals, which melded the philosophy of All Kinds of Minds with clinical practice. He has designed numerous techniques and tools to help educators and clinicians integrate a neurodevelopmental assessment approach into their practices.

About *Revealing Minds*

IN ORDER TO HELP struggling learners you have to understand *why* they are struggling. *Revealing Minds* is a road map for uncovering the factors causing learning problems. Is a language problem behind a student's struggles with writing? Is weak memory undermining math work? Could some aspect of attention be derailing reading comprehension? Without knowing why students struggle, deciding what strategies might help them can be a guessing game.

Revealing Minds describes a positive assessment approach based on the philosophy and framework of the All Kinds of Minds institute and the pioneering work of pediatrician Mel Levine. Written for clinicians and educators who want to delve deep into the potential causes of learning problems, *Revealing Minds* is a practical, how-to guide to assessment. Readers will learn about essential thought processes such as how to connect academic skills to brain-based functions, how to interpret contrasts in a student's performance, and how to identify recurring themes. Much more than a testing manual, *Revealing Minds* contains numerous diagrams to help interpret information gleaned from tests and other information sources. It also contains several case studies to illustrate how students' profiles can be revealed through this approach.

About All Kinds of Minds

ALL KINDS OF MINDS is a nonprofit institute for the understanding of differences in learning. Its mission is to help struggling learners measurably improve their success by providing programs that integrate educational, scientific, and clinical expertise. Based on the work of co-founder and renowned pediatrician Mel Levine, the philosophy of All Kinds of Minds takes a positive view of learning diversity, providing parents, professionals, and students with thought processes and tools for better understanding of brain functioning and academic performance—an understanding that can then lead to increased success in school and life.

Revealing Minds

1

Assessing to Understand

WHAT COLOR IS THE BOTTOM LIGHT of a traffic light? Most of us have been stumped at some point by this incredibly obvious question. We see traffic lights every day, and have for most of our lives, but is that bottom light red or green (or yellow)? Sometimes what seems obvious is not. Sometimes we need to pause and reflect on seemingly common knowledge that we have taken for granted.

Clinicians and educators come across the term *assessment* constantly in the day's work. Assessment is a type of service that we provide, along with therapy and counseling, instruction and remediation, or consultation. But what is assessment? What does it mean to assess?

The dictionary definition of *assessment* is to appraise or evaluate. The etymology of the word stems originally from the Latin *assidere*, "to sit beside." That's a revealing image: to sit *beside* someone as you learn about that person. Regarding work with children and adolescents, the process of assessment should be about sitting beside a student (literally and figuratively) to develop a deeper understanding of the student.

But how often does that actually happen in practice? Let's narrow the parameters to work with children and adolescents who have learning problems (say, difficulty in reading, weak attention, or language delays). How often is an assessment really about *understanding* how a student learns? The answer is—*not often enough*. For various reasons, assessment tends to be an exercise in eligibility and qualification for services. Or about obtaining a diagnosis for insurance reimbursement. Or about exposing what's wrong with a student.

In this book, I describe a different way of thinking about—and conducting—assessments of kids with learning problems. The mind-set and approach is based on a single, simple premise: *The point of assessment is to develop a deeper understanding of the student*.

The Case for Phenomenology

Inherent in this argument that assessment should be about understanding the student is the notion that assessment should be about *more* than determining a label or assigning a diagnosis. For better or for worse, labels and diagnoses have their purposes, although those purposes are fairly narrow and not consistent with understanding the student. So what would take the place, so to speak, of a diagnosis or a category or a label? *Phenomena*.

A phenomenological approach to assessment means making use of phenomena, or bits of information, to better understand the student. Now one could argue that any assessment approach does this. But the key here is that a phenomenological approach puts phenomena front and center, whereas a labeling or diagnostic approach matches phenomena against a list of criteria to make a determination about a label (yes, the student meets the criteria or no, the student does not meet the criteria). To the clinician who is labeling, phenomena are a means to an end. To the clinician who uses a phenomenological approach, the phenomena are the means *and the end*.

To someone new to phenomenological thinking, this may sound like a disorganized mess of a process. How could anyone possibly focus only on phenomena and not have some way to make sense of them? The simple answer is that you're right—no one could do so without some sort of organizing system. When looking at a large number of phenomena, it is vitally important to search for patterns or themes, to let an underlying meaning emerge. Phenomena do need to be organized, and *profiles* are an effective means of organization.

Profiles as Tools for Understanding Students

A *profile* is simply a description of a student's assets and weaknesses. *Assets* may be areas that are strong relative to same-age peers, working appropriately given the student's age, or functioning relatively better than the student's weak areas. *Weaknesses* are abilities that, for whatever reason, are not working as they should and that are having a negative effect on the student's life (usually school life). Profiles can be made up of phenomena that are pertinent to understanding a student's learning; such phenomena relate to *neurodevelopmental functions*, or basic abilities of the human brain. In the next chapter I describe a framework that can be used to conceptualize students' learning, including systems that you are already familiar with, such as attention and memory.

Approaches that rely on labels and categories (for example, special education, or the *Diagnostic and Statistical Manual*—the DSM) tend to lump students together without elucidating individual differences or the factors contributing to learning problems. So how can a profiling approach be more beneficial than a labeling and category-driven approach? Let me first relate a personal anecdote, a true story that I call "A Tale of Two Dishwashers."

SEVERAL YEARS AGO my wife and I lived in a townhouse, our first home together. We inherited a dishwasher from the previous owners, and about a year after we moved in we started having a problem with it. Every time we used it, we'd find a puddle of water on our kitchen floor at the end of the cycle. Upon closer inspection, I saw that during the cycle drops of water collected at the bottom of the door, dropping onto the floor, gradually creating a puddle. I decided to address this problem with textbook masculine aplomb: I called the repairman.

When he arrived I showed him to the kitchen and explained the problem. He then opened the dishwasher, peered into it with a flashlight, then calmly took out a screwdriver and poked it through a small rusted hole that I had not noticed. "There's the problem," he said. "You've got a hole right there in the door." Then he added, "That'll be $85."

A few months later my wife and I moved (not because of the faulty dishwasher) into a brand-new home. It even had a brand-new dishwasher. But after a couple of months, as you might predict, we noticed a puddle collecting on our kitchen floor every time we ran the dishwasher. Having learned my lesson, I quickly grabbed a flashlight and screwdriver and looked for a rusted hole. Stymied by the lack of a hole, or of any rust for that matter, I again resorted to calling the repairman.

A different person came this time (sparing me some embarrassment), and he spent much more time surveying the situation. He looked inside, probed components, looked underneath, and checked the plumbing feeding in and out of the dishwasher. After about twenty minutes he stood up and said, "You've got about five things going on here. The water depth feedback buoy is a little sticky, but that's not the whole story. The in-flow is a bit high, so we need to ratchet that back a bit. There's also too much water collecting near the front, behind the door, so we need to raise the front legs a hair. Don't load pots near the front because you don't want a lot of water splashing into the door. And your water is soft, so use a bit less soap to decrease the amount of suds."

THE TWO DISHWASHERS each had the same problem on the surface, but due to vastly different reasons. One could say that both dishwashers had LD, or leaking disability. But assessment led to understanding what was going on with each, and ultimately dictated the solutions. To further illustrate how profiles facilitate deeper understandings of students, let's consider two brief case studies (students, rather than household appliances).

WILLIAM AND ASHELAY are both thirteen years old, and both are really struggling with the writing demands of eighth grade. Both meet diagnostic criteria for Disorder of Written Expression. Namely, their writing abilities seem to be in stark contrast to their overall abilities, and both are achieving appropriately in reading and math.

William's assets include stellar visual-spatial ability. That is, he is very good at discerning visual patterns and generating nonverbal material such as drawings and models. He has no trouble using a pen or pencil, whether for handwriting or drawing. He seems to be able to understand and produce sequences (for example, in math, science, and social studies). He is adept at reasoning, can use logic to solve math problems, understands concepts, and has good comprehension when listening and reading.

Ashelay also is a good thinker. Whether in math, science, or social situations, she has a nice capacity to solve problems. She also has a solid memory for a variety of information types (for example, math facts, vocabulary definitions, procedures, experiences). Finally, Ashelay has terrific oral expression; in fact, her ability to communicate ideas when speaking is in stark contrast to what she puts down on paper.

Unlike Ashelay, William struggles with oral expression as well as written expression. He does not participate much in class discussions. When conversing he tends to use brief, unelaborated language and relies on non-specific terms such as *things* and *stuff*. His parents report that he reached his developmental milestones for language (for example, putting together two- or three-word phrases) later than usual.

Ashelay has terrible difficulty controlling a pencil. She does not have an adequate sense of where her fingers are during letter formation; as a consequence, she tends to write heavily to get more feedback, and sometimes she even resorts to carefully watching her pencil tip. Handwriting is a protracted, laborious process for her and—despite her efforts—her legibility is poor. Compounding her handwriting difficulty are some attention issues. Specifically, Ashelay does not seem to have sufficient mental energy (or cognitive fuel) for thinking and working. She fatigues during academic work faster than would be expected for a student her age. She also does not have appropriate quality control over her overall academic work, as she seldom checks for mistakes or corrects her own errors.

AS SHOULD BE EVIDENT, William and Ashelay are very different students in terms of their assets and their weaknesses, despite the fact that, on the surface at least, they share a diagnostic label. The "dishwasher logic" holds true—though both students meet criteria for Disorder of Written Expression, it should be obvious how much more we know about them by examining their profiles.

Answering the Question Why? (and Why That Matters)

Assessment should be able to answer a question like "Why is my son struggling with reading?" with a better answer than "Because he has a reading disability." Rather, assessment should be able to reveal factors such as language functioning or memory ability or attention control that are impeding the student's reading. It is critical to go beyond a label or category to uncover the reasons that a student is struggling with an academic skill. For example, how would profiles and deeper understandings about William and Ashelay translate into helping them be more successful in school, and in life?

First, these students (and their parents) would benefit from knowing the reasons for their struggles with writing. Not elucidating their profiles would be akin to a pediatrician seeing a child brought in by a mother worried about an elevated temperature and simply proclaiming, "The kid has fever disorder!" It's merely a restating of the chief complaint to label William or Ashelay as students with writing disabilities. Resiliency theory and research tells us that children are much better equipped to cope with life's challenges when they are aware of their weaknesses and vulnerabilities, as well as their assets and talents (Brooks & Goldstein, 2001). Further, self-awareness has been found to be associated with long-term success of individuals with learning problems, particularly when they know the specifics of their problems and can compartmentalize those aspects of themselves (Raskind, Goldberg, Higgins, & Herman, 1999).

☞ *Demystification* is an ongoing dialogue about the student's learning with the student. The dialogue can take many forms, depending on the student's age and profile (for example, a student with language difficulty may need more visual supports). Parameters are put around weaknesses, assets are highlighted, and a positive message about the future delivered. Demystification is usually initiated by a professional who does the assessment, but should be continued by a parent or caregiver (Levine, 2002).

Werner and Smith (2001) discussed the importance of a supportive adult as a protective factor for resilience. Also, Brooks and Goldstein (2004) described the concept of the "charismatic adult," someone who does not necessarily need to be a parent, but who fosters resilience by helping kids feel special and appreciated. The professional who demystifies learning problems is such an adult, providing critical support for students struggling in school. Successful adults with learning problems have identified the importance of support and guidance from significant others, including mentors, teachers, and therapists (Raskind et al., 1999).

Second, the learning plans for William and Ashelay will differ markedly when we consider their profiles. This point about differential treatment has been made for reading decoding problems, for example (Riccio & Hynd, 1995). William's learning plan will focus on improving oral expression as well as written expression. He has problems putting his ideas into language long before he has a pencil in his hand. In contrast, Ashelay's difficulty occurs when she has to use a pencil to produce writing (as opposed to pure oral expression). Hence, Ashelay's plan will include accommodations and interventions for her handwriting struggles and weak attention. Demystification about the learning plans will be important so that they understand the rationales behind the strategies they use. Regardless of where (regular classroom, special education classroom, tutoring, at the dinner table during homework time) and how these students get their instruction (at various levels depending on their response to intervention), knowing their profiles will be of huge benefit in guiding how they should be taught.

> ☞ *Learning plan* refers to a road map to improved school and life success
> for the student. It addresses weak areas but also describes how to nurture and leverage assets and affinities. Demystification is an aspect of
> learning plans. Every student would have a unique learning plan, just
> as every student has a unique profile.

Identifying Assets (and Why They Matter)

Hopefully it was obvious that assets would be included in the profiles for William and Ashelay. As mentioned earlier, assets are areas that could be strong relative to same-age peers, working appropriately, or even just functioning relatively better than weak areas. All too often, assets are forgotten components of a profile, as there is so much focus on deficits for students who are struggling in school. Why do assets matter?

First, identifying assets can boost self-esteem. Many students with learning problems have experienced failure after failure and have been told only about their deficits. When I was in third grade my family moved to a big city and I attended a large public school. The transition was difficult, but I was bolstered by a particular asset that emerged in my new class; I knew almost all of the U.S. state capitals. (Don't ask me to list them now, though!) So whenever my teacher or a classmate wanted to know the capital of a state, I was the expert who provided the information. Assets can be cultivated both in the classroom and in the family. For example, a student may emerge as the math whiz at school and the electronics hook-up technician at home. (Something many parents need help with!) Assets can take the form of academic topics, skills, or other applied areas (such as art, music, athletics). Research has shown that one of the ingredients for long-term life success for individuals with learning problems is awareness of strengths and talents, both academic and nonacademic (Raskind et al., 1999). In addition, nurturing strengths is consistent with tenets of positive psychology, which emphasizes and promotes happiness, subjective well-being, and character assets (Seligman & Csikszentmihalyi, 2000).

> ☞ *Assets* are aspects of learning, brain functions, or skills that are operating appropriately, if not better. *Affinities* are areas of high interest (sometimes passionate interest), and could be topics or activities. Sometimes assets are also affinities (a great combination). But often what we might be good at (like balancing a checkbook) is not something we enjoy, and what we might enjoy (like golfing) is not something we are good at (just check the handicaps at any municipal course).

The importance of assets is also supported by resiliency research. One feature of resilient children is having an interest or hobby that brings comfort when aspects of their lives are in disarray (Werner & Smith, 1992). Such mastery experiences have also been described as "islands of competence" (Brooks & Goldstein, 2001) and relate to the notion of leveraging assets to bolster resiliency.

Second, exploring assets can help better understand weaknesses, sometimes by ruling out possibilities. Consider a fifth-grade student who is struggling with math, particularly when it comes to solving *word problems*. Say this student also has excellent word decoding skills and age-appropriate reading comprehension. These assets probably rule out a language problem that might be undermining the understanding of math word problems. The reason for the student's math difficulty must, therefore, lie elsewhere.

For these reasons, assessment should also be able to answer positive *why* questions like these:

- "Why is Lee so good at spelling?"
- "Why is Sam able to write so effectively?"
- "Why is Kim so adept at using computers?"

Neurodevelopmental Variation as Normal Variation

Related to the importance of identifying assets is the notion that we need to stop regarding neurodevelopmental variation as a kind of pathology. A student's profile is what it is, and sometimes it is a good match for the demands of the moment (in academic classes, grade levels, courses, sports, or career) and sometimes it is not. Therein lies another problem with a deficit-oriented labeling approach: Is it really valid to claim that students who are suddenly placed in an environment that involves demands not suited to their profiles have a learning disability? Often learning problems emerge late in schooling (or in life). Take the high school student who has always earned adequate grades in math but is now stumped by algebra. Rather than diagnosing this student with a math disability, isn't it more positive (and productive) to explore what it is about algebra that does not sync up with the current profile of strengths and weaknesses?

Professionals always need to look at what is expected of the student, task-analyze the demands, and consider how well the student's profile is set up to meet those expectations. Task-analysis is so important in supporting students with learning problems that I devote Chapter Three to this topic.

A central tenet of this neurodevelopmental approach is that all students (actually, all people) possess unique *profiles*. We all have our own particular combination of assets and weaknesses. Some have their weaknesses exposed (and likely their positives unheralded) more than others, but I see no compelling reason to refer to those unfortunate individuals as disabled. What's more, most schools require students to be generalists, to be adept at a wide range of activities and tasks, which is a tall order for many students. In contrast, adulthood accommodates specialists. Many individuals who struggle in school with specialized minds will flourish as adults when they can focus on their interests and strengths.

Why the Focus on Assessment

The best description leads to the best prescription.

—Mel Levine

The goal of any professional who assesses struggling students is to help them and their families. Clearly, this involves either recommending or providing the most effective learning plan possible. The trick is selecting the right strategies and approaches to recommend. Volumes of teaching techniques and learning strategies are available for struggling learners, but it is incumbent on the professional to sort through the possibilities and make selections for students based on their specific needs, the classroom and other educational settings (such as tutoring), and the family. For example, Gibb and Wilder (2002) demonstrated the importance of linking assessment to treatment regarding teachers' analyzing data, forming hypotheses about causes of reading problems, and then using those hypotheses to guide decision making in the intervention process.

Although some learning strategies are included in this book (including Appendix E, "Learning Plan Resources"), my focus here is on assessment designed to equip you for making decisions about what to recommend. If the assessment process truly leads to a deeper understanding of the student, then the learning plan flows naturally. This held for William and Ashelay (and my two dishwashers, for that matter)—knowing their profiles dictated the selections for their individualized plans. In addition, learning plans need to incorporate ongoing, regular demystification as a major component, and a neurodevelopmental assessment will provide the understanding to the students (and those who work with them) about their individual profiles.

The Approach of This Book

In my experience training clinicians I have been struck by how often people say they are looking for "hands-on learning" about how to help struggling students. I believe that the quest is really for a way to be grounded in the practical world, with plenty of tips to take immediately to a clinical or educational practice. Accordingly, I have written this book to be more of a how-to manual than a textbook (and I hope that it is a more compelling how-to manual than what you might find on setting up a stereo system or constructing a porch). This book is not intended, however, to provide training in test administration. Rather, the focus here will be the thinking involved in assessment, and the material in this book is designed to enhance the way people use the test administration skills they have or will gain elsewhere (that is, discovering new ways to use the tools that are already in the toolbox).

Here are some of the features I have tried to build into this book:

- Hands-on illustrative examples—vignettes, case studies, patterns of data and their potential interpretations
- User-friendly presentation of information in multiple formats—diagrams, tables, text
- Meta-cognitive moments for pondering the thinking of the professional
- Focus on low-severity, high-incidence problems related to academic learning
- A dose of levity, because working with kids should be enjoyable

My attention is mainly on school-age students who are experiencing what some have described as "unexpected underachievement" (Lyon et al., 2001). This approach seems more practical than concentrating on "high-severity, low-incidence" problems, such as mental retardation and autism, as the "low-severity, high-incidence" problems are more commonly encountered in regular education classrooms and certain types of special education classes (such as resource programs).

☞ It is critical to note that most, if not all, of the tenets of this book are relevant to supporting all children and all individuals, even those with severe needs. How the tenets are applied, though, will differ depending on the population. The specific assessment techniques, as well as some thoughts about learning plans, will be focused on the "low-severity, high-incidence" end of the continuum. Also, the phrase "low-severity" should not be taken as minimizing the negative effects of any learning problem.

As I discuss in depth in Chapter Seven, I believe in recurring themes, and this book has several themes that I continually revisit. These are the core ideas:

- *Assess to understand:* Go beyond labels and diagnoses.
- *Think with a theory:* Organize your data and hypotheses.
- *Task-analyze:* Be better than the tests you use.
- *Make linkages:* Connect profiles to schoolwork and life demands.

- *View the student from multiple angles:* Do more than test.
- *Consider key contrasts:* Discrepancies can reveal much.
- *Search for recurring themes:* Identify patterns and make use of them.

Following the thirteen chapters are several other resources, including a glossary, references, and topic index. I have also included several appendices: a sample of supporting research for the neurodevelopmental framework (Appendix A), a guide to assessment task-analysis (Appendix B), an index of potential neurodevelopmental findings (Appendix C), a listing of test batteries mentioned in this book (Appendix D), and resources for generating learning plans (Appendix E).

My Perspective and Background

My fascination with child development and learning goes back to my undergraduate years. I recall that during a course on Piaget's theories I was stunned at what very young minds could accomplish, though constrained by development and limited experience. Rather than heading directly into graduate study, I chose to gain practical experience with children as a classroom teacher. I taught science for three years to students as young as first grade and as old as eighth grade; I got to see, up close and personal, a developmental spectrum in terms of cognitive, emotional, social, and physical development. I then earned a doctorate in school psychology.

I selected school psychology to meld my curiosity about development and learning with a passion for schools. My graduate training in assessment was cut from the traditional school psychology cloth—standardized measures of intelligence and academic skills, ability-achievement discrepancies, eligibility determination for special education—that I lived and breathed in several school systems during field practica and an internship. As a postdoctoral fellow, however, I trained in neuropsychology and new possibilities about assessment opened up for me. Specifically, I saw how an assessment battery could be customized for a student and made up of procedures drawn from several instruments. Also, I experienced linking a profile to academic skills (such as memory to writing) and thinking in terms of phenomena instead of tests.

Working at the All Kinds of Minds institute solidified my belief in an assessment approach based on understanding the student, rather than on labeling, categorizing, or diagnosing. My mentor and the co-founder of All Kinds of Minds, Dr. Mel Levine, has modeled how to think deeply and compassionately about students, to demystify, and to relentlessly search for strengths. Through the Institute's Student Success Program, I conducted or supervised thousands of assessments of struggling learners (kindergartners to college students), employing a nonlabeling, phenomenological approach. I have also provided professional development to thousands of clinicians and educators through presentations, workshops, and individual mentoring.

☞ All Kinds of Minds (www.allkindsofminds.org) is a nonprofit Institute that helps students who struggle with learning make measurable improvements in their success in school and life by providing programs that integrate educational, scientific, and clinical expertise.

Assessment Is Both Complex and Simple

Assessment is a vitally important service for students struggling with learning. Students, parents, and teachers are hungry for clear explanations about learning problems because they want specific suggestions for success. Like all clinical processes, it requires professional training and experience. It is usually a complex process, because learning is complex and students are complex. But at the same time, assessment is also a simple process.

In essence, assessment comprises three steps: collect information, interpret the information, and communicate the interpretation. Though each of these steps takes expertise and time, they are made simpler when you have a system for collecting data, interpreting data, and communicating findings. The conceptual framework I describe in the next chapter can serve as such a system.

2

The Need for a Framework

SUPPOSE SOMEONE ASKS YOU, "What theory guides your work?" What would you say?

For some time now I have firmly held to the opinion that every clinician or educator should have an answer to that question. In the same way that artists or musicians know what influences shape their work, teachers should know what pedagogical theory steers their instruction. Psychologists should know their theoretical roots. All professionals working with struggling learners should be cognizant of the developmental theory that guides their practice. In this chapter I lay out the basics and cover the elements such a theory should include.

The Prepared Mind

In the fields of observation chance favors only the prepared mind.

—Louis Pasteur

Assessment involves observation first, interpretation second, and communication third. A framework about learning provides scaffolding for observing, interpreting, and communicating, preparing your mind for understanding the student. Without a framework, assessment is haphazard, disorganized, and undisciplined. To illustrate, consider the following list of observations made while an elementary student reads a passage aloud:

- Has adequate mental energy level and alertness.
- Decodes sight words accurately.
- Accurately decodes regularly spelled words.

- Pauses at irregularly spelled words and makes guesses based on context.
- Uses appropriate inflection and emphasis.
- Stops to make tangential comments about passage.

☞ *Decoding* is the reading of individual words (for example, calling out), though not necessarily having an understanding of the words. Words can be decoded through segments and sounds—a process called *word attack*—or by recognizing them visually as *sight words. Regularly spelled words* typically can be decoded through word attack, while *irregularly spelled words* require memorization of their visual appearance as sight words.

All these observations may be valuable data for understanding the student. But how is a clinician or educator to make sense of it? Table 2.1 sorts the observations into some categories.

Mental energy and alertness are aspects of attention that are important for sustained cognitive effort and work. Tangential comments can be signs of limited focus on the task at hand, or of an overly active mind that makes too many connections, leading to a type of internal distractibility. Decoding words involves considerable memory, particularly for sight words (which this student could recognize) and irregularly spelled words (which caused more of a struggle). Reading requires language, both in terms of decoding individual words (phonological processing for phonics) and comprehension; the

Table 2.1   Some Phenomena Sorted into Categories

Phenomena Related to Attention	Phenomena Related to Memory	Phenomena Related to Language
• Has adequate mental energy level and alertness.	• Decodes sight words accurately.	• Accurately decodes regularly spelled words.
• Stops to make tangential comments about passage.	• Pauses at irregularly spelled words and makes guesses based on context.	• Uses appropriate inflection and emphasis.

student could readily decode words with regular spellings, and the appropriate inflection and emphasis suggest a generally solid understanding of the passage.

Clearly no firm conclusions about this particular student's profile could be reached based on this handful of data points; these observations would be examined along with other pieces of information from a variety of sources, such as performance on other reading passages, other academic tasks, neurodevelopmental tests, and history. Chapter Five will address the important issue of a balanced approach to assessment.

☞ Two oft-confused terms are *phonological processing* and *phonics.* The former refers to the linguistic capacity to distinguish and manipulate word sounds *(phonemes)* with or without print, while the latter refers to the linking of phonemes to *graphemes,* or printed letters (Cooper, 2000). See Chapter Ten for more discussion.

The categories of attention, memory, and language in this example provide an organizing system for the observations about this student's reading. That is, they serve as scaffolding. A *framework* is a conceptual structure or template that can be used to organize phenomena and data and enhance our understanding of the student. It is vital equipment for assessment because it clarifies what to look for and then guides how to interpret what is found.

The Pitfalls of Being Atheoretical

I learned early on the risks of working without a theory—of being *atheoretical.* After my internship (which was in a large urban school system) I took a postdoctoral fellowship where I was trained by a superb neuropsychologist named Steve Hooper. The first report that I gave to him to review, a write-up of a comprehensive assessment of a student's intellectual functioning and achievement, was constructed using the format I had used successfully in the schools. The body of the report was divided into sections, each devoted to the findings from the individual tests I had administered (for example, an IQ test and an achievement test). Within the sections, I dutifully went through each subtest, describing the task and how well the student performed on a normative basis (that is, using standard scores comparing the student to same-age peers). I was expecting to get rave reviews from my supervisor for my thoroughness and clean writing style.

He ripped it to shreds (metaphorically).

The problem with my report, he told me, was not the findings that I included. He emphasized that I had captured all the important data. What he did not like was the way I organized it according to tests. He wanted me to format it according to *constructs* (such as memory) and *skills* (such as reading) and to be more descriptive of the functions than the tasks. The rationale for his method of organization, he said, was to force me to see patterns in my findings and to confront discrepancies in the data. The format would also help the reader understand the same patterns and discrepancies.

I don't want to seem overly dramatic, but that was a watershed moment in my career. In revising that report I experienced a basic shift in the way I thought about assessment, not just about report formats. I realized that I needed to think construct first, test second. Tests, even the best tests, are merely tools; they are a means and not an end. Without a conceptual framework, I was flying blind with my various tests and scores.

That experience also brought home to me the message of this chapter: for assessment to work, you need to have a conceptual framework—and to be able to describe that framework. This framework need not be confining. On the contrary, it should be liberating. It opens your eyes to new sources of data and deeper levels of interpretation (the ones that involve seeing patterns and themes). What's more, a conceptual framework can and should be adaptable; it isn't something you cling to and defend in the face of new thinking and research.

Conceptual Correctness

In every truth the opposite is equally true.

—Hermann Hesse

Once you buy in to the argument that you need a conceptual and theoretical framework, then the issue is selecting a framework, or combination of frameworks. When it comes to child development, cognitive functioning, and learning, you have many possibilities to choose from. I describe some of these potential frameworks a bit later in this chapter.

But here's an insight that will make the selection process less worrying. Coming on the decision for the first time, people often search earnestly for the *correct* framework. But does a framework need to be correct? The short answer, in my opinion, is no. This apparent paradox stems from the nature of frameworks themselves—that is, of what scholars refer to as *theories*.

Two basic but contradictory assumptions can be made about scientific theories. The first is that theories represent realities of the universe. The second is that theories are simply devices for making the universe more understandable.

Regarding the first assumption, *positivism* is the school of thought that maintains the universe has a structure, and that the task of science is to understand that structure. Similarly, *scientific realism* holds that scientific theories go beyond data to posit the existence of nonobservable entities that actually exist (Cacioppo, Semin, & Berntson, 2004). So a scientific realist would view conceptual frameworks of learning as representations of actual brain functions.

The second assumption, *relativism,* posits that structures are merely imposed on the universe. *Scientific instrumentalism* proposes that scientific theories produce intellectual structures that predict what is observed, and that these frameworks facilitate the answering of questions and the solving of problems (Cacioppo et al. 2004). A scientific instrumentalist, then, would view conceptual frameworks as tools that help organize what is observed.

The choice is by no means limited to scientific exploration. For example, I was an oarsman in college, rowing on eight-man crews, and our coach routinely reviewed videotape of us on the water, discussing technique. What technique is that, you may well ask—from the outside it can look like the choices involved in rowing a racing shell are limited to how much energy to put in. In practice, though, rowers have several different styles of rowing, each with a distinct set of sequenced motions. I recall one of my crewmates asking our coach, "What is the best rowing style?" "The style you row doesn't really matter," our coach replied, "as long as you believe in it."

To a certain extent I feel that the same can be said about learning theory. Whether you subscribe to positivism or relativism, theories are still helpful as organizational frameworks.

Theoretical Frameworks for Understanding Learning

A theory is no more like a fact than a photograph is like a person.
—Edgar Watson Howe

Frameworks for development and learning come from several sources and disciplines, and intelligence theory and neuropsychology are two of the more prominent ones. Intelligence theories date back to the nineteenth century with such pioneering psychologists as Galton, who first proposed that tests could be used to measure psychological differences between individuals. Alfred Binet and others then developed mental ability tests. Several theories of ability were developed in the early twentieth century, and eventually led to the development of the first modern intelligence measures, or IQ (intelligence quotient) tests. Despite some exceptions (for example, Thorndike), most theories of intelligence include g, a term coined by Spearman as a general index of cognitive ability. To varying degrees, intelligence theories also include more specific factors or subcomponents that contribute to g (Bolles, 1993; Fancher, 1990).

Cattell-Horn-Carroll (CHC)

In the past two decades, the Cattell-Horn-Carroll (CHC) theory has drawn considerable attention. It is grounded in decades of factor analytic research from cognitive ability test databases, as well as studies of development and heritability. CHC is actually an amalgam of two bodies of work: Cattell-Horn Gf-Gc theory and Carroll's three-tier model of human cognitive abilities. Carroll (1993) proposed a framework that differentiated abilities by breadth, with the broadest level a general intelligence factor conceptually similar to Spearman's g. This general factor was divided into eight narrower abilities: Fluid Intelligence (Gf), Crystallized Intelligence (Gc), General Memory and Learning (Gy), Broad Visual Perception (Gv), Broad Auditory Perception

(Ga), Broad Retrieval Ability (Glr), Broad Cognitive Speediness (Gs), and Reaction Time/Decision Speed (Gt). These eight abilities were composed of more specific factors, sixty-nine in aggregate. Cattell-Horn's model was similar on several fronts, including its hierarchical structure and varying levels of breadth; several of the factors, including Gf and Gc, were defined similarly. In the 1990s, Carroll's model was combined with Cattell-Horn's work, with the first published hyphenated linking of "Cattell-Horn-Carroll" or CHC appearing in Flanagan, McGrew, and Ortiz (2000).

Like its roots, CHC is also a hierarchical framework with three strata: stratum III is *g*, stratum II consists of broad cognitive abilities, and stratum I consists of narrow cognitive abilities. These are the broad cognitive abilities of stratum II:

- Fluid reasoning (Gf): Forming and recognizing logical relationships among patterns, making deductive and inductive inferences, and transforming novel stimuli

- Comprehension-knowledge (Gc): Using language and acquired knowledge effectively

- Short-term memory (Gsm): Understanding and storing information in immediate awareness and then using it within a few seconds

- Visual processing (Gv): Recognizing spatial relationships and analyzing and manipulating visual stimuli

- Auditory processing (Ga): Perceiving, attending to, and analyzing patterns of sound and speech

- Long-term retrieval (Glr): Storing and readily retrieving information in long-term memory

- Processing speed (Gs): Performing simple cognitive tasks quickly, especially when under pressure to maintain focused attention and concentration

Stratum II abilities are further subdivided into numerous narrow cognitive abilities, or stratum I (Evans, Floyd, McGrew, & Leforgee, 2001). The CHC can be very useful for organizing findings and understanding learners, and its research base is extensive. However, the fact that it is organized around *g* may limit its applicability for a phenomenological approach aimed at developing profiles. It should be noted, though, that proponents

Table 2.2   Guilford's Structure of Intellect (SOI) Model

Content Dimension	Operations Dimension	Products Dimension
1. Visual 2. Auditory 3. Symbolic (numbers, letters, symbols, designs) 4. Semantic (the meaning of words, ideas) 5. Behavioral (people's actions and expressions)	1. Cognition (recognizing and discovering) 2. Memory (retaining and recalling the contents of thought) 3. Divergent production (producing a variety of ideas or solutions to a problem) 4. Convergent production (producing a single best solution to a problem) 5. Evaluation (critiquing the intellectual contents)	1. Units (a single number, letter, or word) 2. Classes (a higher-order concept, say, men + women = people) 3. Relations (connections between concepts) 4. Systems (classifications of relations) 5. Transformation (altering or restructuring intellectual contents) 6. Implication (drawing inferences between separate pieces of information)

of CHC are engaging in ongoing discussion about g's importance in the framework.

Structure of Intellect (SOI)

The Structure of Intellect (SOI) model (see Table 2.2) includes an impressive array of variability, while still incorporating a way to organize concepts. In SOI, phenomena are placed along three axes (with five or six possible types per axis) that form a cube; because each of these three dimensions is independent, the theory has room for 150 different components of intelligence (Guilford, 1982). Clearly, this model provides for wide-ranging individual variation while offering a framework for categorizing and interpreting phenomena.

Luria's Work and the PASS Model

In contrast to most intelligence theories, neuropsychological frameworks usually are not centered on a single, central factor of g. Rather, neuropsychologists have sought to map various mental abilities onto brain structures. In so doing they have created frameworks that include factors and subcomponents that can be quite compatible with a profiling approach. A highly influential thinker in the field was the Russian neuropsychologist Alexander Romanovich Luria. In his seminal book *The Working Brain,* he first describes basic brain anatomy, including the functions of the various cortices and lobes. Then he organizes brain functions into familiar categories, such as attention and memory (Luria, 1973).

A more recent theory is the PASS model from Das, Naglieri, and Kirby (1994). PASS is an acronym for "planning, attention, successive, and simultaneous." *Successive* refers to information that is perceived, interpreted, or remembered in a serial order (for example, language), whereas *simultaneous* refers to material that is perceived, interpreted, or remembered as a gestalt (for example, visual-spatial information). PASS combines features of neuropsychological and *g*-based theories, in that the model yields a global index of ability while emphasizing specific cognitive processes. Its derivation drew heavily from neuropsychology (including Luria), as well as factor analysis and studies of academic achievement. Mental abilities such as memory are integrated into the model in several ways. For example, information committed to short- and long-term memory can be coded successively or simultaneously. Strategy use is a significant consideration in this model, and is incorporated under the planning factor.

A Neurodevelopmental Framework

Another way to organize phenomena is to apply an adaptable neurodevelopmental framework. The framework I emphasize in this book draws heavily from the model developed by Melvin Levine (1998). It is similar to neuropsychological frameworks and is influenced by Luria, who conceptualized brain function as consisting of several related areas: perception (including for verbal and spatial information), movement and action (muscle tone through complex actions), memory (including for verbal and spatial information), speech (receptive and expressive), thinking (analysis, development of strategies and tactics, consideration of results), and attention. Luria divided attention into three units: Unit 1 (the brain stem and related areas) regulates cortical activity and levels of alertness, while Unit 2 (the lateral and posterior regions of the neocortex) analyzes and stores newly received information, and Unit 3 (the frontal lobes) programs and regulates activity (Luria, 1973).

In addition to Luria, this neurodevelopmental framework also draws from disciplines such as speech-language pathology, occupational therapy, and physical therapy. Aspects of this framework are similar (in name or definition, or both) to those of other theories, including those described earlier. At a macro level, it consists of eight constructs (sometimes referred to as systems), many of which have names that are familiar to parents, teachers, and even students—an important benefit. Here are the eight constructs:

- *Attention:* Control of cognitive functioning (regulating mental energy, processing incoming information, and managing output)
- *Memory:* Storage and retrieval of information temporarily, over extended periods, or while using the information
- *Language:* Understanding and use of linguistic sounds, words, sentences, and discourse
- *Spatial ordering:* Processing and production of material that is visual, spatial, or both
- *Temporal-sequential ordering:* Processing and production of material that is serial (including the understanding and management of time)
- *Neuromotor function:* Control over movement of large muscles, hands, and fingers (including for handwriting)
- *Higher-order cognition:* Complex and sophisticated thinking
- *Social cognition:* Navigation of interaction with others, including verbal and nonverbal tactics

In addition to the eight constructs (see Figure 2.1), this framework includes several "cross-construct" phenomena that interact with all of the constructs and their component parts:

- *Rate of processing and production:* The speed with which material is processed (as in reading) or generated (writing)
- *Chunk size:* The amount of material processed or generated
- *Metacognition:* The level of understanding about one's mind and learning abilities (that is, the degree of thinking about thinking)
- *Strategy use:* The capacity to solve problems and complete tasks in systematic ways

Figure 2.1   A Neurodevelopmental Framework

Attention	Memory	Language	Spatial Ordering	Temporal-Sequential Ordering	Neuromotor Function	Higher-Order Cognition	Social Cognition
Cross-Construct Phenomena (Rate, Chunk Size, Metacognition, Strategy Use)							

At a micro level, some of the constructs are divided into subsystems (see Figure 2.2):

Attention

- *Mental energy control system:* For initiating and maintaining the cognitive fuel needed for optimal learning and behavior
- *Processing control system:* For handling information entering through the senses
- *Production control system:* For regulating thinking for academic and behavioral output

Figure 2.2   A Neurodevelopmental Framework, Constructs, and Components

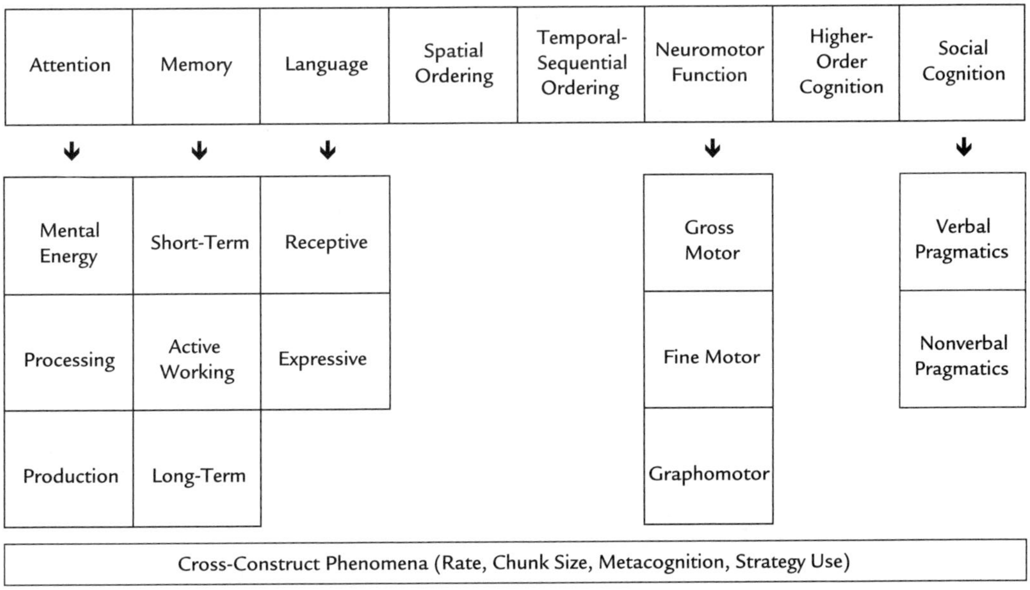

Attention	Memory	Language	Spatial Ordering	Temporal-Sequential Ordering	Neuromotor Function	Higher-Order Cognition	Social Cognition
↓	↓	↓			↓		↓
Mental Energy	Short-Term	Receptive			Gross Motor		Verbal Pragmatics
Processing	Active Working	Expressive			Fine Motor		Nonverbal Pragmatics
Production	Long-Term				Graphomotor		
Cross-Construct Phenomena (Rate, Chunk Size, Metacognition, Strategy Use)							

Memory

- *Short-term:* Registering information for a brief time
- *Active working:* Mentally suspending information while using or manipulating it
- *Long-term (storage and access):* Placing information in memory that can be retrieved after a delay

Language

- *Receptive:* Processing and understanding incoming oral and written information
- *Expressive:* Communicating and producing ideas orally or in writing, or both

Neuromotor

- *Gross motor:* Controlling the body's large muscles
- *Fine motor:* Controlling hands and fingers (that is, manual dexterity)
- *Graphomotor:* Controlling hands and fingers for the purpose of handwriting

Social cognition

- *Verbal pragmatics:* Use and understanding of language within social contexts and for the purpose of fostering optimal relationships with others
- *Nonverbal pragmatics:* Behaviors and nonverbal tactics that foster optimal relationships with others

---

☞ Chapters Eight, Nine, and Ten provide more in-depth discussion about the components of attention, memory, and language, respectively, along with specific approaches for assessing each. Chapter Eleven similarly addresses the other constructs.

This neurodevelopmental framework has a number of features that make it attractive for understanding students with learning problems. First, it is an amalgam of research and theory, and so can be readily adapted as new science warrants; Appendix A includes some of the supporting literature for the components of the framework as it now stands. Second, its constructs and subcomponents are linked to academic skills; in other words, the framework represents a broad range of brain functions that are germane to school performance. Chapter Four focuses on connecting academic skills and subskills with the neurodevelopmental functions that undergird them. Third, as mentioned earlier, the framework is relatively user-friendly in that it has symmetry and includes terms likely to be familiar (for example, most everybody knows about memory, at least in general terms). Since assessment should be about improving the understanding of students among their parents and teachers, as well as among the students themselves, an understandable framework can be extremely useful.

A few other remarks should be made about this neurodevelopmental framework. Since it is a conceptualization of brain function with the purpose of organizing findings, its organization is somewhat arbitrary; in other words, components of one construct could just as easily be considered as components of another construct (having what amounts to dual citizenship between them). For example, *graphomotor function* involves recall of letter appearance as well as motor sequences to produce letters. So should *graphomotor function* sit under memory rather than under neuromotor function? As long as we are aware of these kinds of interfaces between functions, it shouldn't really matter as we assess students.

Again, this framework is a tool for organizing (and then communicating) assessment findings. When assessing learning problems, the priority is to link neurodevelopmental functioning to academic performance, as opposed to linking behavior to brain anatomy (which would be the focus of traditional neuropsychology). For the "low-severity, high-incidence" population I mentioned in Chapter One—the ones teachers and school psychologists deal with every day—mapping functions onto brain anatomy is rarely fruitful, particularly in terms of building learning plans.

Other Factors That May Impede Learning

When assessing students with learning problems, it is critical to consider not only the brain (and how its various functions are organized) but also other factors that may be hindering (or aiding) learning. One such factor is the student's environment, which typically can be subdivided into home and school environments. Regarding the home, it is important to appraise the level of support that the family is able to provide (how much time the parents have for the student, for example) and to identify the presence of disruptive factors (such as family discord or parental pressure). Regarding school, the clinician needs to know about the instruction the student is receiving, such as how reading or math are taught, as well as such basic variables as classroom size, student-to-teacher ratio, individualized services available at the school, and classroom social dynamics. Dudley-Marling (2004) discussed the need to consider the student's learning environment in terms of social constructivism—locating learning (and learning problems) within the context of human relations and activity.

A second general factor to assess is the student's emotional-behavioral status. When adults run into trouble on the job or face career crises, stress usually follows. For children and adolescents, school is a career, so it can be expected that school difficulty often leads to emotional difficulty. A considerable amount of research has substantiated that students who struggle with learning also have behavioral and emotional problems (Yasutake & Bryan, 1995), including feelings of low self-worth (Nowicki, 2003); loneliness and victimization (Sabornie, 1994); depression and sense of inadequacy (Martinez & Semrud-Clikeman, 2004); and increased levels of stress, less peer support, and poorer adjustment (Wenz-Gross & Siperstein, 1998). Furthermore, students with learning problems report school-related loneliness, even though they may feel part of a social network (Pavri & Monda-Amaya, 2001). Gender should also be considered, as girls may show more internalized problems, such as depression and social stress, whereas boys may show more externalized problems, such as school maladjustment (Martinez & Semrud-Clikeman, 2004).

It is often difficult to tell whether emotional problems are causing learning problems or being caused by them, and the two sets of problems may well exacerbate each other. For example, math-related anxiety has been found to erode attention and working memory capacity; poor math performance can be caused by a student's ineffective efforts to divert focus away from the worry and back to the task, as opposed to the experience of worrying itself (Hopko, Ashcraft, Gute, Ruggiero, & Lewis, 1998). The potential for problems to build on one another supports the argument that learning problems and emotional issues should be addressed in parallel, through a learning plan that includes instructional interventions and accommodations as well as supports for emotional needs (such as counseling). In fact, one of the predictors of long-term success for individuals with learning problems is emotional stability, such as being able to cope with stress and frustration (Raskind et al., 1999).

Medical issues represent a third factor that may impede learning. Obviously, severe medical problems disrupt overall quality of life for both students and their families. But several other, more subtle issues can greatly hinder learning if undetected (and untreated). For example, lack of sleep or disturbances in sleep can significantly sap energy levels during the day and diminish academic performance (Dornbusch, 2002). Seizure disorders can cause lapses of awareness, resulting in missed information (Coulter, 1999); such lapses may be misinterpreted as attention problems. Though rare in incidence, an underlying neurologic or genetic condition such as Fragile X syndrome can manifest as a learning problem (Harris-Schmidt & Fast, 1998). More common conditions are allergies and asthma that, again, can encumber learning if not treated sufficiently (Bender, 1999).

These other factors that can affect learning will be discussed further in Chapter Eleven, along with strategies for assessing them.

Selecting a Framework: A Choice for the Professional

Professionals who assess learning problems have several frameworks from which to choose (or from which to strategically select components for an amalgam). As long as the frameworks have scientific support for their validity, they will be useful whether they conform to scientific realism or serve scientific instrumentalism. In addition to being thoroughly knowledgeable about your chosen framework, you also need to believe in it. Having a framework prepares the mind for assessment, and is a pathway to the more sophisticated thinking about students and learning introduced in the next chapter.

3

The Art of Task-Analysis

WITH A THEORETICAL FRAMEWORK in hand as a road map, it is much easier to look critically at what is involved in performing academic skills. Careful consideration of the mental ingredients necessary for an academic task is the art of *task-analysis*.

Actually, task-analysis can be done with any skill or process, in or out of the classroom. Grocery shopping, for example. This task usually begins with looking over your kitchen to see what items you are running low on (attention processing control system), planning ahead for what you need for upcoming meals (attention production control system), then writing a shopping list (graphomotor function). At the grocery store you need to read the food labels and understand announcements about specials broadcast over the public address system (receptive language). Even though you have a list, you often have to recall what food you already have at home (long-term memory access), and you need to keep a running track of roughly how much your total purchase will cost (active working memory). Having a good sense of the physical layout of the store can be helpful (spatial ordering). As you shop you often need to avoid impulses to buy things, such as junk food or items that are on sale but not really needed (attention production control system). Finally, sometimes key ingredients are out of stock, requiring you to improvise ways to adjust a recipe or change the menu altogether (higher-order cognition).

Really, anything we use our brains for (which is just about everything!) can be task-analyzed in terms of the neurodevelopmental functions typically required. It's important to bear in mind, though, that the same task may be approached distinctly by different individuals, meaning that different mixes of neurodevelopmental functions may be involved.

Back to grocery shopping, for example—some people do not plan their shopping or make lists ahead of time. Some people rely more heavily on memory or shop with their families, requiring social cognition. Task-analyzing for clinical purposes is, in a sense, an exercise in probability: identifying the neurodevelopmental functions most commonly involved. When working with students, it's always best to be aware of unique approaches and individual variation.

Two Types of Reasoning

When the mind is thinking, it is talking to itself.

—Plato

It's time for the first of the "meta-cognitive moments" I promised in the first chapter. When it comes to assessment, the work calls for two general types of reasoning: *deductive* and *inductive. Deductive reasoning* involves thinking from the general to the specific. For example, starting with breakdowns in one or more neurodevelopmental constructs and then predicting the symptoms that might be caused by those breakdowns is deductive. This type of reasoning is important when creating learning plans for students, especially when preparing for upcoming challenges (say, the next school year). Perhaps an assessment has yielded the information that Benjamin, a fifth grader, has memory difficulties but strong spatial ordering. Using deductive reasoning, a clinician or educator works with Benjamin's parents and teachers to review the sixth-grade curriculum for its memory demands, then sets up the necessary interventions (applying the student's spatial ability when studying by converting notes to cluster diagrams) and accommodations (asking the teachers to incorporate many recognition questions, such as multiple-choice, into tests and quizzes). Deductive reasoning also comes into play when adults are learning a new framework themselves; in the later chapters of this book we will discuss memory, for example, and the various tests, tasks, and procedures for assessing its components.

In contrast, *inductive reasoning* involves thinking from the specific to the general. In this context, it starts with symptoms (the things that occur during academic work) and then hypothesizes about the breakdowns in one or more constructs that might be causing them. Obviously, much inductive reasoning

Figure 3.1   Deductive and Inductive Reasoning

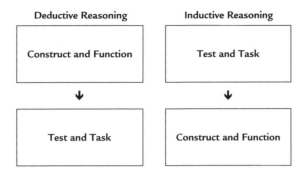

happens during assessment. We make observations and then induce (generalize) the student's neurodevelopmental profile from those observations. Inductive thinking is used with analyzing performance patterns and student behaviors in a search for recurring themes (see Chapter Seven).

In a sense, deductive and inductive reasoning are opposites, as Figure 3.1 illustrates. They involve thinking that goes in reverse directions: specific to general or general to specific. For assessment work, deductive reasoning starts with constructs and functions and then goes to tests and tasks (both neurodevelopmental and academic), whereas inductive reasoning starts with tests and tasks and then goes to constructs and functions.

Task-analysis involves extensive use of deductive reasoning in that you start with aspects of a framework and then deduce the task components related to that framework. Being adept at task-analysis raises your game, taking clinical thinking to another level of sophistication. Incidentally, task-analysis can be done with whatever theoretical framework or combination of frameworks you may choose. In this book, though, I stick with the neurodevelopmental framework outlined in Chapter Two.

Analysis of Academic Skills

Any academic skill can be analyzed in terms of its typical neurodevelopmental underpinnings. It is useful to be able to task-analyze academic skills because helping students with a learning problem requires understanding how learning is supposed to work, just as a mechanic first needs to know how an engine works before being able to diagnose one that is not working properly.

Table 3.1   Task-Analysis of Long Division

Neurodevelopmental Ingredients	Task Component
Attention production controls (previewing, self-monitoring)	Estimating what the ballpark answer will be before starting to solve the long division problem, then self-checking against this estimate at the end
Long-term memory	Storing and then recalling the various steps (in the correct order) that comprise the long division procedure
Graphomotor function	Writing numbers legibly
Spatial ordering	Keeping columns aligned properly so that place values are accurate
Temporal-sequential ordering	Performing the steps in the proper order
Higher-order cognition	Understanding the conceptual logic behind the process of long division (that it is the opposite of multiplication), rather than simply using rote memory and an algorithmic approach

To demonstrate, let's task-analyze an academic task that just about everyone was taught in school (though many of us have forgotten since): long division. Using *deductive reasoning,* we will work our way through the neurodevelopmental framework, starting with attention, and list the constructs and functions that play a major role in this academic task (see Table 3.1).

Task-analysis identifies the major factors typically involved for successful completion of that task. To solve a long division problem, not all of the listed ingredients necessarily need to be in place. For instance, it is possible to generate a correct answer without first estimating the answer (previewing), writing numbers legibly (graphomotor function), keeping columns aligned (spatial ordering), or understanding the conceptual logic behind long division (higher-order cognition). However, long division is made far easier when these neurodevelopmental factors are in place. In addition, some factors may support other, weaker factors; highly accurate long-term memory may make up for tenuous higher-order thinking (and vice versa).

Now let's take on a task that can be challenging to many students—writing a book report—and focus on what this task entails for a fifth grader (see Table 3.2).

Table 3.2   Task-Analysis of Writing a Book Report

Neurodevelopmental Ingredients	Task Component
Attention production controls (previewing, pacing, self-monitoring)	Planning the report's organization and use of evidence from book, working at the right pace (that is, not rushing), self-checking, and revising
Memory	Recalling important facts to include from the book, mentally suspending information while writing
Expressive language	Retrieving the right words and using them correctly, constructing sentences, placing sentences together in a cohesive way to generate discourse
Graphomotor function	Writing notes and outline legibly
Fine motor function	Keyboarding
Higher-order cognition	Forming a logical argument, linking and explaining concepts

Effective task-analysis requires being very specific with the task elements. Writing a book report is not merely writing; this task incorporates many components that come into play before, during, and after the student puts pencil to paper or finger to keyboard. Task-analysis also requires careful consideration of the various task elements, some of which may be obvious and some not. For writing a book report, expressive language is probably an easy neurodevelopmental function to identify, while memory and attention may not be as apparent. As mentioned earlier in connection with grocery shopping, one has to be open-minded about how different people may approach the same task differently, requiring flexible task-analysis. For instance, a fifth grader may use cluster diagrams or graphic organizers (spatial ordering), rather than more traditional outline formats, to plan a book report. (And not just a fifth grader; I actually visualize my writing as differently shaped pieces of text and make extensive use of various color fonts as I produce drafts.)

Task-analyzing an academic skill requires specifying the grade level, since the task demands can change markedly as children progress through school. For instance, writing a book report in the third grade may not require fine motor function for keyboarding. It might rely more heavily on graphomotor function for writing out the report by hand, and it might require less higher-order cognition in terms of the sophistication of the writing involved. Similarly, an eleventh grader may need even more previewing than a fifth grader since a book report might unfold over a longer period and require more planning.

Analysis of Assessment Tasks

The burden is on the test users to be "better" than the tests they use.

—Alan Kaufman

The process of assessment usually involves the use of tasks or tests. Such measures can vary widely in what they are designed to assess, and in their degree of structure and standardization; these types of tasks are discussed further in Chapter Five. Assessing to understand requires a high level of expertise with the tasks and tests in use. Simply knowing administration and scoring procedures is not sufficient. Expertise with assessment tools involves really knowing the factors that contribute to task performance, and just as academic skills can be task-analyzed with deductive reasoning, so can assessment methods.

Let's illustrate task-analysis of an assessment tool by considering *elision* (see Table 3.3), in which the student is read a word (say, "west"), repeats the word, then hears a phoneme from that word (for example, /s/) and is asked to delete that phoneme from the word to say a new word (in this case, "wet"). Elision involves *segmenting* (breaking apart word sounds) and then *re-blending* (putting word sounds together).

Elision tasks are often found in batteries, such as the Comprehensive Test of Phonological Processing (Wagner, Torgesen, & Rashotte, 1999) to assess advanced levels of phonological processing. However, as the example of elision illustrates, task-analysis requires going beyond what is advertised about a test; elision involves a great deal more than just phonological processing. It is actually very difficult to picture any assessment task that does not tap several neurodevelopmental constructs and functions. Some tasks isolate functions more narrowly than others, but all tasks are multi-factorial in terms of their neurodevelopmental underpinnings. Again, to task-analyze effectively, one needs to be open-minded in considering all of the possible factors involved, including those that are not readily apparent.

Table 3.3   Task-Analysis of Elision

Neurodevelopmental Ingredients	Task Component
Attention processing controls (processing depth)	Listening attentively enough to hear the word and phoneme accurately
Attention production controls (pacing, self-monitoring)	Segmenting and re-blending at a good pace, not rushing; reviewing what one is saying to determine if the new word sounds correct
Active working memory	Mentally suspending word and phonemes while segmenting and re-blending
Receptive language (phonological processing)	Actually segmenting and re-blending the word sounds; discerning and then manipulating the individual phonemes
Receptive language (sentence comprehension)	Understanding relatively obscure task instructions (elision is not a task that students normally are asked to complete in classrooms)
Temporal-sequential ordering	Having an accurate sense of the sequence of the phonemes

Let's conduct another task-analysis with a complex form copy (see Table 3.4), such as the Rey Complex Figure and Recognition Trial (Meyers & Meyers, 1996). In such a task the student is shown a relatively abstract geometric figure and is asked to copy it (with the original on hand for reference). Figure 3.2 contains a mock complex figure, to give you a better sense of this type of task without actually reproducing live test material.

On the surface, copying a complex form appears to be a rather daunting spatial ordering challenge. Again, there is much more to this type of task. Copying is made much easier when ingredients such as previewing and self-monitoring are in place, though it is possible to be successful without them.

An assessment battery often includes tasks or tests that are similar (for instance, spelling), but that have important differences (spelling isolated words and spelling words in context). Comparing performance across such tasks can be very revealing about a student's profile, and task-analysis is critical when interpreting key discrepancies in assessment data. I discuss this essential thought process further in Chapter Six.

Table 3.4   Task-Analysis of Complex Figure Copy

Neurodevelopmental Ingredients	Task Component
Attention processing controls (processing depth)	Picking up all the details from the figure, including the smaller ones
Attention production controls (previewing, pacing, self-monitoring)	Coming up with a good plan for constructing the figure (for example, starting with major elements, then adding smaller details); not rushing through; comparing copy with original for accuracy
Fine motor function and graphomotor function	Pencil control
Spatial ordering	Accurately perceiving the spatial elements (for example, proportions, part-to-whole relationships, intersections) of the figure and then generating the copy
Cross-construct phenomena (chunk size, strategy use)	Handling a large amount of visual input; going about copy in a systematic way, possibly by converting the information into another modality (for example, thinking aloud about what the figure looks like)

Constructing Learning Plans

As noted, deductive task-analysis is important when developing learning plans for students with academic difficulties. Once a student's profile has been established, you can then turn to current demands to understand where the difficulties lie and generate appropriate interventions and accommodations—and if all goes well, prevent future problems.

Figure 3.2   Mock Complex Figure

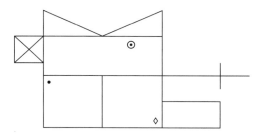

Sienna, for instance, is a fourth grader whose assessment reveals receptive and expressive language dysfunction but solid to strong functions in other neurodevelopmental constructs, including memory and attention. By comparing her profile to the task-analyses conducted earlier in this chapter, it becomes clear that long division shouldn't be an issue, since language is not a major ingredient of this particular academic task. In contrast, writing a book report would be a challenge for Sienna because of the numerous expressive language demands of writing from the word level to the discourse level. On the other hand, Sienna's assets might be engaged to help her with writing. She has the higher-order cognition to form arguments and understand concepts, even though converting her thinking into words is problematic; she may need coaching in techniques such as graphic organizers so that she can better translate her ideas into a visual format, which she can then start putting onto paper.

Sometimes task-analysis needs to look at upcoming academic demands. As a fourth grader, Sienna may not be writing book reports yet, but in fifth and sixth grades she will. Anticipating such challenges can go a long way toward planning, accommodating, and heading off worry about school. In addition, you can and should consider tasks that may not be hard for a student, or that may even be easy or enjoyable. Sienna might like to hear that although language arts classes in middle school will require a lot of support and effort, other classes such as math and science will be far less taxing. Also, Sienna might benefit from learning about extracurricular activities that she might want to try, such as swimming (a team sport that does not require much in the way of language). Similarly, high school students may need consultation on college and career options, and task-analyzing possibilities can help forge a life game plan.

At this point it is important to emphasize that we never want to tell a student a task or goal is out of reach. Perhaps Sienna aspires to writing for the middle school newspaper. Who's to say that she won't make it happen? Task-analysis does not provide a crystal ball, but it can help with preparations for the challenges ahead. So Sienna might be told that it will be even more important to find some good strategies for coping with her language issues so that she can be the best writer she can be. Task-analysis can also be used to find alternative interests and goals. In a conversation about why she wants to write for the school paper, Sienna might reveal that she looks forward to the excitement of journalism, wants to inform people, and likes working on a team. Maybe being a photographer for the school paper would be a better fit for her profile, while providing her with what she really wants out of the experience.

To be able to task-analyze, one obviously needs a theoretical framework, but also a working knowledge of the discrete components of a task or skill, the subskills that it involves. Such working knowledge can be derived from several sources, such as national academic standards, local norms, professional experience, and simply asking educators about curriculum. Incidentally, task-analysis can be even more effective when done collaboratively; engaging teachers, parents, and even students in a dialogue about academic demands can be both fruitful and powerful.

Task-Analysis as an Assessment Tool

Though this book will review many assessment tasks and academic skills, it would be simply overwhelming to task-analyze the entire universe of available tasks. The key is to have the skill to task-analyze whatever tests and skills are necessary for understanding individual students. Appendix B contains a task-analysis guide for reviewing the assessment tools that will be discussed more in later chapters—but it's not the final answer. Look at Appendix B as a form of scaffolding, a way to structure and organize your thinking.

Task-analysis helps you build a deep understanding of what students need to learn and perform academic skills. It provides a platform for authentic descriptions of what's going on and facilitates development of customized learning tactics. It makes it necessary to think with a theory, since it relies on an organizational framework for identifying the factors involved with a task or skill. Task-analysis is what allows you to be "better than the test" that's in use; it takes your thinking to another level of sophistication and paves the way to making linkages between neurodevelopmental functions and academic skills.

4

Making Linkages

MAKING LINKAGES IS THE CORE of assessing to understand. Once you can see the connections between skills and the neurodevelopmental factors that contribute to them, you can tell why a student may be finding any given skill troublesome or easy. Of course, many different theoretical frameworks will support the process of making linkages; any of the theories described in Chapter Two could be employed to organize and scaffold the ingredients of academic skill development and school performance. You don't have to stick with the neurodevelopmental framework emphasized in this book, but bear with the explanations because they illustrate the process to be used with any workable framework.

Many experts in the field advocate an approach that considers academic skills along with domain-specific factors (such as language) correlated with those skills (for example, Fletcher et al., 1998; Lyon et al., 2001), especially Levine (1998). An "inside-to-outside" approach to assessment views academic skill deficits as outcomes arising from associated fundamental deficits (Denckla, 1996a).

Functions Versus Skills

To understand the principle of making linkages, it is necessary to clarify the distinction between an academic skill and a neurodevelopmental function. *Academic skills* stem from human civilization and culture. They involve traditional tasks such as reading text, writing, and solving math problems. Such skills have emerged relatively recently in terms of human history and can be broken down into subskills. An *academic task*—having a student read or spell words or solve math problems, for example—is designed to assess an academic skill.

In contrast, a *neurodevelopmental function* is a more innate mental ability that humans had in some form or fashion long before the advent of academic skills. Foorman (1995) made the point that humans are biologically specialized to produce language but not to read and write. Literacy is not a natural act in the same sense as speaking, so education plays a much larger role in the learning process for reading and writing than it does for language itself. Neurodevelopmental functions enable the performance of academic skills, but also of all the other things that people do in their daily lives.

A *neurodevelopmental task* is designed to assess neurodevelopmental functions in as pure a form as possible; such tasks make as little use of reading, writing, and math as possible. An example of a neurodevelopmental task is *listening comprehension,* which can help you assess a student's receptive language ability without mixing up the results with the student's skill at decoding while reading.

It is helpful to think of skills and functions in terms of layers (see Figure 4.1). *Skills* are at the top layer because they are undergirded by their respective subskills and by functions. In addition, skills comprise the top layer because they are more visible, especially to students and parents. Put differently, students and parents know about skills such as spelling and math, and usually have some sense of how well the student is performing in those

Figure 4.1   Layers of Academic Skills and Neurodevelopmental Functions

Reading Decoding	Reading Comprehension	Spelling	Written Expression	Math Operations	Math Reasoning

↑   ↑   ↑   ↑   ↑   ↑

Academic Subskills

↑   ↑   ↑   ↑   ↑   ↑   ↑   ↑

Attention	Memory	Language	Spatial Ordering	Temporal-Sequential Ordering	Neuromotor Function	Higher-Order Cognition	Social Cognition

Cross-Construct Phenomena (Rate, Chunk Size, Metacognition, Strategy Use)

Figure 4.2   Linkages Between Academic Skills and Neurodevelopmental Functions

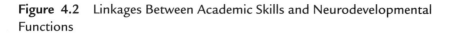
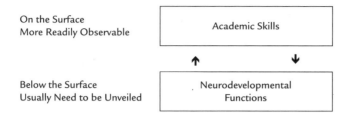

On the Surface
More Readily Observable

Academic Skills

Below the Surface
Usually Need to be Unveiled

Neurodevelopmental
Functions

areas. Parents and students may not know much about memory, for example, or how well it is functioning for a student. So while skills are on center stage, constructs and functions are backstage and out of sight.

Linkages

In separating skills and functions this way and viewing them in a sort of hierarchy, we make them relative terms. Some might argue that listening, speaking, and getting along with others are critical skills for school, for instance, even though they do not involve reading, writing, or math. Still, this hierarchy between skills and functions is a useful scaffolding for professionals who want to assess to understand (see Figure 4.2).

Being able to think in terms of both academic skills and neurodevelopmental functions is akin to being able to translate between two languages. Fluency comes when you can work smoothly in both directions. Similarly, a well-versed assessor can both task-analyze skills in terms of functions (see Figure 4.3) and describe a function in terms of the skills it supports (see

Figure 4.3   Linkages Between an Academic Skill and Neurodevelopmental Functions

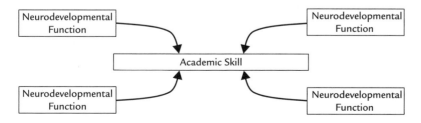

Neurodevelopmental
Function

Neurodevelopmental
Function

Academic Skill

Neurodevelopmental
Function

Neurodevelopmental
Function

Figure 4.4   Linkages Between a Neurodevelopmental Function and Academic Skills

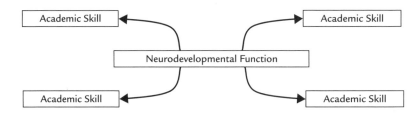

Figure 4.4). For example, in Chapter Three we task-analyzed long division and identified functions involved in this math subskill: attention production controls, long-term memory, graphomotor function, spatial ordering, temporal-sequential ordering, and higher-order cognition.

Translating in the reverse direction would involve taking a function or construct such as spatial ordering and identifying the skills that it undergirds (such as geometry and other math subskills, or aspects of science).

Note that linkages can apply across the range of grades and ages, helping to explain what may appear to be different problems. For example, difficulty with active working memory will usually show different symptoms in a third grader than in an eighth grader. Also, linkages can differ depending upon the subject area (for example, sequencing problems may affect math class in one way and language arts in quite another).

Why Linkages Matter

Linkages are an integral part of assessing to understand because they help explain why a student is adept at—or struggling with—an academic skill. Put differently, capacity with an academic skill can usually be explained in terms of a neurodevelopmental function or set of functions. For example, reading decoding can be undermined by weaknesses in any of several different neurodevelopmental functions, just as fever can result from several different causes. Pediatricians need to be well-versed in the common causes of fever so they can assess the possibilities through differential diagnosis. Making linkages is analogous to diagnosing the cause of a fever; knowing the cause then guides the treatment plan.

Figure 4.5   Reading Decoding Subskills and Neurodevelopmental Functions

Reading Decoding					
↑	↑	↑	↑	↑	↑
Subskills: Word Attack, Sight Word Recognition					
↑	↑	↑	↑	↑	↑
Attention	Memory	Language	Spatial Ordering	Temporal-Sequential Ordering	Cross-Construct Phenomena
Processing Production Controls	Short-Term; Active Working	Phonological Processing; Semantics	Visual Processing of Letter Patterns	Rapidly Processing Sequenced Information	Rate of Processing

Figure 4.5 includes the primary subskills for reading decoding, *word attack* and *sight word recognition,* along with the main neurodevelopmental functions involved in the development and performance of decoding. Each of the major academic skill areas (decoding, reading comprehension, spelling, written expression, math operations, and math reasoning) can be conceptualized this way. In addition, other aspects of schooling, such as organization and socialization, can be broken down into their component parts and associated functions.

Linkages matter for two main reasons. First, the explanation of a linkage is one of the critical components of demystification. Students (as well as parents and teachers) should know why they are struggling with an academic skill or an aspect of learning. Knowing why helps to overcome low self-esteem born of misplaced attributions. ("I don't get math because I'm stupid" gives the student nothing to work with, while "I don't get math easily because I'm not used to seeing patterns at a glance" is more optimistic and includes an explanation for the pattern-matching exercises the student is practicing.) Knowing why boosts buy-in to a learning plan since everyone involved can see the rationale for the strategies it includes.

Second, linkages guide treatment planning and the development of learning plans. Those who assess learning problems need to take the next step and help parents and teachers make decisions about instruction based on the student's unique learning profile. This elegantly simple point was drawn by

Stecker, Fuchs, and Fuchs (2005), who looked at the research on curriculum-based measurement and concluded that frequent and regular progress monitoring alone is not enough to improve achievement; teachers need to tailor instruction to student needs—and consultation helps teachers accomplish this. Put differently, students have individual characteristics that influence the degree of success they have with particular intervention programs (Lyon et al., 2001). Even when public schools use response to intervention as the mechanism for identifying students for special education and for determining their level of service (such as pull-in service in the regular classroom, pull-out service, self-contained special education classroom), it will still be important to use linkages to guide instructional decision making in those various settings.

> ☞ The assessment approach described in this book is compatible with *response to intervention,* a system that can identify many learning problems early and closely monitor student progress in some skill areas (such as decoding). Revealing why certain students are struggling, or are not responding to intervention, will be the critical role for this approach in terms of guiding instruction (Fiorello, Hale, & Snyder, 2006; Flanagan, Ortiz, Alfonso, & Dynda, 2006; Hale, Kaufman, Naglieri, & Kavale, 2006; Holdnack & Weiss, 2006; Willis & Dumont, 2006). Response to intervention can be viewed as a wide-lens telescope and individual assessment as a microscope (Mather & Kaufman, 2006).

To illustrate, let's revisit William and Ashelay, the thirteen-year-old eighth graders I described in Chapter One, who are struggling with writing for very different reasons. William's writing difficulty stems from weak expressive language, and he also has trouble communicating when speaking. In contrast, Ashelay is an effective oral communicator, but because of graphomotor dysfunction and some weak attention controls, she cannot get her ideas down on paper (see Table 4.1).

For William, the key is to improve his oral expression as well as his written expression. There are numerous ways to do this, but one strategy is to prompt him to elaborate even during casual conversation (that is, expand a one- or two-word reply into a complete sentence). It would help to engage him in conversation about something he likes a lot; at the outset some students have an easier time practicing elaboration when discussing their *affinities,* or areas

Table 4.1   Profiles for William and Ashelay, Eighth Graders Struggling with Writing

	William	Ashelay
Academic weakness	Written expression	Written expression
Neurodevelopmental assets	Spatial ordering, graphomotor function, fine motor function, temporal-sequential ordering, higher-order cognition, receptive language	Higher-order cognition, memory, expressive language
Neurodevelopmental weaknesses	Expressive language	Graphomotor function, attention—mental energy control system; self-monitoring
Learning plan approach	Focus on improving oral expression, such as by prompting him to expand his one-word responses to full sentences during conversation	Accommodations and interventions for weak graphomotor function and attention, such as learning keyboarding and staging her writing

of strong interest. For Ashelay, the key is to remove the barrier between her expressive language and her writing. Keyboarding is a logical accommodation for bypassing her graphomotor difficulty, and voice recognition software is another possibility. Emphasizing and segregating the stages of the writing process (brainstorm, outline, first draft, second draft, final edit) will help her maintain her mental energy (writing can be an exhausting task) and to self-monitor for mistakes.

Major Linkages Between Skill Deficits and Neurodevelopmental Functions

This section provides a sample of available research for the major linkages between neurodevelopmental constructs and academic skills. Complex as it is, it's just a taste of what's out there—a truly comprehensive review would be overwhelming to compile and to read. All I've done here is pull in a sample of the literature that supports linkages. Put differently, here are the usual suspects when it comes to neurodevelopmental breakdowns underlying

Table 4.2   Reading Decoding Linkages

Construct	Supporting literature
Attention	• Found evidence for a general attention deficit for visual stimuli related to reading problems (Heiervang & Hugdahl, 2003) • Attention problems can result in reading difficulty (Cohen, 1994)
Memory	• Verbal short-term memory is related to phonological decoding; phonological short-term memory plays a less important role in early reading skill than other functions, such as phonology and rapid automatic naming (Torgesen, 1996) • Poor immediate recall is a deficit commonly found in students with decoding problems (Riccio & Hynd, 1995) • Working memory demands are significant for decoding unfamiliar words (Fiorello, Hale, & Snyder, 2006) • Visual-verbal paired associate memory is predictive of reading skill above and beyond phonemic awareness and short-term memory (Windfuhr & Snowling, 2001) • Weak memory for sound-symbol associations was found in a group of weak readers (Gang & Siegel, 2002) • Strong relationships found between orthography and decoding, and working memory and decoding (McCallum et al., 2006) • Orthographic memory problems had a negative effect on reading (Badian, 2005) • Orthographic ability found to be an even better predictor of decoding than phonology (Holland, McIntosh, & Huffman, 2004)
Language	• Phonemic awareness is highly correlated with reading achievement (Snider, 1995) • Phonological awareness is a prerequisite for developing reading skill (Foorman, 1995) • Phoneme awareness is a correlate of reading skill (Joshi, 1995) • One of the deficits most commonly found in children with decoding problems is phonological insensitivity (Riccio & Hynd, 1995) • Measures of phonological awareness, rapid naming, and vocabulary separate good and poor readers (Fletcher et al., 1998) • Word reading was directly and significantly predicted by rapid letter naming and rapid object naming (Neuhaus & Swank, 2002)
Spatial ordering	• While decoding problems are primarily rooted in phonology, the ability to process rapid visual information is an additional factor and accounts for a significant portion of reading outcome variance (Eden, Stein, Wood, & Wood, 1995) • Reading, first and foremost, involves visual processing of letters (Foorman, 1995) • Visuo-perceptual system dysfunction (logographic or simultaneous processing) leads to decoding problems, often an overreliance on phonology (Riccio & Hynd, 1995)

Table 4.2   Reading Decoding Linkages (*Continued*)

Construct	Supporting literature
Temporal-sequential ordering	• Processing and retaining rapidly sequenced bits of information is important in learning to read; students with reading disabilities had difficulty processing both verbal and nonverbal rapidly presented material (Boden & Brodeur, 1999)
Cross-construct phenomena	• Rapidly processing and retaining sequenced bits of information is vital in learning to read; students with reading disabilities demonstrated difficulty processing both verbal and nonverbal information that was presented rapidly (Boden & Brodeur, 1999) • While decoding problems are primarily rooted in phonology, the ability to process rapid visual information is an additional factor and accounts for a significant portion of reading outcome variance (Eden et al., 1995) • Slow speed on continuous or discrete naming tasks is commonly found in students with decoding problems (Riccio & Hynd, 1995)

academic difficulty. Some sources explore more than one construct or skill, so citations may appear in multiple places.

Reading has two major components: the ability to pronounce the written word (either aloud or in the mind) and the ability to understand the meaning of words and text (Joshi, 1995). The former is known as *reading decoding* (or *decoding*) and the latter is referred to as *reading comprehension.*

☞ Two parallel literacy components can be described as *inside-out* (code based on phonology and letter-sound connections) and *outside-in* (aspects of oral language such as semantics, conceptual knowledge, and understanding of narrative) (Whitehurst & Lonigan, 1998). Obviously, early literacy instruction emphasizes inside-out (Storch & Whitehurst, 2002).

Reading decoding involves phonics (the system of sound-symbol associations) and sight word recognition (recognizing words, especially short and high-use words such as *the,* based on their visual configurations). Decoding is typically assessed by having the student read words aloud, in isolation or in context. Table 4.2 lists support for linkages related to decoding.

Reading comprehension requires an understanding of what printed words mean, either alone or a part of an extended piece of text. Reading

Table 4.3   Reading Comprehension Linkages

Construct	Supporting Literature
Attention	• Attention deficits have implications for some reading problems; for example, teachers may observe difficulties in comprehension only when the passage is long, or the student may have a strong vocabulary but weak comprehension—since vocabulary does not involve sustained attention (Zentall, 1993) • Attention problems can result in reading difficulty (Cohen, 1994) • Successful readers monitor their comprehension while reading and make immediate decisions about what is important in text (Keene & Zimmermann, 1997) • Students with a planning weakness substantially improved their reading comprehension after instruction designed to develop planning (Haddad et al., 2003)
Memory	• Students with small active working memories extract less precise new word meanings from context; drawing inferences depends on the reader's ability to integrate successively encountered contextual cues, a process made harder when earlier cues are no longer accessible to working memory (Daneman & Green, 1986) • Students with reading problems appear to have an active working memory deficit that affects memory for words (Siegal & Ryan, 1989) • Performance on reading tasks requires working memory (Swanson, Cochran, & Ewers, 1990)
Language	• Most students with language comprehension problems also have difficulty with reading comprehension (Johnson, 1993) • Skilled reading requires comprehension, a higher level of information processing that includes listening comprehension and vocabulary (Aaron, 1995) • Unitary view of comprehension holds that the same processing takes place when both reading and listening; a general comprehension problem is suggested when both reading and listening comprehension are significantly below grade-level expectations, possibly due to problems in linguistic development (Carlisle, 1991) • Except for differences in modality, reading comprehension and listening comprehension stem from the same cognitive process; vocabulary is an important correlate of comprehension and one of the best predictors of reading ability (Joshi, 1995)
Spatial ordering	• A strategy for reading is to create visual images from text (Keene & Zimmermann, 1997)
Higher-order cognition	• Teaching techniques that employed concept mapping significantly improved reading comprehension of low-achieving seventh graders (Guastello, Beasley, & Sinatra, 2000)

Table 4.3 Reading Comprehension Linkages (*Continued*)

Construct	Supporting Literature
	• *Conceptual understanding of text structures was reinforced via story-mapping with students with reading problems, resulting in an improvement in the number of story elements included in students' recall of stories (Vallecorsa & DeBettencourt, 1997)* • *Research has shown that overt identification of concepts along with the deliberate use of graphic organizers reduce reading comprehension demands placed on struggling students (McCoy & Ketterlin-Geller, 2004)*
Cross-construct phenomena	• *Metacognition is a component of reading comprehension (Joshi, 1995)* • *Proficient readers think about their thinking while reading (Keene & Zimmermann, 1997)*

comprehension is assessed by probing the student's understanding of the text (for example, via comprehension questions or asking the student to summarize), as well as by considering reports from school and home. See Chapter Ten for further discussion of reading assessment; Table 4.3 lists linkages for reading comprehension.

Spelling (see Table 4.4) is a multifaceted skill that is not a literal phonetic transcription of speech. Instead, it includes a large number of exceptions in terms of rules and phonology (Moats, 1994a).

Writing is a problem-solving process in which authors reflect their declarative knowledge in written form (Hooper et al., 1994). See Chapter Ten for further discussion of writing assessment; Table 4.5 lists linkages for writing.

Table 4.4 Spelling Linkages

Construct	Supporting Literature
Attention	• *38 percent of students with attention deficits also have spelling disabilities (Zentall, 1993)*
Memory	• *Performance on spelling tasks requires working memory (Swanson et al., 1990)* • *Orthographic memory and memory for sound-symbol relationships are needed for spelling (Moats, 1994a)* • *Auditory memory found to be predictive of spelling skill (McCallum et al., 2006)*
Language	• *Phonology is a prerequisite for spelling (Foorman, 1995)* • *When assessing spelling skills, distinguish between awareness of phonemes (analyzing and isolating sound units in words) and discrimination of phonemes (determining whether two phonemes sound alike) (Joshi, 1995)* • *Spelling requires phonology, morphology, and semantics (Moats, 1994a)*

Table 4.5 Written Expression Linkages

Construct	Supporting Literature
Attention	• Planning is an important phase in writing and weak writers tend to generate disorganized text; good writers make revisions to their work, whereas weak writers do not (Hooper et al., 1994) • Performance on planning tasks is related to written composition quality (Johnson, Bardos, & Tayebi, 2003)
Memory	• Producing words in context (as for sentence production) reflects differences in active working memory capacity (Daneman & Green, 1986) • Declarative and procedural memory are used in writing (Hooper et al., 1994)
Language	• Oral and written language are related; students generally do not write more complex grammatical constructions than they use orally (Johnson, 1993) • Written language difficulty could be a language issue (Waber & Bernstein, 1994) • Semantic and syntactic processes are involved in writing (Hooper et al., 1994)
Temporal-sequential ordering	• Correct minus incorrect word sequences was the most reliable and valid predictor of student writing proficiency, as measured by teacher ratings and a district writing test (Espin, Shin, & Deno, 2000) • Instruction that included coaching on sequencing ideas led to improved schematic structure of stories and longer papers for students with writing difficulty; improvements generalized to persuasive essay writing and were generally maintained over time (Troia, Graham, & Harris, 1999)
Neuromotor function	• Writing difficulty for students with weak attention may be due to fundamental problems in graphomotor control in conjunction with or independent from the organizational and language demands of writing (Marcotte & Stern, 1997) • Written language difficulty could be a motor issue regarding inefficiency of output (Waber & Bernstein, 1994) • The motoric or muscular process is involved in writing (Hooper et al., 1994)
Higher-order cognition	• Conceptual understanding of text structures was reinforced via story-mapping with students with writing difficulty, resulting in improved writing performance (Vallecorsa & DeBettencourt, 1997) • Writers need to understand how to adapt to different audiences (Hooper et al., 1994)
Social cognition	• Audience awareness is an important component of writing; techniques such as assigning storytelling from different perspectives and role-switching activities can enhance social cognition among writers (McAlexander, 1996) • Several characteristics differentiated a successful collaborate writing group (ninth graders) from the other two groups, including engagement during the writing process, level of cognitive conflict, and kinds of social interactions; successful coauthors used authentic conversation about emerging text and felt comfortable enough with each other to engage in productive cognitive conflict (Dale, 1994)
Cross-construct phenomena	• Strategy use is a component of written comprehension (Hooper et al., 1994)

Math operations constitute the basic framework of math and include computations, facts, and relatively rote skills and axioms. *Math reasoning* refers to the thinking and conceptualization that are especially important for sophisticated math work; it requires use of knowledge of operations and axioms, quantitative concepts, and numerical relationships (Proctor, Floyd, & Shaver, 2005). Math operations rely more on constructs such as memory and attention, whereas math reasoning relies more on higher-order cognition for the understanding of math. Much of the research on neurodevelopmental functions involved in math performance has not cleanly differentiated between operations and reasoning; hence, Table 4.6 represents a sample of the literature related to general math linkages.

To this point I have focused on some general principles involved with a neurodevelopmental assessment approach, including how to conceptualize and categorize phenomena, task-analyze skills and assessment methods, and understand the relationship between a neurodevelopmental profile and academic performance. In the next chapter I begin to concentrate on the assessment process itself, starting with the importance of gathering a wide spectrum of data.

Table 4.6   Math Operations and Reasoning Linkages

Construct	Supporting Literature
Attention	• Students with an inattentive type of attention deficit showed greater incidence of math calculation errors than students with the hyperactive type of attention deficit (Marshall, Hynd, Handwerk, & Hall, 1997) • Planning and self-monitoring are necessary for mathematics (Hale, Fiorello, Bertin, & Sherman, 2003)
Memory	• Students who find math difficult show a specific working-memory deficit for tasks involving counting and numbers (Siegal & Ryan, 1989) • Performance on mathematics tasks requires working memory (Swanson et al., 1990) • One of the main differences between high- and low-ability math groups was speed of identifying numbers, which are representations retrieved from long-term memory; a high-ability math group used direct memory retrieval of math facts significantly more frequently than a low-ability math group (Bull & Johnson, 1997)

(continued)

Table 4.6   Math Operations and Reasoning Linkages (*Continued*)

Construct	Supporting Literature
	• *Long-term memory is needed for math, including storage and retrieval of math facts and paired associations (Hale et al., 2003)*
	• *General math achievement has been linked to the CHC broad cognitive ability clusters of comprehension-knowledge and short-term memory (Proctor, Floyd, & Shaver, 2005)*
Language	• *One type of developmental dyscalculia is verbal, or a disruption in the ability to name math terms and relations (Kosc, 1974)*
Spatial ordering	• *Math research has identified one type of acalculia as spatial (Rourke & Conway, 1997)*
	• *Impairment of the ability to read math symbols represents a subtype of dyscalculia; difficulty manipulating real or pictured objects for math purposes is another subtype (Kosc, 1974)*
	• *Math difficulties were frequently noted in students with weak visual-spatial function, presumably due to difficulty with spatial relations (for example, place value, tracking) (Gross-Tsur, Shalev, Manor, & Amir, 1995)*
	• *Visual-perceptual processes are needed for math, such as column alignment, place value, and attention to visual details (Hale et al., 2003)*
Temporal-sequential ordering	• *Sequencing ability was an area in which a low-ability math group showed weak performance, relative to a high-ability math group (Bull & Johnson, 1997)*
Neuromotor function	• *A subtype of dyscalculia is graphical, or difficulty with writing numbers and operational symbols (Kosc, 1974)*
Higher-order cognition	• *Math reasoning is just one dimension of the more general concept formation and problem solving needed for learning (Rourke & Conway, 1997)*
	• *A subtype of dyscalculia involves impairment of the ability to understand math ideas and relations required for mental calculation (Kosc, 1974)*
	• *General math achievement, especially math reasoning, has been linked to the CHC broad cognitive ability cluster of fluid reasoning (Proctor, Floyd, & Shaver, 2005)*
Cross-construct phenomena	• *Speed of processing is a major factor in explaining math difficulties (Bull & Johnson, 1997)*
	• *General math achievement has been linked to the CHC broad cognitive ability cluster of processing speed (Proctor, Floyd, & Shaver, 2005)*

5

Assessing from Multiple Angles

IMAGINE BEING IN A JOB REVIEW, listening to your supervisor judging your performance over the past fiscal year on the basis of a single piece of information. Of course, this would not be a valid way of evaluating your work, and it certainly would not be fair. You'd be unhappy if your supervisor didn't mention several pieces of information; even if the review was favorable, too narrow a base would probably be worrisome.

Assessment should likewise include a spectrum of information, a balanced portfolio of findings that are cross-indexed and integrated. Individual pieces of evidence that are inconsistent with other information should be thoroughly questioned. To really understand the student you need to consider a variety of things: test-derived sources of data, historical information, presenting problems (also known as *referral concerns and questions*), observations, interview results, and information from other sources to tease out the competing possibilities (Meyer et al., 2001). Figure 5.1 displays the primary components of assessment, including testing and other techniques.

Assessment and Testing

Assessment is not the same thing as testing. As should be evident at this point in the book, *assessment* is the process of collecting and interpreting a broad range of data for the purpose of understanding the student's learning profile. *Testing*, on the other hand, is the use of an instrument (often standardized) for collecting data, and is one potential aspect of assessment. Testing usually involves structured clinician-student interactions and standardized procedures and materials. Test items often are analogs of tasks students face in real life (such as reading, listening, memorizing). However, many test tasks

Figure 5.1   Primary Components of an Assessment

Assessment				
↑	↑	↑	↑	↑
Testing	History Gathering	Interviewing	Observation	Student Work Pattern Analysis
↑	↑		↑	
Standardized, Quantitative	Past		Product	
Dynamic, Qualitative	Current		Process	

seem quite dissimilar to academic work, as is the case with many neurodevelopmental tasks (see Chapter Four).

The assessment-testing distinction was made by Gregory Meyer and his colleagues (2001), regarding psychological testing and psychological assessment, in particular. This group defined psychological testing as having a narrow objective of obtaining a specific score by administering a particular scale. Psychological assessment, by contrast, involves taking a variety of test scores—usually obtained by multiple methods—and considering the data in the context of history, referral information, and observed behavior to understand the patient, to answer the referral questions, and then to communicate findings to the patient and family.

Multi-Method Assessment

Though not every neurodevelopmental function can be tested, all can be assessed. The process of assessment, for many functions, must rely on qualitative techniques such as parent reports and observation. In addition, no single instrument can assess the breadth of neurodevelopmental functions, and there isn't even a single battery that can do it. Therefore, a multi-method approach is usually necessary. *Multi-method assessment* refers to incorporating elements (for example, subtests) from various tests and batteries into a customized battery for a student. The customization would stem from the referral concerns and history. For instance, if the student is struggling with reading decoding, then the battery would probably need to include measures of phonological processing. (Customization from history is discussed further later in this chapter.) Considering the spectrum of neurodevelopmental functions that might need to be assessed across various age ranges, it would be rare to use the same battery with two different students with a multi-method approach.

A *fixed battery* is a much different approach to test selection. It involves a consistent set of procedures used for every student (perhaps differentiated by age or grade level), regardless of the referral question. Fixed batteries, in their pure form, are not customized for the student or targeted on areas to explore. Though a fixed battery may seem rigid and impractical, it actually has several virtues. First, using the same procedures on a consistent basis allows the professional to garner more experience with those procedures, facilitating the development of personal norms (for example, knowing how students typically approach tasks from a qualitative perspective). Second, having a regular battery usually results in a comprehensive appraisal of the student's profile, or casting a wide net; assessing with a fixed battery may not yield depth in particular areas in question, but may yield breadth (see Table 5.1).

It is actually possible to combine customized and fixed batteries and take advantage of the benefits of each type. For general age or grade ranges (say, early elementary, late elementary, middle school, high school), you can have a small set of tasks that constitute the core of every battery. Beyond that core,

Table 5.1 Pros and Cons of Multi-Method, Customized Batteries and Fixed Batteries

Multi-Method and Customized Batteries		Fixed Batteries	
Pros	Cons	Pros	Cons
• Customized for student needs	• May not yield sufficient breadth	• Can provide more breadth	• Not customized for student needs
• Can provide more depth in target areas	• Hinder development of personal norms	• Facilitate development of personal norms	• May not yield sufficient depth in target areas
	• Require time to plan assessment	• Efficient for assessment planning	
	• Require experience to learn how to use	• May be easier to learn	

customize according to what needs to be assessed. This combined approach to battery building enables development of personal norms through extensive experience with certain tasks. Such experience can pay dividends in terms of being able to readily identify typical and atypical approaches to tasks, develop useful interview questions (see next section), and have "limit testing" techniques at the ready (see section later in this chapter). At the same time, the combined approach allows for considerable customization of the battery, considering referral questions and the student's history.

Qualitative and Quantitative Findings

Qualitative and quantitative assessment both serve a purpose in an assessment, and each has its own set of advantages and disadvantages.

One defining feature of a qualitative finding is that it is not a numerical score. Rather, qualitative data describe observations made about phenomena and student behavior. They can focus on either process or product. *Process observations* involve how the student arrived at a response or completed a task (for example, work rate, planning, use of strategies, self-monitoring, enthusiasm for tasks). *Product observations* appraise features of the student's response or output (such as accuracy, types and patterns of errors, organization of work).

Watch out for the temptation to focus on test administration at the expense of making process observations and spending time talking with each student. Observations of behavior and nuances of how a student approaches a task help you read between the lines and develop a real understanding. Similarly, you can gain a great deal of insight by simply asking students about their learning. Interview questions obviously need to be gauged developmentally, but even very young students can provide revealing answers.

Many opportunities for interview questions arise spontaneously, in response to what the student is doing in the moment. During math work, for instance, a student can be asked questions about incorrectly solved problems. (For example, you can ask, "How did you get your answer?" or "Is this answer right?" "Why is it wrong?" "Where is the mistake?" "Is there a better way to solve it?") However, it can also be useful to have a list of questions to ask in certain situations. For example, Vaughn and Wilson (1994) described how math interviews can be used to determine how students solve problems.

They suggested that three variables should be considered when interviewing about math problems. First, delve into the student's experience with discriminating problem types by asking questions like these: "Have you seen this kind of problem before?" "How is this kind of problem different from this other type?" Second, appraise the student's understanding of math terminology: "When you see 'of' in a word problem, what are you supposed to do?" "What is a hypotenuse?" Third, explore how well the student can use differing examples to demonstrate understanding of concepts: "Tell me how you'd find the perimeter of this table, that window, and this room." "What are some situations when a bar graph would be useful?" Appendix C includes some example student responses that can be gained via interview questions, as well as how these findings relate to neurodevelopmental constructs and functions.

Product observations often take the form of student work pattern analysis. This involves analyzing student work output to explore the thought processes that went into solving the problem, including how the answers developed (Vaughn & Wilson, 1994). The idea is to look for specific phenomena, observations that inform functioning or skill level. Certain academic subjects lend themselves much better to pattern analysis than others. Math, writing, and spelling are well-suited to pattern analysis because they yield a tangible product that can be reviewed. Reading, on the other hand, generally does not result in a product, meaning that you have to rely on process observations instead.

To make sense of qualitative findings, you need to develop your own *personal norms*, that is, your experience with the task and your cumulative expectations for typical student performance, as well as for the kinds of questions to ask during interviews. In general, academic tasks are well-suited for qualitative data because grade-level standards can make it easier to shape personal norms. For example, seventh graders' math skills can be compared against grade-level standards (for a school, district, state, or nation) to judge where they stand next to those of other seventh graders.

Personal norms are an important aspect of assessment with neurodevelopmental tasks, as well. For example, in Chapter Three I described the complex form copy task, akin to the Rey Complex Figure and Recognition Trial (Meyers & Meyers, 1996). Though such a task is often accompanied by a structured system for scoring, including norms for rating performance level, personal norms are very important when using such a task. Once you've administered numerous complex form copies, you are in a position to judge whether the student's approach to the copy (say, working left to right, top to bottom, inside-out, or large structure then details) is typical or atypical. Scoring systems and norms, though important and useful, cannot capture all the nuances related to how students work. In short, personal norms help to fill in the gaps.

Quantitative findings provide a different perspective on students. Quantitative assessment data are often normative, meaning that the developers of the test administered the task to numerous students (usually at different ages and grade levels) to generate means, standard deviations (an indicator of how much scores vary from the mean), and *standard scores*. Probably the best-known example of a quantitative finding is an IQ score, which, for most intelligence tests, has a mean of 100 and a standard deviation of 15. Norms facilitate comparisons with same-age peers. If a student earns an IQ score of 105, that basically indicates that compared to other students of the same age, this one scored a bit higher than the average.

> ☞   A *standard score* is a comparison between a student's ability level in a defined area or skill with that of other students of a similar age. Standard scores enable developmental judgments about performance levels.

Normative information is particularly helpful for assessing performance on neurodevelopmental tasks for which personal norms are difficult to develop. Whereas academic tasks can be anchored by grade-level expectations, tasks like recalling series of orally presented numbers are hard to judge without comparing performance to same-age peers. A standard score, in essence, is a comparison between the student's performance on a task and that of same-age peers.

It should be clear that both qualitative and quantitative data are important for assessing to understand. One type of data is not inherently better than the other, and one does not trump the other. However, each serves a different purpose in an assessment, with quantitative findings used more to compare a student's performance to same-age peers (especially on neurodevelopmental tasks) and qualitative findings providing critical insight into the student's work process. So these data types should not be viewed as being in opposition, but rather should be used in conjunction with each other. Using a

Table 5.2   Qualitative and Quantitative Findings

Qualitative Findings		Quantitative Findings	
Pros	Cons	Pros	Cons
• Elucidate subtle aspects of student learning • Can emerge spontaneously	• Comparisons with same-age peers more difficult • Require experience to identify and interpret	• Anchor comparisons with same-age peers • Usually easier to learn how to interpret	• May not reveal subtle aspects of student learning • Usually emerge from structured testing

mix of information helps to avoid the mistake of being bound by, or overrelying upon, any single piece of data, such as a test score; no clinical question can be answered solely by a test score (Meyer et al., 2001). Combining, comparing, and cross-indexing findings facilitate really grasping a student's learning profile. Table 5.2 summarizes some of the pros and cons for both kinds of assessment findings.

The idea of a balanced portfolio of assessment information may seem obvious. However, the learning disabilities field has an unfortunate history of overreliance on test data. Though most medical and mental disorders are diagnosed using a spectrum of data, qualitative and quantitative, for years most learning problems have been assessed by the numbers (see Chapter Six for a discussion of the ability-achievement discrepancy), an approach that made diagnosis ultimately about subtraction (IQ minus standard achievement score). Public law and regulations facilitated a testing mind-set and a gate-keeping mentality regarding eligibility for special education services for students with learning problems. This led to an erosion of confidence in the professional judgment of clinicians such as school psychologists, who had to show numerically that a student had a learning disability rather than make a case using a portfolio of assessment findings. Further, relatively few clinicians had the training and experience in the art of assessment to go further than merely testing, so they wound up using testing so much that it has become synonymous with assessment. Fortunately, the field (and federal law) is shifting toward an approach that looks more closely at the student's learning needs.

Dynamic, flexible assessment procedures generally yield qualitative information. Quantitative findings generally come from standardized procedures ("psychometric measures") and yield standard scores. The next section provides more depth about dynamic and standardized techniques, including the benefits of each for assessment.

Dynamic and Standardized Techniques

Assessments should combine dynamic and standardized assessment. Dynamic, flexible procedures make it easier to elicit the best possible performance and search for effective management strategies. After all, one of the prime objectives of an assessment should be developing a learning plan. Standardized procedures permit reliable comparisons of task performance with skill levels of same-age peers.

Normed or *standard* scores can be useful as measurements of phenomena, but not as measurements of students. In essence, a standard score is a comparison; it allows one to compare how a student's ability level in a defined area or skill compares to that of other students of a similar age (Meyer et al., 2001). Hence, standard scores enable developmental judgments about a student's performance level in specific areas. One might argue that standard scores would not be needed for a given test if the clinician has sufficient experience with that test to judge the student's performance level against same-age peers. Given the complexity of most psycho-educational measures, as well as the significant developmental changes that occur in students, this "internal norming" is seldom feasible. Hence, standard scores can be quite useful in determining level of performance, as long as they are considered along with the qualitative data that are available.

☞ "Although psychological tests can assist clinicians with case formulation and treatment conditions, they are only tools. Tests do not think for themselves, nor do they directly communicate with patients. Like a stethoscope, a blood pressure gauge, or an MRI scan, a psychological test is a dumb tool, and the worth of the tool cannot be separated from the sophistication of the clinician who draws inferences from it and then communicates with patients and other professionals" (Meyer et al., 2001, p. 153).

On the other hand, interactive methods incorporate teaching into the assessment process in a deliberate and strategic effort to produce improvement in the student's performance (Moats, 1994b). The overarching goal is to learn as much as possible about each student's skills in order to inform an appropriate instructional plan. *Dynamic assessment* is the most commonly used term to describe such an approach.

Lidz (1991, 1995) delineated several critical features of dynamic assessment:

- *Interactive nature:* The clinician actually functions as an assessment tool.
- *Test-intervene-test format:* The clinician assesses a skill, provides necessary support to the student, and then retests to determine whether the student incorporated the teaching.
- *Focus on learner change:* The clinician observes the student's response to supports and implementation of metacognitive processes (for example, thinking aloud).
- *Goal:* The clinician works to derive information for the development of interventions.
- *Emphasis:* The clinician focuses on cognitive functions and processes (such as attention and strategy use).

More than anything, dynamic assessment represents an attitude or a way of thinking about assessing students (Lidz, 1995). With dynamic assessment, the clinician acts more like an interactive guide, mediating tasks as a teacher and coaching the student on problem-solving strategies. Rather than focusing on the outcome, the emphasis is on the learning process and the strategies used by the student (Vaughn & Wilson, 1994). Consequently, a dynamic assessment can look and feel very much like a tutoring session, and the clinician like a teacher.

Dynamic assessment puts a premium on the how. How does the student approach a task? Use strategies? Think about this problem? How does the student write, spell, read, memorize, or solve math problems? Not only is this focus critical for generating a learning plan, it also helps everyone avoid getting bogged down in the why. Such why questions ask about the root causes of a learning breakdown. Why does Jay have weak memory? Why does Lee have a language difficulty? Such questions of etiology are seldom useful to a professional, who needs to focus on the student in the present. The current profile is what it is, and the student needs to be addressed through a learning plan based on that profile. These kinds of why questions are critical for research and ultimately for prevention programs. But for most assessments, probing into etiology is not helpful and may even be detrimental in terms of leading parents to blame themselves for factors long since passed (such as infant health, day care, language exposure during early childhood), and subtly conveying to the student that the damage has been done and there's little hope for improvement now.

Limit Testing

One interactive assessment technique is *limit testing*, which can be described as stretching the way a testing instrument or procedure is administered to learn as much as possible about a student's neurodevelopmental functions and academic skills. Limit testing requires expanding on the usual demands of a task to test hypotheses about functions and skills. Often testing the limits is necessary to go beyond information gleaned from a standard score for a test or subtest.

One type of limit testing is interviewing the student following the task. Was the vocabulary in the test questions familiar? What strategy was the student trying to use? Did the geometric objects to be copied look like anything in the real world? Which items were difficult or easy, and why?

More often, limit testing involves appending additional procedures to a task in an effort to test hypotheses. For instance, open-ended test questions could be followed with multiple-choice versions to contrast recall and recognition memory. Task instructions might be reworded to explore whether receptive language accounted for an error. Paper and pencil can be provided after a purely oral task (such as mental math) to factor out active working memory demands. Put differently, limit testing is about creating varying conditions under which the student works so you can explore hypotheses. How to interpret contrasts in a student's performance under different task conditions is the topic of Chapter Six.

To test limits effectively, you need a thorough understanding of the assessment task, including the possible neurodevelopmental functions that undergird performance on it; this is another reason that task-analysis is such an important skill (see Chapter Three). It takes flexible thinking and creativity to create new ways to test hypotheses; the same task could conceivably be used dozens of different ways depending on the student and the hypotheses that need to be explored.

Limit testing can be done in such a way as to protect normative scores, especially if done after standardized procedures are completed. For example, at the completion of a standardized subtest, a couple of items could be explored through changing the task demands, such as turning an open-ended question into a multiple-choice format. The accuracy of the student's original responses would not need to be revealed, and original responses could be retained for scoring purposes. However, important additional information could be gained through the limit testing.

What History Can Reveal

Much of contemporary developmental psychology is the science of the strange behavior of children in strange situations with strange adults for the briefest possible periods of time.

—Urie Bronfenbrenner (1977, p. 33)

Assessments should incorporate both past history and current history, two oddly phrased terms that warrant clarification. *Past history* (a tautology) refers to student information that is relatively dated, though still potentially relevant. When assessing learning problems, an arbitrary cut point for past history is the beginning of the current or most recent (in the case of summertime) academic year. So reports from parents and teachers from preceding years, including early childhood and infancy, would be considered past history. On the other hand, *current history* (an oxymoron) refers to information that is relatively current (that is, from the current or most recent academic year). History can be gathered in a variety of ways, including through checklists designed for such a purpose, reviewing student records, or interviewing. Appendix C includes historical information connected to neurodevelopmental constructs and functions that is typically useful when assessing learning problems.

History brings into the assessment the perspectives of those who know the student best. Research has shown that history reports can be reliable sources of information. Faraone, Biederman, and Milberger (1995) found that diagnoses drawn from mothers' descriptions of psychopathology in their children were accurate and reliable for a variety of mental health problems including attention-deficit/hyperactivity disorder (ADHD), major depression, bipolar disorder, separation anxiety disorder, and other anxiety disorders.

Past history related to prenatal conditions, infancy, and early childhood needs to be used judiciously because it may not be particularly relevant to the student's learning plan and, as mentioned earlier, can be very troubling and guilt-inducing to parents if they come to think that their years-old decisions have led to their child's current learning problems. Primary causal factors include prematurity, poor nutrition in early childhood, head injury, genetics, environmental and educational shortcomings, and ear infections. Such factors need to be elucidated through research and targeted in prevention efforts (such as public health and early intervention), but can be distracting and potentially detrimental to working relationships with parents if they shed no light on what should be done to help the individual student now. A tenet of this book is that assessment should reveal the underlying causes of a learning problem, but the causes to focus on should be neurodevelopmental functions and other factors that describe the student's current learning abilities; these are what help you understand the student, form the foundation for demystification, and drive the generation of the learning plan.

☞ Doctors have an expression that goes, "Treat the patient in front of you." This sentiment also applies to assessing learning problems. It's best to focus your history-gathering efforts on factors relevant to the student's current status and learning plan, and to avoid pondering primary causes.

History helps reveal what students can do in their usual learning and working environment. Testing situations are inherently artificial and tests are, even in their best form, merely imperfect analogues of real-life tasks. Data from testing must be cross-indexed with descriptions from parents, teachers, and others who might know the student. Comparing test results with history helps validate what was observed in a clinical situation. When discrepancies emerge, they may not invalidate certain findings so much as illuminate factors that could be important to consider. For example, a parent may describe a student's oral expression as being appropriate or strong, whereas a teacher may report oral language difficulty. Both can be true, because students have to generate qualitatively different language in the classroom than they do in family or social settings. This makes sense because academic or literate language is more detail-laden and sophisticated, whereas social language is more lingo-driven and free-form.

As mentioned earlier in this chapter, an important use of history relates to targeting and customizing batteries. Every student has a unique profile, so it follows that each student should participate in a unique assessment (even if, as discussed previously, the battery contains a fixed core of procedures for the student's age or grade). More to the point, each student has unique referral concerns that need to be explored, such as "Why is writing so difficult?" or "How come getting organized is so much trouble?" History helps you decide where to start with forming a battery. For example, a student with a history of writing problems probably warrants a range of assessment methods to get at areas such as expressive language, the production control system (attention), active working memory, and graphomotor function. Further, history can help focus a battery. Taking the current example, if history suggests that the student met early developmental language milestones appropriately (such as saying the first word between twelve and eighteen months, and forming two- or three-word sentences and having a fifty-word vocabulary around twenty-four months) and is currently reasonably comfortable with oral expression (participation in classroom discussions), then expressive language is less likely to be the culprit and more time could be devoted to other potential weaknesses. The case study that follows shows how history can direct and focus a battery.

CASE STUDY

Sam is a ten-year-old who is about to enter the fifth grade, the last year in elementary school for him. His parents and teachers have been concerned about his *reading comprehension*, which seems to be lagging behind that of his peers. Everyone wants to get him help before he gets to middle school, when his reading assignments will be lengthier and more complex. He seems to decode well when reading words in isolation, and his written work is grade-appropriate (though he has not had to compose very long or complex reports yet). He also has very good math skills. His teacher notes that his attention seems to wane during class discussions, though he is very engaged in small group work.

Based on the referral concerns and history, it seems important to explore Sam's language. His receptive language could definitely be behind his reading comprehension issues, and might also account for the way his attention fades when he has to listen. In addition, his expressive language might also have weaknesses that have not yet been revealed in the basic written work of elementary school. Because he can decode, his phonological processing and automaticity are likely intact, and his good math suggests strengths in higher-order cognition and aspects of long-term memory; testing in these areas is less of a priority than getting a handle on his overall language. Finally, his attention should be appraised, probably through asking more questions of his parents and teachers (and Sam himself), as well as with observation during academic work and tasks designed to tap attention (see Chapter Eight for examples).

An important point of this chapter is that a battery should include a balance of techniques, both dynamic and standardized. Striking a good balance and making effective choices about components of a battery all depend on professional judgment. As the case study of Sam illustrates, thinking with a theory is critical to the process. In other words, think first about what is to be assessed (say, receptive language) and then think about how it is to be assessed (for example, with listening comprehension tasks). Once the findings are gathered from the testing, they should be interpreted along with the history in an effort to view the student from multiple angles. So history is a starting point for developing a battery and then is interpreted alongside the data gleaned from the battery.

Assets and Affinities

An important objective of assessment is determining the causes of a learning breakdown—to both demystify the student and customize the learning plan. It is extremely easy, though, for that objective to overwhelm another, equally important assessment objective: highlighting and revealing assets and affinities. To be sure, uncovering the reasons for a student's learning problems is critical. But understanding the student has to involve a careful look at what is going well and what topics are passionate interests.

☞ To review, *assets* are aspects of learning, brain functions, or skills that are operating appropriately or very well. *Affinities* are areas of high interest (sometimes passionate interest), and could be topics or activities. Ideally, *assets* are also *affinities* (that is, the students tend to be good at things they enjoy, and vice versa), but this is not always the case.

For many students with learning problems, the focus has been on their deficiencies and their struggles. Every student has assets, even if they show up only in comparison to weak areas or fall beyond the neurodevelopmental framework (or whatever theory is being used by the professional). Assets can include character traits such as curiosity, perseverance, self-reliance, motivation, the ability to adapt to different situations, empathy, supportiveness, and willingness to accept help or constructive criticism. Students may have strengths in nonacademic areas like cooking, drama, music, sports, child care, mechanics, electronics, carpentry, and computers.

Risk and resilience theories posit that assets can be critical protective factors for students who are suffering from the frustration, disappointment, and loss of self-esteem that so often accompany learning problems. Many, if not most, students with learning problems have never had their assets revealed or their affinities affirmed as important and unique. So illuminating assets and affinities is crucial for the demystification process and for helping the student feel more optimistic and empowered. Further, assets and affinities are vital components of a learning plan and can be used in two distinct ways. First, they should be nurtured and strengthened through specific tactics and activities. (For example, a student who is skilled at working with younger students could become a camp counselor.) Second, they can be drawn upon to bolster weak areas. (For example, a student with solid language but weak math could be coached to use language to think through math problems.)

Revealing assets and affinities often requires imagination from the clinician or educator. A student's strengths may not be readily apparent, but looking closely and engaging in lateral thinking will always reveal something positive. Additionally, using assets and affinities usually involves creativity in terms of generating ways to nurture and strengthen these areas and taking advantage of them to address weak functions and skills.

The Case for Teamwork

Great discoveries and improvements invariably involve the cooperation of many minds.

—Alexander Graham Bell

It is possible for a single professional to conduct an assessment of a student's learning. In fact, the single-professional model does have certain advantages. Working alone broadens your perspective on the student, since you're administering all the tasks (neurodevelopmental and academic) and thus have a good chance of seeing subtle connections in the student's performance across tasks. Also, the single-professional model can be efficient, as you need not build time into the assessment schedule for a team meeting, and writing a report is far simpler with one author than with a committee.

Despite the advantages of the single-professional model, I strongly favor a team assessment model for several reasons. I believe that having more than one person work with the student provides important insights, particularly when it comes to interpreting findings and generating the student's learning profile. Teamwork provides multiple sets of eyes for viewing and then understanding how the student learns.

The team configuration that has worked well in my experience includes a learning specialist assessing the student's academic skills while hypothesizing about neurodevelopmental functions, and another clinician (or pair of clinicians) assessing functions while hypothesizing about skills. Figure 5.2 shows how the learning specialist operates more on the surface (assessing academics, which are more visible to the student and others) but thinks downward to functions, and the focus of the rest of the team is below the surface—thinking about functions and extending the resulting insight upward to skills. The real collaboration comes in connecting the hypotheses, linking skills with functions. Communication within the team is obviously a crucial element for understanding the student. Also, clinicians working on a particular level of

Figure 5.2   Team Approach to Making Linkages Between Skills and Functions

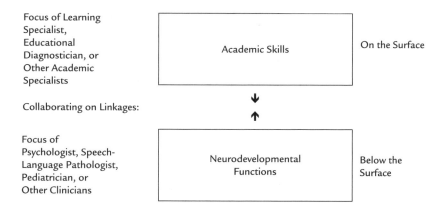

assessment need to be able to reverse their usual thinking. For example, a psychologist needs to be able to hypothesize about functions based on historical information regarding a student's reading and writing skills.

The team approach usually means that clinicians become specialists with not just a set of assessment procedures (academic or neurodevelopmental), but also with a primary direction of thinking (skills to functions, or vice versa). Specializing builds up experience with batteries and facilitates the development of personal norms. Finally, a clinical team can provide the student with a change of pace (and face) that is likely to boost rapport and evoke an optimal performance. Professionals have unique working styles that mesh differently with students; using a team increases the probability of connecting with the student (and the tactics for connecting with the student can be shared among the team members).

Assessment as a Process

Another way to think about the multiple angles of assessment involves the time dimension. Even with the help of history, an assessment session that is circumscribed by a single day or two-day period can be a relatively narrow window for understanding the student. Ideally, assessment should be an ongoing process so that the understanding of the student can unfold over time. A primary way of accomplishing ongoing assessment is through the follow-up process. Follow-up (sometimes referred to as aftercare) is the consultation provided to families after the assessment sessions, often after the family has had the opportunity to read the written report. Families almost always have questions about the written findings, especially about how to implement tactics included in the learning plan. Follow-up is an important process for continuing demystification and for supporting implementation of the student's plan. But in addition, follow-up can give the professional additional assessment information.

As discussed in Chapter Thirteen, the assessment process offers no absolute certainty. At best, professionals can look to supporting evidence for a hypothesis; they cannot actually prove anything about a student's learning. Looking at the student over time, though, can provide additional evidence for a hypothesis and increase the probability that findings have really captured the student's learning issues. In a sense, a learning plan can become a controlled experiment. For instance, a clinical team may conclude that Sam (from the case study earlier in this chapter) has receptive and expressive language weaknesses that are undermining his reading and writing. Further, the team recommends several tactics for improving his language (listening comprehension exercises, drawing out his oral language at home). Monitoring his progress through follow-up will help to determine the efficacy of such tactics. If Sam improves, then the hypothesis that his language was the culprit is supported. But if he does not improve, the team may need to rethink the findings and, possibly, assess further in order to understand what is really going on with his profile.

Comparing and Contrasting Angles

An important reason to assess from multiple angles is that comparing different types of findings can help to understand a student. In some cases, the contrast between two pieces of information is actually more revealing than the pieces themselves. The next chapter covers comparing and contrasting findings, along with ways to interpret comparisons.

6

A Better Use of the Discrepancy Concept

ANYONE WHO HAS WORKED in the field of learning disabilities or special education in the last few decades is all too familiar with the *discrepancy formula*, the difference between a student's IQ score and at least one standardized achievement score. If this difference is big enough (usually fifteen points), then the criterion is met for determination of learning disability. In short, IQ serves as a proxy for what a student should be able to achieve, if only the learning disability weren't in the way. The discrepancy formula was adopted as a standard for eligibility determination (only one standard, but certainly the primary one) in 1977, soon after the passage of the Education for All Handicapped Children Act of 1975 (EAHCA). The idea was to bring objectivity to the differentiation of students with and without learning disabilities (Lyon et al., 2001). The formula has served as a gatekeeping mechanism for special education, with students whose scores meet the criterion qualifying for services.

Though it has been the standard in the diagnosis of learning disabilities and the major criterion for special education eligibility, for some time the discrepancy formula has come under considerable fire from the scientific community. Several criticisms have been voiced in terms of both its theoretical validity and its practical limitations. Discrepancy formulas have actually differed from state to state, meaning that a student may lose or gain services merely as a result of a family move (Lyon et al., 2001). Another problem is that the discrepancy method does not capture all the students who have learning problems. Because of regression to the mean, students with lower IQ scores tend to be underidentified; in contrast, regression to the mean results in overidentification of students with higher IQ scores. Discrepancy methods often delay identification and treatment because students need to achieve poorly through early elementary school until they finally meet criteria for an IQ-achievement split; as a result the average age of a student identified with a learning disability is ten, despite evidence that after age eight, reading problems are much harder to deal with (Fletcher et al., 1998). G. Reid Lyon and his colleagues (2001) describe this as the "wait-to-fail" model.

☞ *Regression to the mean* is a statistical principle asserting that if two variables are less than perfectly correlated and a subsample is selected with extreme scores on the first variable, then the subsample's mean of the second variable will almost always be less extreme than the mean of the first variable; the second variable's mean will regress toward the mean of the total sample (Darlington, 1990).

Because of these and other criticisms, the field has been gradually moving away from the discrepancy formula and toward a diagnostic approach that turns out to be more in line with assessing to understand. Most notably, the 2004 Individuals with Disabilities Education Improvement Act (IDEA) reauthorization has added language that now allows local education agencies to abandon the discrepancy formula altogether (Apling & Jones, 2005).

Nonetheless, many things in the world that are problematic and undesirable have, at their core, something of value, and the discrepancy formula is no exception. Though subtracting students' standardized achievement scores from their IQ scores is becoming an increasingly dated practice, the notion of comparing and contrasting aspects of a student's abilities and skills is actually quite sound. This chapter explores the significant value of the discrepancy concept to the goal of assessing to understand.

Clinical Contrasts

The *discrepancy concept* is about much more than just a formula, IQ-achievement splits, and gatekeeping for special education. The discrepancy concept is the clinical thought process of comparing one aspect of a student's mind to another aspect. Is language different from memory? Are spatial abilities different from attention?

An assessment for learning problems almost always involves tests or tasks, which could target academic skills or neurodevelopmental functions, and can be task-analyzed (see Chapter Three). Students almost always vary in how well they perform with the various tasks that make up a given assessment battery. When a discrepant performance on two tasks can be used to reveal or isolate components of a student's profile, we have what I refer to as a *clinical contrast*.

The technique of comparing a student's performances across certain tasks has been described by Denckla (1996b) within the context of assessing *executive functions* (mental abilities that include self-regulation, inhibition, planning, and organizing). In effect, a problem with executive functions needs to be identified by first establishing adequate processing of the material (for example, language-based or visual) involved in a task. Since content-free tasks do not exist, it is necessary to compare tasks that share content but that differ in their executive demands; the result would be intraindividual performance pairings on content-matched tasks. An example would be to compare how well a student copies a complex figure with the results of a task that involves copying basic figures (both tasks involving similar content—abstract geometric designs); this example is discussed in more detail later in this chapter.

The first step in this particular thought process is to task-analyze the tasks or skills to be compared. Once the neurodevelopmental ingredients have been established, the second step is to compare how the student performed on the tasks or skills to factor out potential explanations for variable performance. In the following sections I illustrate three general kinds of *clinical contrasts:* comparing an academic task or skill to another academic task or skill, comparing a neurodevelopmental assessment task to another neurodevelopmental task, and comparing an academic task or skill to a neurodevelopmental assessment task. Many neurodevelopmental phenomena (for example, aspects of memory and language) will be mentioned in these sections in connection to the particular contrast being discussed; these same phenomena are also listed in Appendix C, which should make it easier to look them up later as you work on a student assessment.

Academic Task to Academic Task

As described in Chapter Four, an academic task is designed to assess an academic skill, the way having a student spell words assesses the student's skill at spelling. Drawing clinical contrasts requires thinking of academic performance in novel ways. For example, a skill as seemingly straightforward as spelling can be broken down into different kinds of tasks: spelling words in isolation (akin to a traditional spelling test), spelling words in context (either sentences or passages), and spelling recognition (identifying the correct spelling of a word when it sits alongside several misspellings). Each of these types of spelling tasks share important neurodevelopmental underpinnings, but they also involve key differences, as Figure 6.1 illustrates.

Comparing performance on these different types of spelling tasks can yield some important clinical contrasts. For instance, if the student is a more accurate speller when the words are isolated than when they are in context, active working memory and self-monitoring are the likely culprits. If the student spells better orally than in writing, then graphomotor function might be the undermining factor. Similarly, a student who is more adept at reciting the alphabet than at handwriting the alphabet probably has graphomotor dysfunction.

Some students show differences in their reading decoding and reading comprehension. When decoding is stronger than comprehension, the usual explanation is that phonological processing, paired associate memory, and automaticity are operating well, but receptive language is weak; the student can call out words but struggles to derive meaning from the overall text. When comprehension is stronger than decoding, the opposite pattern is generally true: good receptive language but weak phonological processing and other functions associated with phonics.

Math operations are the framework of math and involve computations, basic skills, math facts, and calculation procedures. Operation problems usually do not contain language (unlike word problems). The patterns in operation problems are more obvious; for example, it's relatively easy to look at a problem like $72 \div 12$ and identify it as a division problem. Finally, a math operation problem usually requires rote calculations, rather than a great deal of logic.

In contrast, *math reasoning* is the more advanced thinking and conceptualization necessary for solving applied and sophisticated math problems.

Figure 6.1   Spelling Tasks, Shared and Unique Neurodevelopmental Functions
[1] Especially for long words
[2] Orthographic recognition is also used in decoding.

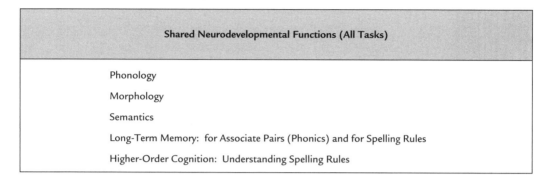

Shared Neurodevelopmental Functions (All Tasks)
Phonology
Morphology
Semantics
Long-Term Memory: for Associate Pairs (Phonics) and for Spelling Rules
Higher-Order Cognition: Understanding Spelling Rules

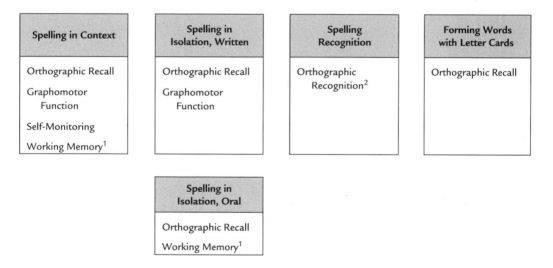

Spelling in Context	Spelling in Isolation, Written	Spelling Recognition	Forming Words with Letter Cards
Orthographic Recall	Orthographic Recall	Orthographic Recognition[2]	Orthographic Recall
Graphomotor Function	Graphomotor Function		
Self-Monitoring			
Working Memory[1]			

Spelling in Isolation, Oral
Orthographic Recall
Working Memory[1]

Such problems require more sorting of essential information from nonessential information, and the computations required can be harder to identify. Take this problem as an example: "Over the next 5 hours the 12 pollsters will call 72 homes. How many homes will each pollster need to call?" The key numbers are 12 and 72 (5 is a distracting item), and one has to identify the pattern of the question as a division problem (72 ÷ 12). Unlike most math operations problems, math reasoning requires setting up problems for solution prior to calculation. Finally, math reasoning puts more of a premium on generalization in terms of knowing the basic patterns of problems and their required procedures. It is important to recognize that comparisons

Table 6.1   Shared and Unique Neurodevelopmental Functions for Math Operations and Math Reasoning

Functions for Math Operations and Math Reasoning	Shared	Emphasized for Math Operations	Emphasized for Math Reasoning	Shared, More for Math Reasoning
Saliency determination			•	
Processing depth	•			
Previewing[1]				•
Facilitation and inhibition	•			
Pacing	•			
Self-monitoring[1]				•
Short-term memory	•			
Active working memory				•
Paired associate memory[2]		•		
Procedural memory	•			
Semantic understanding			•	
Sentence comprehension			•	
Discourse processing			•	
Temporal-sequential ordering	•			
Spatial ordering	•			
Problem solving				•
Rule use				•
Conceptualization			•	
Strategy use				•
Rate of processing and production	•			

[1]Estimating and checking reasonableness of answers more important in math reasoning.
[2]For learning math facts.

between math operations and math reasoning are relative. Table 6.1 depicts the major linkages between each category of math skill and neurodevelopmental functions.

The quality of a student's writing may vary as a function of the length of the writing. Writing a passage and writing a sentence share some core neurodevelopmental functions (see Figure 6.2) in terms of language at the word and sentence levels, active working memory, memory for rules, and graphomotor function. However, a student who also has language weaknesses at the discourse level has trouble extending or elaborating thoughts through language, and one who has limits in attention (mental energy control system or

Figure 6.2   Writing a Passage Versus Writing a Sentence, Shared and Unique Neurodevelopmental Functions
[1] Demands on attention controls decrease with size of output

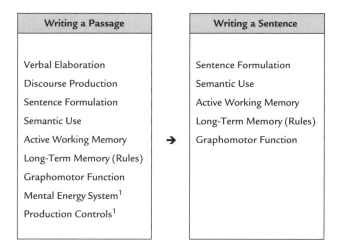

production control system) could have writing difficulties that do not manifest when writing small pieces like a sentence but are problematic for longer pieces.

Table 6.2 is the first of three in this chapter that present some of the major clinical contrasts to look for when assessing students with learning problems, along with some potential explanations from a neurodevelopmental standpoint. This table focuses on contrasts between academic skills. It is important to note that a clinical contrast, in and of itself, is not sufficient evidence to judge how well a function or construct is operating. As was discussed at length in the preceding chapter, assessment needs to consider multiple angles and cross-index findings from various sources.

Neurodevelopmental Task to Neurodevelopmental Task

As discussed in Chapter Four, a neurodevelopmental task is designed to assess functions with minimal use of academic skills. An example of such a task is copying a complex form, such as the model shown in Chapter Three (repeated in Figure 6.3).

One of the intraindividual performance pairings described by Denckla (1996b) is copying complex geometric figures with copying basic geometric

Table 6.2   Clinical Contrasts Between Academic Tasks

Academic tasks	Potential Explanations
Decoding better in isolation than in context	• Intact functions for decoding (such as phonology, paired associate memory, automaticity) with weak active working memory, self-monitoring, or chunk size capacity undermining word attack in context • Weak receptive language (sentence or discourse levels) undermining use of context cues
Decoding better in context than in isolation	• Good receptive language (sentence or discourse levels) enabling use of context cues to compensate for weak word attack
Reading decoding stronger than reading comprehension	• Good phonology (bolstering phonics and word attack), but weak receptive language at the higher levels (words, sentences, discourse) • Limited chunk size (student struggles with extended pieces of information) • Weak active working memory for extended text
Reading comprehension stronger than reading decoding	• Good receptive language at the higher levels (words, sentences, discourse), but weak phonology undermining phonics (student compensates by using context cues and prior knowledge) • Good higher-order cognition (for example, understanding of concepts) compensating for weak decoding
Spelling better in isolation than in context	• Intact functions for spelling (such as phonology and paired associate memory) with weak active working memory, self-monitoring, or chunk size capacity undermining spelling in context
Spelling better in context than in isolation	• Good morphology or semantics (enabling better use of context and meaning for accurate spelling)
Spelling better than decoding	• Good orthographic memory for letter patterns and whole words, compensating for weak functions undermining word attack (for example, phonology, paired associate memory, automaticity)
Decoding better than spelling	• Intact functions for word attack (for example, phonology, paired associate memory, automaticity), with long-term memory storage better than access for orthographic patterns (recognizing letter patterns better than recalling letter patterns)
Decoding nonsense words better than decoding real words	• Intact functions for decoding (for example, phonology, paired associate memory, automaticity) with weak orthographic memory for irregularly spelled words

Table 6.2   Clinical Contrasts Between Academic Tasks (*Continued*)

Academic tasks	Potential Explanations
Reading comprehension stronger than written expression	• Receptive language stronger than expressive language • Weak graphomotor function • Disparity in attention: intact processing control system and weak production control system • Overall faster rate of processing than rate of production
Written expression stronger than reading comprehension	• Expressive language stronger than receptive language • Overall rate of production faster than rate of processing
Math operations stronger than math reasoning	• Good rote memory (such as paired associate and procedural) with tenuous conceptualization, reasoning and logic, or rule use, or all three • Weak receptive language (semantic, sentence, discourse) undermining success with word problems • Difficulty with word problems due to weak saliency determination, previewing, or self-monitoring, or all three • Difficulty handling extended problems due to weak active working memory or strategy use, or both
Math reasoning stronger than math operations	• Weak rote memory (for example, paired associate, procedural) with good conceptualization, reasoning and logic, or rule use, or all three • Good receptive language (semantic, sentence, discourse) enabling success with word problems • Good saliency determination (finding key details in problems) • Relative difficulty with decontextualized information • Good strategy use

Figure 6.3   Mock Complex Figure

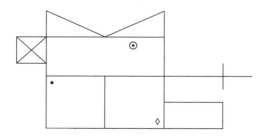

Figure 6.4   Mock Basic Geometric Figures

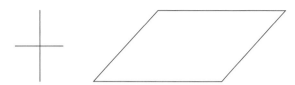

figures. A complex figure is obviously visual, unfamiliar to the student, and relatively large (that is, filling most of a page). It contains numerous elements and requires the student to organize the page when copying. In contrast, basic figures are also visual and unfamiliar, but are smaller (that is, several to a page), have fewer elements, and are copied on a structured page (one that is subdivided into sections). Figure 6.4 contains two examples of basic figures that a student might be asked to copy.

> ☞ The initial copying of a complex figure is often followed by short- and long-term recall tasks in which the student is asked to draw the figure from memory; in addition, the long-term recall task may be followed by a recognition task requiring the student to differentiate components of the complex figure from shapes that were not in the figure. All such tasks obviously tap into memory for visual information.

A matching and identification task would involve similar basic figures, but would eliminate output and graphomotor demands. The student would be shown a figure, for example, along with several other similar figures with the same target figure embedded (see Figure 6.5); the student then has to match or identify the correct figure, in a multiple-choice format.

Figure 6.5   Mock Basic Geometric Figure Matching

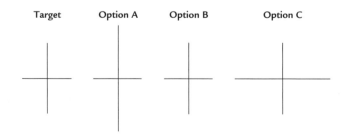

Figure 6.6   Comparative Task-Analysis, Complex Figure, Basic Figure, and Figure Matching
[1] Example: Rey Complex Figure Test (Meyers & Meyers, 1996).
[2] Example: Beery-Buktenica Developmental Test of Visual-Motor Integration (Beery & Beery, 2004).
[3] Example: Beery-Buktenica Developmental Test of Visual Perception (Beery & Beery, 2004).

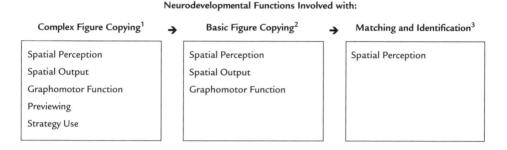

Neurodevelopmental Functions Involved with:

Complex Figure Copying[1]	→	Basic Figure Copying[2]	→	Matching and Identification[3]
Spatial Perception		Spatial Perception		Spatial Perception
Spatial Output		Spatial Output		
Graphomotor Function		Graphomotor Function		
Previewing				
Strategy Use				

Though these three tasks share some core features, they become progressively narrower in terms of functions that are involved (see Figure 6.6). Copying a complex figure clearly is the most complicated of the three tasks, followed by the basic figure copying, and then the matching and identification task.

Clinical contrasts across these three tasks can be very revealing. Let's assume that a student does well with copying the complex figure. Such a performance provides evidence of intact or strong functioning in spatial perception and output, graphomotor function, previewing, and strategy use. However, if a student struggles with copying the complex figure, determining which functions were undermining the performance would require comparison with performance on the basic figure copy task. Copying a basic figure places far fewer demands on the student's previewing and strategy use. A student who struggles with a complex figure but performs adequately (or well) with a basic figure probably has weak previewing or strategy use, or both. Now extend the comparisons further and assume that a student has difficulty copying both the complex and basic figures; if that student is successful with matching and identifying the basic figures, then spatial perception is probably intact but graphomotor function is undermining the output. This example illustrates how a clinical contrast can be a process of elimination, helping to isolate functions related to the student's performance.

Figure 6.7   Long-Term Memory: Better Storage Than Access

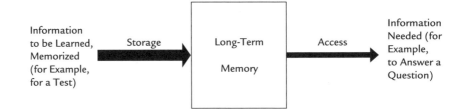

Another clinical contrast involving neurodevelopmental tasks relates to the two aspects of long-term memory: storage and access. Difficulty with long-term memory typically takes one of two forms. The first is a storage problem, meaning that the person has trouble consolidating information for later use. If storage is problematic, access is then problematic; how can information be accessed if it was not first stored? Second, storage is intact (or strong) but access is problematic. In other words, information is getting in, but the person has trouble getting it out later. This second scenario is depicted in Figure 6.7 and can be elucidated through a clinical contrast.

When someone can store information but has trouble accessing it, free-recall or open-ended questions are especially difficult. An example of a free-recall question is "What is the term for a warm-blooded vertebrate?" In contrast, recognition questions are far easier for someone who has stored information and has trouble with access. Here is an example of a recognition question: "Is a warm-blooded vertebrate called a mollusk, mammal, or chordate?" Recognition questions can take many forms, but common examples are matching and multiple-choice; such questions provide a prompt or cue that bypasses long-term memory access and taps more directly into long-term memory storage. Hence a student who struggles with recall questions but is more successful with recognition questions probably has long-term storage that is relatively stronger than long-term access.

Some interesting sentence construction tasks can assess expressive language separate from written expression. Let's compare two such tasks, neither of which requires the student to write anything with a pen or pencil. In the first task, the student sees the words in Figure 6.8 displayed on an easel and is asked to create two sentences with them (speaking the sentences aloud).

Figure 6.8 Mock Sentence Generation Task

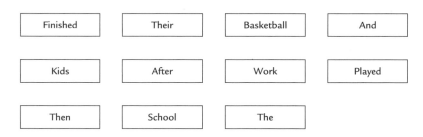

Finished	Their	Basketball	And
Kids	After	Work	Played
Then	School	The	

Here are some potential correct responses:

After school the kids finished their work and then played basketball.
The kids played basketball after school and then finished their work.
The kids played basketball and then finished their work after school.

Constructing the sentences from the displayed words obviously requires language (sentence formulation and semantic use). This particular task also requires active working memory; the student cannot write anything down, and so must mentally shuffle the words and remember what the first sentence was while making a second, different sentence. Now imagine a second sentence construction task in which the student is asked to create two sentences with the same set of words, but each word is on a separate card and the sentences are to be constructed by moving the cards around on the table, which drastically reduces the demand on working memory. This clinical contrast would provide data about the student's active working memory and its effect on communication.

☞ Administering the range of neurodevelopmental tasks described here would be unrealistic for most assessments—and usually unnecessary as well. Often the best course is to pick tasks that tap numerous functions (like a complex figure copy) and employ related tasks (such as basic figure copy) only if the student shows difficulty on the initial task; this approach enables the clinician to investigate the causes of difficulty on a multifaceted task.

Higher-order cognition tests can be sorted into verbal (primarily language-based thinking) and nonverbal tasks. Comparing a student's

Figure 6.9   Mock Matrix Analogy Item

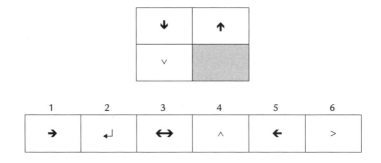

performance on these two different kinds of tasks can be quite useful, especially if language difficulty is suspected. Also, some students demonstrate much stronger higher-order thinking when solving nonverbal problems than when grappling with complex linguistic material, perhaps due to relatively strong spatial ordering. A common task of nonverbal higher thinking is the matrix analogy. Similar to a verbal analogy, a matrix analogy requires the student to determine the relationship between two pictures (of either abstract figures or real objects) and then to apply that relationship to two other pictures. In Figure 6.9, the student needs to identify that the two figures in the top row of the matrix are identical, except that they are inverted; then the student needs to select from among the six potential responses the figure to go in the shaded box (option number 4 is correct because it is an inverted version of the figure in the bottom-left quadrant in the matrix). Other than some initial instructions to the student, this task involves no oral language.

A verbal analogy requires the student to determine the relationship between two words (presented orally or in written format, or both), and then to apply the relationship to two other words. Sometimes possible responses are provided in a multiple-choice format. Here is an example of a verbal analogy:

"Turtle is to shell as porcupine is to___."

   a. Claws

   b. Spines

   c. Eyes

   d. Forests

Selecting the correct answer (b) requires a conceptual understanding of animals' protective features. Much like verbal analogies are similarity tasks, in which the student is asked to describe (or select a response that describes) how two words are related or alike. For instance, an item may ask, "How are turtle shells and porcupine spines alike?" A correct answer would be a description of how both provide protection to the animal.

If a student performs better with verbal analogies or similarities tasks than with matrix analogies, possible explanations include relatively stronger language or weaker spatial ordering (leading to difficulty perceiving the visual elements of the matrices). In contrast, a student who is more successful with matrices probably has relatively weaker language or stronger spatial ordering. As with all clinical contrasts, such discrepancies merely provide one piece of data that needs to be interpreted in the context of all available data, including history and other test findings related to language and spatial ordering.

As in the preceding section, Table 6.3 lists some major clinical contrasts and possible neurodevelopmental explanations. This table focuses on performance comparisons between neurodevelopmental tasks. Again, these clinical contrasts need to be considered along with other findings in the assessment of constructs and functions.

Neurodevelopmental Task to Academic Task

This particular kind of clinical contrast is really central to the concept of making linkages in a neurodevelopmental assessment approach. As discussed in Chapter Four, academic skills can be conceptualized as being on the surface, since parents, students, and teachers can readily observe them. Also, academic skills are undergirded by neurodevelopmental constructs and functions (see Figure 6.10).

Although much can be learned by comparing academic skills and tasks to each other, and neurodevelopmental tasks to each other, comparing academic skills and tasks to neurodevelopmental tasks is a major aspect of a neurodevelopmental approach to assessment. The routine I have typically used is for a learning specialist to first conduct an academic assessment with the student. The learning specialist assesses from multiple angles, task-analyzes,

Table 6.3   Clinical Contrasts Between Neurodevelopmental Tasks

Neurodevelopmental Tasks	Potential Explanations
Complex form copying weaker than basic form copying	• Intact spatial perception and output and intact graphomotor function with weak previewing or strategy use • Limited chunk size (student struggles with extended pieces of information) • Superficial processing depth (difficulty handling all the details in the complex figure)
Basic form copying weaker than matching or identifying forms	• Intact spatial perception with weak spatial output or graphomotor function
Better performance on recognition tasks than free-recall tasks	• Long-term memory access weaker than long-term memory storage • Problematic mental energy control system (recognizing usually requires less effort than recalling)
Better performance on free-recall tasks than recognition tasks	• Excessive cognitive activation (recognition items trigger tangential thoughts) • Difficulty with decontextualized information • Weak saliency determination (differentiating correct recognition items from distracter items)
Sentence formulation with word cards better than sentence formulation with easel	• Intact sentence formulation with weak active working memory for mentally shuffling the words displayed on the easel • Weak self-monitoring (checking for accuracy is easier when using the cards)
Stronger performance with matrix analogies than with verbal analogies	• Better reasoning and logic with nonverbal information • Spatial ordering stronger than language
Stronger performance with verbal analogies than with matrix analogies	• Better reasoning and logic with verbal information • Language stronger than spatial ordering
Differential between capacity to interpret, recall, and generate verbal information and visual material	• Language stronger than spatial ordering (or vice versa) • Verbal memory stronger than visual memory (or vice versa)
Listening comprehension for narrative discourse stronger than for expository discourse	• Weak saliency determination or processing depth (narrative text usually has fewer details to filter and process) • Weak semantic understanding (especially technical terms) • Relative difficulty with decontextualized information (better able to relate narrative to personal experience)

Table 6.3   Clinical Contrasts Between Neurodevelopmental Tasks (*Continued*)

Neurodevelopmental Tasks	Potential Explanations
Listening comprehension for expository discourse stronger than for narrative discourse	• Weak social cognition, difficulty understanding characters and their interactions • Excessive cognitive activation (story details trigger distracting thoughts) • Strong memory and knowledge base • Strong conceptualization (abstract ideas)
Comprehension of contextualized information stronger than decontextualized information	• Weak conceptualization (abstract ideas) • Superficial processing depth (trouble with high density detail) • Weak memory and knowledge base
Comprehension of decontextualized information stronger than contextualized information	• Strong conceptualization (abstract ideas) • Weak saliency determination or cognitive activation leading to being distracted by contextualized information • Strong memory and knowledge base

looks at clinical contrasts across academic skills, and then shares hypotheses about linkages to neurodevelopmental functions. For example, the learning specialist may have learned from history that the student struggles with word decoding, then observed that the student did make numerous errors when decoding in context but performed much better when the words were in isolation; from that history and observed clinical contrasts the learning specialist has a hypothesis that the student has weak active working memory that is undermining the ability to decode while reading for meaning. The next clinician's role, then, is to employ neurodevelopmental tasks to explore active working memory (among other functions) in its "pure" form (that is, when

Figure 6.10   Linkages Between Academic Skills and Neurodevelopmental Functions

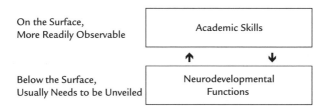

not *confounded*—that is, influenced by reading ability) to test the learning specialist's hypothesis.

I should note here that although I am a proponent of team assessment, it is possible to go through the same type of reasoning process I just described as a sole professional working with a student. Under those conditions it is even more important to be open-minded about different possibilities. When you're on your own, you really have to be willing to challenge your initial ideas about a student.

A major category of neurodevelopmental task involves listening comprehension. Such tasks, obviously, require the student to listen to orally presented information (at the word, sentence, or discourse levels) that must be comprehended. The information can vary in complexity from basic vocabulary to multistep directions to complex and ambiguous material. Though listening comprehension requires a number of functions, including attention and memory, receptive language is the primary neurodevelopmental ingredient.

Listening tasks are very useful for comparison with reading skill (Aaron, 1995). Reading comprehension requires first decoding printed text and then assigning meaning to that text. In contrast, listening comprehension is the understanding of spoken language without having to use phonics (decoding sound-symbol associations). Also, a reader can control the input speed, which enables rereading and checking back in the text for details. A listener usually cannot control speed of input (Carlisle, 1991), which places higher demands on attention and processing rate for receptive language (see Table 6.4).

Written expression is the communication of verbal ideas on paper (or via word processing software), whereas oral expression is entirely oral. Both require expressive language, but writing also requires graphomotor function and active working memory, among others. Let's compare written and oral output, looking first at the sentence level (see Figure 6.11). Writing a sentence obviously involves language functions in terms of correct word usage, word order, and execution of grammar rules; handwriting sentences also requires graphomotor function and active working memory in order to simultaneously manage all the sentence components and writing tasks (letter formation, spelling, grammar). The preceding section compared two types of language tasks: one in which the student creates sentences from words displayed on an easel, and another in which the student creates sentences from

Table 6.4   Reading Comprehension Versus Listening Comprehension, Shared and Unique Neurodevelopmental Functions

Neurodevelopmental Constructs and Functions	Used for Reading Comprehension	Used for Listening Comprehension
Mental energy control system	•	•
Processing control system	•	•
Previewing	•	•
Short-term memory	•	•
Active working memory	•	•
Long-term memory access	•	•
Semantic understanding	•	•
Sentence comprehension	•	•
Discourse processing	•	•
Higher-order cognition	•	•
Rate of processing	•	•
Chunk size	•	•
Paired associate memory[1]	•	
Orthographic recognition[1]	•	
Phonological processing[1]	•	
Morphological use[1]	•	
Rule use[1]	•	
Strategy use[1]	•	
Automaticity[1]	•	
Pacing[1]	•	
Self-monitoring[1]	•	
Facilitation and inhibition[1]	•	

[1]Used for phonics and reading decoding.

Figure 6.11   Comparative Task-Analysis for Sentence Formation

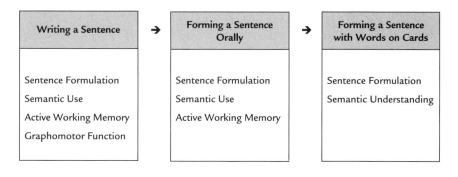

Figure 6.12   Comparative Task-Analysis for Discourse Formation

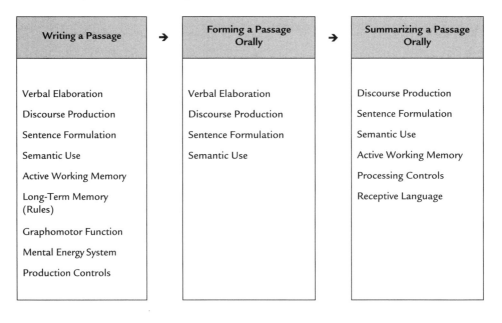

words displayed on individual cards. Both these language tasks eliminate graphomotor demands, and the card task also decreases working memory demands. Comparing all three ways to construct a sentence (writing, oral from words on easel, by sequencing words on cards) creates contrasts that can help to isolate the effects of graphomotor dysfunction and limited active working memory, or to determine if the student has a particular language problem. The process of elimination is similar to comparing complex figure copying to basic figure copying and to matching and identification of basic figures.

Turning now to the discourse level, a student can generate a passage in several ways: via handwriting, orally creating new material, or orally summarizing material already read or heard (see Figure 6.12). As with the sentence-level examples, the oral tasks eliminate graphomotor function and are far less demanding in terms of attention and memory because writing involves so many conventions, such as spelling and punctuation, which must be recalled and monitored. Orally creating new material is heavily dependent on expressive language at multiple levels, as is summarizing orally, though summarizing also requires taking in (attention processing control system and receptive language) and recalling the material (active working memory).

In the preceding section I discussed matrix analogies in contrast with verbal analogies and the similarities task. Performance on matrix analogies can also be contrasted with math reasoning to isolate the logical aspects of solving math problems. A student who understands the logic and concepts involved will have a much easier time solving most math problems. Math problems, especially word problems, require several neurodevelopmental functions in addition to higher-order cognition. Details need to be selected and filtered, approaches planned, and accuracy checked, all of which involve different aspects of attention. Memory demands include procedural memory for algorithms and active working memory for mentally suspending all the task components. Word problems require decoding and reading comprehension, which means that receptive language is needed. So the student who performs well with matrix analogies but has trouble with math reasoning probably has the higher thinking (reasoning and logic, conceptualization) needed for math, but is undermined by other neurodevelopmental weaknesses in areas such as attention, memory, or language.

Table 6.5 discusses clinical contrasts between academic tasks and neurodevelopmental tasks. To reiterate, such contrasts are merely one of many multiple angles that should inform the assessment process.

Clinical Branching Logic

Another way to think about clinical contrasts is through *branching logic*. Such logic involves a series of if-then possibilities or yes-no questions in a decision tree. Earlier in this chapter I contrasted the copying of complex figures with copying basic figures and with matching and identifying basic figures. The decision tree in Figure 6.13 traces the major clinical contrasts and depicts the various neurodevelopmental possibilities for the each.

The decision tree in Figure 6.14 depicts the important contrasts to consider when a student has trouble writing. The first question, "Can the student communicate effectively orally?" should be asked initially in most instances of weak written expression, since this helps to establish whether or not expressive language is at the root of the problem. The answer to the question will help structure the assessment as well as the development of the learning plan.

Table 6.5   Clinical Contrasts Between Academic and Neurodevelopmental Tasks

Clinical Contrasts: Academic and Neurodevelopmental Tasks	Potential Explanations
Listening comprehension stronger than reading comprehension	• Intact receptive language, except for weak phonological processing (affecting decoding) • Weak orthographic memory or paired associate memory, or both (affecting decoding) • Weak facilitation and inhibition or pacing (listening can slow a student down since the reader and speaker is dictating the pace)
Reading comprehension stronger than listening comprehension	• Intact receptive language with slow rate of processing (when listening the speed is determined by the speaker, whereas one can regulate speed when reading) • Intact receptive language with superficial processing depth (deeper processing is easier when reading through rereading and cross-checking)
Oral expression stronger than written expression	• Intact expressive language with weak graphomotor function or active working memory • Weak attention in terms of mental energy control system or production control system • Weak long-term memory access for things like spelling rules and writing conventions (such as punctuation) • Weak phonological processing or paired associate memory affecting phonics and spelling
Written expression stronger than oral expression	• Intact expressive language with slow rate of production (relatively slower act of writing accommodates rate issues) • Intact and strong graphomotor or fine motor function (leading to efficient handwriting or keyboarding) • Intact mental energy control system (sufficient fuel for writing)
Performance with matrix analogies better than math reasoning	• Intact reasoning and logic with weaknesses in attention, memory, or receptive language undermining solution of applied math problems
Math reasoning better than performance with matrix analogies	• Weak reasoning and logic with intact long-term memory storage and access supporting a rote approach to solving problems (memorizing algorithms and recognizing when to use them despite tenuous understanding of them) • Intact attention or receptive language bolstering solving applied problems

Figure 6.13   Branching Logic for Complex Figure Copying
[1]Example: Rey Complex Figure Test (Meyers & Meyers, 1996).
[2]Example: Beery-Buktenica Developmental Test of Visual-Motor Integration (Beery & Beery, 2004).
[3]Example: Beery-Buktenica Developmental Test of Visual Perception (Beery & Beery, 2004).
[4]Note that student may also have weaknesses in other areas that should be identified via different tasks.

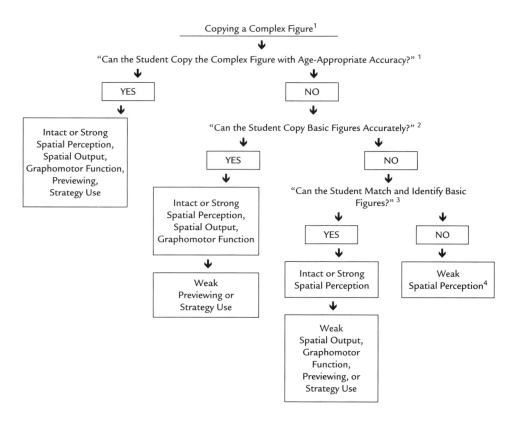

When considering why someone may be a weak speller (see Figure 6.15), an initial question to ask is, "Can the student spell isolated words better than words in context?" If the student can spell better in isolation, then active working memory is often the culprit (the process of writing incorporates numerous tasks that must be juggled mentally, and spelling is sometimes a ball that gets dropped). If the student also struggles with spelling in isolation, then the capacity to recognize correct spellings of words (for example, in a multiple-choice format) can help sort out whether or not orthographic

Figure 6.14   Branching Logic for Writing
[1]Student may have weaknesses at multiple levels of expressive language.
[2]Student may have additional weaknesses (such as working memory or attention).

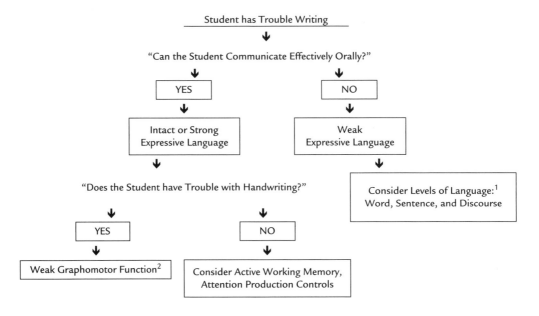

patterns are properly stored in long-term memory. Manipulation of word sounds (phonological processing tasks) is important to consider with the student who is unsuccessful with recognizing word spellings. Finally, paired associate memory may be affecting the student's linking of letter-sound pairs (phonics), even if the student has intact phonological processing. See Chapter Ten for further discussion of the differentiation of phonological processing and phonics.

The next example of a decision tree (see Figure 6.16) involves reading and is more complicated because of the wide range of possibilities for explaining a reading problem. An initial question to ask is whether the student understands when listening, which can help you assess receptive language capacity apart from reading comprehension. If repetition helps the student with weak listening comprehension, then the attention processing controls may be an issue. Nonsense words are non-words that follow the conventions of phonics (for example, *brem*) and can help get at the heart of a decoding problem. Just

Figure 6.15   Branching Logic for Spelling
[1]Student may have additional weaknesses (e.g., paired associate memory).
[2]Paired associate memory is needed to link graphemes with phonemes.

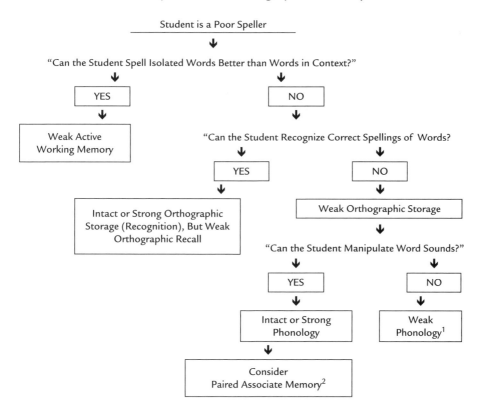

as in the assessment of spelling, manipulation of word sounds can help tease out the role of phonological processing.

These decision trees include the main questions to ask about learning breakdowns and cover just the major neurodevelopmental possibilities; including every possibility or combination of factors would make the diagrams overwhelming. The purpose of the decision trees is to illustrate a way of thinking about assessment findings—how to employ clinical contrasts to help you understand why a student is struggling.

The questions posed on the decision trees can be answered in a variety of ways. For example, direct testing can inform how well the student can copy complex versus basic figures. A question such as "Can the student

Figure 6.16   Branching Logic for Reading
[1]At least at the upper levels of receptive language: word, sentence, and discourse.
[2]Student may have weaknesses at multiple levels of receptive language.
[3]Student may have additional weaknesses (for example, paired associate memory).
[4]Paired associate memory is needed to link graphemes with phonemes.

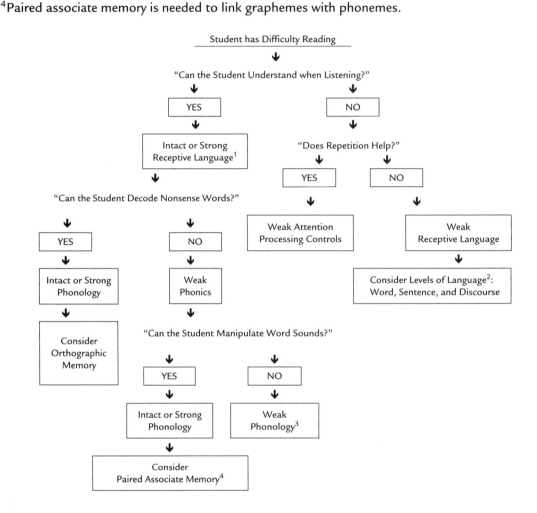

understand when listening?" can be answered, at least in part, through history reports. Reviewing work samples could help to compare how the student spells in isolation and in context. As was discussed in Chapter Four, you usually need a variety of data sources to uncover the reasons behind a student's learning breakdowns.

Contrasts in History Reports

In Chapter Five I discuss the importance of history in this assessment approach. When reviewing information from several people who see the student in different settings, inconsistencies often abound. But it's not often the case that one person is right and one person is wrong. Rather, both are right in their own way. So the discrepancy concept can be useful with interpreting history data, in conjunction with task-analytic thinking. What is it about the two reporters' settings that could account for their differing perspectives? A common example involves descriptions of a student's attention. Consider the following students:

CASE STUDIES

Breston is a sixth grader whose parents are concerned about his attention. Getting him off to school in the morning is a struggle, as is organizing him to do his homework in the evenings. However, his teachers report that he shows good behavior at school and gets his work done. This type of contrast is not uncommon and can be caused by a number of factors. Sometimes students respond well to the particular structure (or teachers) at school better to their parents' behavior management. Also, certain students seem to have just so many good hours of attention per day, which they might expend at school, making early mornings and evenings problematic at home.

Khari is a seventh grader who has difficulties in several of her classes. Her teachers report a number of signs of weak attention, including distractibility and impulsivity. Khari's parents, though, question the validity of her teachers' reports because they do not see attention as a problem at home. Again, this type of contrast is often found in assessment work. In such instances, the explanation usually has to do with the differing demands of the environments in question. Khari may be the kind of student who performs much better when she is in a less-stimulating environment with fewer distractions. Classrooms are replete with potential distractions, whereas the home may be (but isn't always!) relatively calmer.

The assessments for both Breston and Khari should probe into the reasons for the contrasts in history reports. The first determination should be whether attention is really at the root of their respective difficulties. Weak language, for example, can manifest as behavior difficulties that can be misinterpreted as signs of weak attention (see Chapter Eight for further discussion of secondary attention deficits). Let's assume, though, that Breston and Khari both have weak attention controls. For both students, understanding exactly what is happening in the classroom and at home can help to identify effective strategies for their attention that can be transferred across settings. Furthermore, knowing what is happening where their attention is reported to be weak can help parents, teachers, and the students themselves do a better job of managing their attention.

A Tool for Better Understanding

In Chapter Two I told a story from early in my career, when my supervisor criticized my test-bound report and had me rewrite it in a construct-bound manner. One of the reasons that he wanted me to organize my findings according to constructs was to force me to confront discrepancies in my data. Rarely if ever are assessment findings straightforward and clean. Almost every case includes discrepancies in the findings and data outliers. Discrepancies can be critical avenues into a student's assets and weaknesses, however, if they are probed to understand the reasons for the variation. When you think *with a theory* you'll find it easier to take a close look at clinical contrasts, because a theory provides the organizational structure against which the contrasts emerge and can be explained. Contrasts can then, in turn, help in the search for recurring themes, which is the subject of the next chapter.

7

Searching for Recurring Themes

AN ACADEMIC BREAKDOWN MAY STEM from any of several neurodevelopmental weaknesses. Trouble following directions in class, for example, may be observed in students who have a weak processing control system, receptive language, or short-term memory (or problems with some combination of these or other functions). That means five students may have difficulty following directions for five different sets of reasons.

Similarly, any assessment technique represents just part of what it is designed to measure (Meyer et al., 2001). For instance, a vocabulary task (for semantic understanding) will merely sample the words the student knows or may have been exposed to—it can't address all of them. And isolated data from assessment measures do not reflect the dynamic qualities of learning; emerging patterns across a variety of areas are needed to understand complex systems (Kelso, 1995; Zera, 2001).

The key to revealing the cause of a breakdown is to search for recurring themes: multiple pieces of evidence that fit together to make a case or support a hypothesis. Themes can be effective ways of organizing findings, which can really bolster your understanding of the student. Not only can themes help you, they can make assessment results much easier to comprehend for parents, teachers, and students themselves.

Making the Case

Get the facts first. You can distort them later.

—Mark Twain

After collecting information from different sources (such as history, testing, and interviewing), assessment requires sorting through the information and compiling evidence about assets and weaknesses. As I mentioned, one data point can mean multiple things. Let's look at an example involving digit span, a task in which numbers are read to a student who repeats them in the same order or in reverse order; reciting numbers in the same order is considered to be a test of short-term memory, whereas reversing the numbers involves active working memory.

Suppose Lucy, a fourth grader, scored below the expected range for her age both when reciting the numbers forward and when reversing them. Can we then conclude that her short-term and active working memory are both weak?

Not yet, because Lucy's performance on this task only makes sense when we look at it along with her other findings. Reports from her teacher indicate that she has a hard time following oral directions, that she tends to miss a lot of small details when she works (for example, misreading function signs on a math assignment), and that her accuracy across the board is rather inconsistent. She also participated in a multiple learning trial task in which she heard the same list of words several times, and she was expected to recall as many words as possible after each trial; on this task she scored low after the first time she heard the list, but her performance was solid on subsequent trials and after an extended delay. Finally, during the assessment she frequently asked to hear task directions a second time, but was able to follow directions after the repetition.

So looking at these multiple findings, weak processing depth (a component of the attention processing control system) is a recurring theme and appears to be a better hypothesis for Lucy than weak short-term and active working memory. She has a history of struggling with details (skimming over material) and inconsistency (picking up things intermittently). She also really benefited from repetition of information on the multiple learning trial task and when she was presented with directions for tasks. If her memory were really the issue, she would probably have more trouble recalling information even after hearing it a second time.

Have we proved that processing depth is the issue for Lucy, or that memory is not the issue for her? No, we have not proved it, but we have identified this recurring theme based on several pieces of evidence from different sources. It is a hypothesis that makes sense because it can be defended by the findings. Identifying recurring themes is akin to making a legal case in that evidence is collected and organized in support of an argument. But the process is also akin to the scientific method in that available information is used to generate a working hypothesis, which leads to research questions and experimentation to test the hypothesis. As discussed in Chapter Five, the assessment process really should extend into treatment and remediation, as the efficacy of the learning strategies can further inform the student's profile. For Lucy, an important set of recommendations based on this recurring theme is that she not only should get directions repeated, but that she should have ready access to material (for example, written directions) so that she can have a second pass at it. She also could use some structured practice on picking up detail, such as highlighting function signs in an explicit initial step when doing math work. If such ideas make a difference for Lucy, we have even more evidence (but not proof) that her processing depth is the culprit. If the ideas do not make a difference, we have reason to reconsider her profile and our initial hypothesis and go in a different direction with her learning plan.

To reiterate, single, isolated pieces of evidence are seldom useful in an assessment. Clinicians or educators should embed data points in patterns of other data points. Put differently, a weak (or strong) function should emerge from multiple angles, such as assessment procedures, pieces of history, interview responses, or work sample analysis. No single finding should be conclusively interpreted without other pieces to corroborate that finding.

Searching for recurring themes reduces the likelihood of rigidly depending on rules or algorithms for interpreting findings and makes assessment work more intriguing. Writing a term paper about a novel or poem also involves recurring themes. First comes a careful reading (collecting data), identifying a recurring theme (organizing findings), formulating a thesis based on the recurring theme (initial hypothesis), and then supporting it with examples from the text (validating hypothesis). Struggling students are like fascinating novels, and both deserve a rich and detailed understanding.

CASE STUDY

Jin is sixteen years old, and his parents are perplexed by his inconsistent performance in school. They believe him to be very bright, but the quality of his work does not seem to match up with his capabilities. His parents note that he "just does things without thinking about them, which causes him trouble." During assessment of his academic skills, Jin was observed to jump right into math problems; sometimes his initial approach was successful, but often he needed to renavigate midway through problems. When interviewed about his schoolwork, he acknowledged that he seldom outlines before writing ("I like to just get going when I write and not waste time with outlines") and he could not describe any systematic methods for studying ("I basically just review the material that will be on the test"). This lack of a systematic tactic was observed firsthand when he was asked to memorize a word list; Jin relied on rote memory and did not attempt to reorder the words into meaningful categories. When copying a complex geometric figure, he worked from left to right, rather than by starting with the main structure and adding smaller details.

Weak previewing emerged as a recurring theme in the findings. Jin's limited planning for tasks showed up in parent reports, academic skill assessment, neurodevelopmental tasks, and, interestingly, in conversation with Jin himself. This aspect of attention does not come naturally to Jin, and a major emphasis in his learning plan will be to make planning an explicit step anytime he confronts academic work.

Examples of Recurring Themes

Recurring themes come in two types—*narrow* (related to a specific function or construct) and *global* (a pattern across the student's profile). Narrow themes center on one aspect of a student's learning and emerge from different findings. For instance, evidence for limited active working memory usually surfaces from multiple sources, including reports from the classroom and home (for example, trouble with multistep instructions, mental math), review of work samples (better spelling in isolation than in context), and testing (difficulty simultaneously alphabetizing and reordering series of letters and numbers). Lucy represented this kind of recurring theme with her weak processing depth.

Searching for narrow recurring themes can help refine the assessment in terms of revealing functions within a construct that are particularly problematic or strong. For example, we may have considerable evidence that Mekhi, a seventh-grade boy, has weak receptive language, such as delayed reading comprehension and listening comprehension. But looking across the findings we find that he could identify word meanings and has good word decoding. He also showed fairly good comprehension during listening tasks in which he had to answer questions about passages read to him. Where Mekhi had considerable trouble, though, was at the sentence level. Listening tasks involving complex sentence structures (questions that were really statements, ambiguous statements, convoluted pronouns) really confused him. Looking carefully at his reading, he tended to make more mistakes around such complicated sentences in the text. So a key theme for Mekhi was weak sentence comprehension. His receptive language can handle word sounds (phonological processing) and individual words (semantic understanding), but gets overloaded at the sentence level. Interestingly, he seems to have good discourse processing, perhaps because he can use clues in large pieces of text to piece together meaning that escapes him in intricate sentences. In any event, his learning plan will need to focus on bolstering his understanding of multifaceted sentence structures.

Narrow recurring themes represent a thought process that is attuned to patterns across multiple angles (perhaps including test scores, but also going beyond such quantitative findings), making connections, and organizing evidence in support of a hypothesis. After gathering data, you need to pull the lens back so you can trace how a recurring theme (say, weak sentence comprehension) runs through the findings.

CASE STUDY

Casey is a seven-year-old second grader who is delayed with her reading decoding. She completed a variety of tasks during the assessment, and a recurring theme was weak *word retrieval*. For instance, she was asked to quickly name pictures of common objects (for example, light bulb, cat, boat), and though her responses were accurate, she was slow in responding for someone her age. She also generated relatively few members of a semantic category (say, things to play with) in a short time frame. Her writing samples reflected this theme as she employed a fairly narrow vocabulary and a number of nondescript filler words, like *stuff* and *things*. Reports from her teacher suggested that she is somewhat hesitant to respond when called on in class, acting like what she wants to say is "on the tip of her tongue," and this was also observed in conversations with Casey during the assessment.

Global themes span a student's profile, encompassing several neurodevelopmental constructs, academic skills, or both. Identifying a global theme involves pulling the lens back even further so you can see a pattern on top of other patterns. Global themes can reveal particular breakdowns that occur when certain functions or constructs interface. Looking at the findings for Nina, another second grader, we find that she has trouble self-monitoring (a component of the attention production control system) within her expressive language (when writing and speaking); she generates language but has a hard time checking whether or not it is accurate or makes good sense. However, she self-monitors effectively during math work and when the material is visual or spatial. She also seems to be able to monitor herself in social settings. Again, assessment should pave the way to the learning plan, so Nina will need to be demystified about this theme in her learning and her plan will need to provide her with tactics to improve her self-monitoring with language production.

Table 7.1 describes some of the global themes encountered when assessing students with learning problems. However, this list certainly should not be viewed as exhaustive. Keep an open mind, watching for chances to see things in different ways, and recurring themes are such opportunities. Given the complexities of the developing brain and the myriad interplays between different learning environments, it is really not surprising at all that any particular student could display a unique pattern of abilities.

CASE STUDY

Erlana is nine years old and is in the fourth grade. Her mother notes that she was "a star" early in elementary school, but that things started to unravel for her in third grade. Learning to write paragraph-length text has been onerous. Though Erlana used to enjoy math, she now finds it very frustrating. A recurring theme in her profile is difficulty with multitasking, or the capacity to handle complementary tasks simultaneously. This theme emerged whenever she was asked to do several things at once: listen and take notes, recall passages while answering questions about them, solving multistep math problems. In contrast, Erlana was quite adept at isolated tasks: decoding words, composing individual sentences, performing single math operations. Multitasking becomes much more prevalent later in elementary school when academic work takes on manifold facets. Understanding this theme helped Erlana to realize that she was not "stupid" (as she had called herself). Her learning plan included accommodations to separate work steps, as well as structured and supported practice in handling multiple work demands.

Table 7.1   Some Recurring Themes in Student Profiles

Theme	Description	Implications for Learning Plan
Better with visual info than with verbal info	More readily understands, generates, and remembers visual material than language-based info; could include relatively better performance on nonverbal higher-thinking tasks (such as matrix analogies) and with visual recall (for example, drawing a geometric figure after a delay); often related to strong spatial ordering and weak language	Given how important verbal material is in school, will likely need interventions (for example, reading remediation, language therapy) to bolster capacity to handle language-based info; visual strengths can be brought into play by converting verbal info to visual formats (as with cluster diagrams); visual strengths should also be nurtured through activities such as art classes and design software
Better with verbal info than with visual info	More readily understands, generates, and remembers language-based info than visual material; may be confused by nonverbal concepts such as fractions and area; better able to store and retrieve verbal info (such as a word list) than visual material (such as a geometric figure); often related to strong language and weak spatial ordering	For better or for worse, this profile is fairly well-suited for most academic work; may need support in subjects like geometry and more specific skills like using maps, charts, and diagrams; talking through problems involving visual material so the use of language can be helpful
Trouble with abstract material	Has relatively little difficulty understanding, generating, and remembering info that is somehow connected to personal experience (that is, concrete, contextualized), but struggles with the abstract (such as symbolism, nonverbal concepts); often related to weaknesses in higher-order cognition	To a large extent this theme is about making connections, even when they are not obvious; students may need explicit coaching and practice in this (for example, using graphic organizers to diagram concepts, defining features, and examples); students may have more initial success with abstract material that is within an affinity area (say, a student who loves cars working with the concept of transportation and related ideas); symbolism can be taught as a way to use "code words"

(continued)

Table 7.1   Some Recurring Themes in Student Profiles (*Continued*)

Theme	Description	Implications for Learning Plan
Trouble with large chunk sizes	Across tasks, skills, and modalities, breakdowns begin to appear when the student has to grapple with larger amounts of material (for example, paragraphs instead of sentences, word problems instead of simple calculations, large geometric figures instead of basic shapes); may appear late in elementary school or middle school, when students are confronted with bigger chunks	Accommodations may be necessary in terms of shortening some assignments or limiting the scope of materials and problems; interventions should initially target chunk sizes just big enough to give the student difficulty, establish improvement, then move up to even bigger chunk sizes
Top-down thinker, trouble with detail	More drawn to the big picture (the forest) than to minutiae (the trees); usually coupled with good creativity and understanding of concepts, but work quality is undercut by minor mistakes	Demystification needs to affirm importance of "big picture" thinking, while explaining how details are the infrastructure of work; the student may need checklists or other scaffolds to prompt self-review of work quality
Input better than output	Pattern also described by Levine as "output failure" (2003), refers to general difficulty accomplishing tasks and completing work, despite intact understanding of the material; may manifest as weak attention production control system, long-term memory access, and expressive language	Demystification is particularly important for such students and those who work with them, as they may have faced unfair accusations of laziness; their good input functions (for example, receptive language, long-term memory storage) should be highlighted; scaffolding and positive reinforcement may be necessary to elicit more productivity

Potential Hazards in the Search for Recurring Themes

Thinking with a theory goes hand in hand with searching for recurring themes, since theoretical frameworks provide the scaffolding that lets you organize your findings and see themes emerge. But while a framework can be a useful tool, it should not put up boundaries to understanding students. A student may show a pattern that is unique or that does not fit neatly into constructs or functions. Sometimes it is necessary to pull the lens back far enough to see beyond the current framework. Put differently, you need to be open to seeing new things and to seeing things in new ways.

When searching for recurring themes it is important to bear in mind that there is no certainty in the assessment of learning problems. The best anyone can do is identify a theme and provide a balance of supporting evidence. Proving a theme, as with an individual finding, is simply not possible, but you can present a data-based rationale for conclusions.

Another pitfall to consider relates to Occam's Razor (also known as the Law of Parsimony), which states that the simplest explanation is usually the best. Doctors have a saying—if you hear hoofbeats, do not look for a zebra. Try to avoid overcomplicated interpretations of findings. In other words, the hoofbeats you hear will be made by horses (not zebras) the vast majority of the time.

Finally, the search for recurring themes should include assets as well as weaknesses. The thought process behind narrow themes is the same for an intact or strong function as for a weak one. In addition, global themes can center on positive aspects of a student's learning. Several of the global themes listed in Table 7.1 (for example, input better than output) describe both positive and problematic features of a student's profile.

Tactics for Organizing Findings

The first step in identifying a recurring theme is organizing the information about the student. Again, the optimal way to organize data is within a theoretical framework. It is very helpful to have a road map for arranging data points (from history, testing, observation, and so on) into the constructs and functions of the framework being used. The idea is to have methods for laying out the findings to facilitate thinking about constructs (rather than tests) and to identify themes.

One tactic for organizing findings is to have a consistent form for notes. I prefer notes that list the various constructs and functions, with space to insert the different findings. This method would be in contrast to a test-bound form, or a form that is organized by information source (one section for history, a section for each test administered, and so on). Collecting notes according to constructs and functions can be very effective in clarifying thinking and can facilitate interpretation.

Figure 7.1   Example of Construct-Bound Clinical Notes

	Weak/Problematic	Intact/Solid	Strong/Asset
Memory: Short-Term	Digits Forward (Test); Remembering Instructions (Parent)	Hand Movements Forward (Test)	
Memory: Active Working	Digits Backward (Test); Doing Several Things at Once (Student)		Hand Movements Backward (Test)
Memory: Long-Term	Recalling Word List (Test); Fact Recall on Tests (Teacher)		Drawing Complex Figure After Delay (Test); Recall of Charts and Maps (Teacher)

Figure 7.1 presents an example of a construct-bound form for assessment notes. Each row of the form represents a component of the neurodevelopmental framework (just a few are depicted); elements of other frameworks (such as factors or systems) could be substituted. Each column represents a level of functioning from "Weak/Problematic" to "Strong/Asset"; this set of three levels could be replaced by however many levels you wanted to differentiate. Filling out the form would basically be an exercise in plotting data points. For example, a finding related to the short-term memory that suggests intact or solid functioning would be plotted in the center column. In considering multiple angles, both qualitative and quantitative findings would be plotted on the same form. So a low score on an active working memory task (such as reversing orally presented numbers) would be noted in the "Weak/Problematic" column along with a student's comment that he has a hard time when teachers tell him to do several things at once (it can be helpful to also note the source of the findings, as displayed in Figure 7.1).

Although this approach may seem rigid and formulaic, it is far more than a simple cookbook. Instead, it requires considerable expertise on several fronts, starting with making the linkages between the various assessment findings and the constructs or functions (that is, the rows of the table). Resources in other parts of this book, including Appendix C, can help in making such linkages. Second, it calls for a determination about the level of functioning (that is, the columns of the table) for each individual finding. Making level determinations involves much more than reading test scores; it requires personal norms stemming from experience with the assessment methods and pieces of historical information. For instance, sometimes scores can be misleading, such as when a student obtains a high score due to good accuracy but worked slowly or inefficiently (which may not have been captured in the score). So it is sometimes necessary to look past the numbers to make a determination about the student's level of performance.

As I discuss at length in Chapter Six, discrepancies in a student's performance can be extremely revealing. Laying out findings in a construct-bound way makes it easier to see and then interpret such discrepancies. Suppose a student struggles with recalling a list of words thirty minutes after initial learning trials; this data point would be plotted in the "Weak/Problematic" column in the "Memory: Long-term" row. In contrast, the student did very well with drawing a complex figure from memory thirty minutes after the initial copy trial; this finding would be placed in the "Strong/Asset" column in the "Memory: Long-Term" row. We also plot teacher reports that the student has a hard time with factual questions on tests, but seems to remember information from charts, graphs, and maps. Some themes start to emerge from the table: this student's long-term memory does not operate well with verbal information, but is very good with visual information (the same could also be said for short-term and active working memory).

Forms like the one in Figure 7.1 can serve as scaffolding for notes and, more important, for thinking with a theory. There is no magic to the particular format displayed here; columns could represent constructs (rather than levels of functioning) and rows could represent levels of functioning (rather than constructs), or rows and columns could be abandoned altogether in favor of some other format. The key is to find something that works for organizing and viewing findings.

Another useful tactic relates to how professionals communicate findings with each other. In Chapter Five I make the case for team assessment because of how useful multiple perspectives can be. When working in a team, people usually have a conference during which each shares findings so that the team can reach a mutual understanding of the student's profile and linkages. The typical way of sharing information is for each clinician to present a set of findings in their entirety. ("Here is what I found. . .") In contrast, a format that facilitates collaboration and construct-bound thinking is to structure the meeting around a theoretical framework. So the team members discuss all of their findings about attention, for example, and then move on to memory and other constructs. This format helps the meeting be a dialogue among professionals rather than a set of individual presentations. It helps the team see connections in the findings and identify recurring themes. It also puts each member of the team on a more equal footing for the assessment, since each individual contributes to each area of the assessment (rather than certain areas being the purview of certain individuals). For instance, a team should not single out one person for the assessment of attention, since the entire team got to view several of the attention controls when working with the student.

Change in Course

The emphasis of this book to this point has been on general principles of assessing learning problems. Now that the groundwork has been laid, our focus shifts to more specific assessment techniques. In other words, we're getting down to the nuts and bolts of assessment.

The next three chapters are devoted to the assessment of attention, memory, and language, respectively (see shaded portions of Figure 7.2). Though there are some differences in how the field conceptualizes them, these three constructs are universally accepted across theories of learning and brain development. In addition to being theoretically well-established as constructs, weaknesses in them are highly prevalent in learning problems (particularly low-severity, high-incidence problems). Finally, discussion of these three constructs demonstrates the thought process that can be applied to other neurodevelopmental constructs, regardless of their theoretical framework of origin.

Figure 7.2   A Neurodevelopmental Framework

Attention	Memory	Language	Spatial Ordering	Temporal-Sequential Ordering	Neuromotor Function	Higher-Order Cognition	Social Cognition
Cross-Construct Phenomena (Rate, Chunk Size, Metacognition, Strategy Use)							

Each of the next three chapters begins with a description of the construct, including its component functions, background theory, and some important distinctions for conceptualizing the constructs. The bulk of the discussion centers on general assessment techniques for the particular construct, including multiple types of findings (for example, qualitative and quantitative). The chapters include lists and descriptions of tasks designed to assess the constructs, as well as considerations for task-analysis. After a discussion of potential signs of weakness in the construct, the chapters conclude with illustrative case studies.

8

Assessing Attention

A TENET OF THIS BOOK is that clinical thinking should be undergirded by theory, and this is no more important for any aspect of learning than attention. Attention has been a touchstone in education for the last couple of decades, mainly as the centerpiece of ADHD. Although it enters into the discussion about many students with learning problems, many professionals in the field have relatively minimal understanding of attention as a theoretical construct. A conceptual understanding of attention makes every step of assessment and demystification easier, and ultimately students and families need to understand what attention is (and what it is not).

So what is *attention?* It is a multifaceted construct (Sergeant, 1996) that regulates mental energy, processes and filters incoming information, and controls output (Levine, 1998). It interfaces with all other neurodevelopmental functions and is involved in every academic area in some way or another. Though critically important, attention is not a sophisticated process in and of itself. Rather, attention supports the more complex neurodevelopmental functions, such as language and higher-order cognition.

Attention is not a list of behaviors (like the ones described in the ADHD diagnostic criteria), and it's not a lack of behaviors, either. Attention is an aspect of cognition that affects physical actions (such as controlling impulses), but it emanates from mental functioning. The next section extends the discussion of attention as a construct, focusing on its cognitive processes.

The Construct of Attention

The true art of memory is the art of attention.

—Samuel Johnson

Interestingly, many models of intelligence (such as Cattell-Horn-Carroll, or CHC, and Structure of Intellect, or SOI) do not explicitly list attention as a component (that is, as a broad or narrow ability, factor, axis, or dimension). However, the concept of attention is usually infused into aspects of intelligence theories. CHC, for example, includes short-term memory and visual processing, and the definitions of each incorporate ideas of filtering information (Evans et al., 2001). SOI discusses the functions of recognizing and producing (Guilford, 1982), which are akin to input (processing) and output (production) aspects of attention. The PASS model (Das et al., 1994) of intelligence, however, does explicitly include planning ("P") and attention ("A"). The attention component of PASS handles input, or information entering the senses (for example, sight and hearing). The planning component controls output (for example, thinking, communication, action) and use of strategies.

The term *executive functions* has gained prominence in recent years and refers to a domain of cognitive abilities that includes self-regulation, selective inhibition of responding, response preparation, cognitive flexibility, and organizing (Reader, Harris, Schuerholz, & Denckla, 1994). Executive functions are inherently self-regulating (as opposed to working on external stimuli) since they serve to change subsequent behavior (Barkley, 1996). Many researchers support a close connection between these functions and active working memory, which is necessary for suspending information online while previewing, planning, or self-monitoring (Barkley, 1996; Roberts & Pennington, 1996). Barkley (2000) has hypothesized that the hyperactive subtype of ADHD is an output disorder of impulsivity and self-control stemming from executive dysfunction. Interestingly, research has shown that improvements in executive functions through childhood coincide with growth spurts in frontal lobe development (Anderson, 1998); components of young brains make more and better connections, enabling them to better regulate and direct thinking.

As mentioned earlier, the Russian neuropsychologist Luria described three anatomical and functional units of attention (1973). Unit 1 refers to the brain stem and related areas, all of which are lower in the brain's structure. This unit regulates levels of alertness by bringing about gradual changes in cognitive functioning (rather than the all-or-nothing changes brought about by Unit 2). It is activated by the body's metabolism, stimuli from the external environment, and the cerebral cortex (which houses higher brain functions).

Luria's Unit 2 refers to areas that are in higher regions of the brain's structure, such as the lateral and posterior regions of the neocortex (occipital-visual, temporal-auditory, parietal-general sensory). This unit analyzes and stores newly received information and, in contrast to Unit 1, operates via the all-or-nothing principle (that is, as a switch that is either on or off, rather than a dial). Also, Unit 2 is organized into three hierarchical zones (primary, secondary, and tertiary) that become decreasingly specialized in modality and progressively lateralized and overlapping; in other words, the higher zones are set up to make more connections, allowing for conversion of concrete perceptions into abstract thinking and formation of schemes.

Luria's Unit 3 also refers to areas that are in higher regions of the brain's structure, but at the front of the brain, or the frontal lobes. This unit programs and controls mental activity. It is essentially a superstructure above other components of the cerebral cortex. It formulates plans, strategies, and actions; controls behavior; coordinates problem-solving; inhibits impulse; and self-monitors.

To summarize Luria's attention model, Unit 1 regulates alertness like a thermostat, Unit 2 analyzes input like a filter and sorter, and Unit 3 oversees brain functions and output like the conductor of an orchestra. Regarding Unit 1, research has shown that students with attention deficits can show a suboptimal level of arousal (Banaschewski et al., 2003; Brandeis et al., 2002). Problems with Unit 2 appear similar to the inattention category of symptoms for ADHD (for example, does not seem to listen), whereas problems with Unit 3 seem related to the hyperactivity (fidgeting, squirming) and impulsivity (blurting out) categories of symptoms. Unit 3 also bears several similarities with executive functions in terms of self-regulation, inhibition, and organization of thought and action.

The neurodevelopmental framework emphasized in this book (Figure 8.1) incorporates a model of attention that resembles Luria's attention paradigm (see Appendix A for additional background). Levine (1998) divided attention into three control systems that are similar to Luria's three units. The advantages of this paradigm of attention are that it is multifaceted and yet organized in such a way as to facilitate understanding (especially for students and families).

Figure 8.1   Three-System Model of Attention

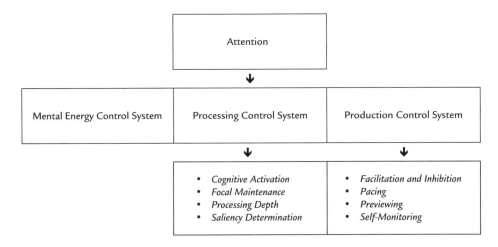

The mental energy control system initiates and maintains the cognitive fuel needed for optimal learning and behavior. Like Luria's Unit 1, the mental energy control system controls appropriate levels of alertness, sufficient and consistent mental effort, and sleep/wake cycles. This system is analogous to a fuel tank.

The processing control system (akin to Luria's Unit 2) handles information entering through the senses. It can be useful to further divide the processing control system into specific controls:

- *Cognitive activation:* Linking incoming information with prior knowledge and experience
- *Focal maintenance:* Sustaining concentration for the appropriate period of time (also referred to as attention span or sustained attention)
- *Processing depth:* Focusing with sufficient intensity to capture details (such as instructions)
- *Saliency determination:* Discriminating between important and unimportant information; avoiding distractions (also known as selective attention)

Finally, the production control system regulates thinking for academic and behavioral output and resembles Luria's Unit 3 as well as executive functions (though there are some distinctions that will be discussed in the next section). As with the processing controls, the specific production controls can be delineated:

- *Facilitation and inhibition:* Selecting the best option before acting or starting a task (facilitation) and suppressing inappropriate decisions and behaviors (inhibition)
- *Pacing:* Working at the most appropriate speed, without rushing
- *Previewing:* Anticipating and predicting likely outcomes of actions, events, and problems; planning how to solve a problem before starting to work
- *Self-monitoring:* Tracking one's output and making necessary revisions; finding and correcting mistakes in one's work

☞ Levine (1998) describes an additional processing control related to regulating satisfaction level; weakness with this control leads to boredom, insatiability, or an extreme attraction to exciting topics and activities. He also describes reinforceability, or the capacity to use feedback and draw from past experience, as another production control. Problems with either can lead to behavior problems, but they are not as closely linked to academic performance as the other processing and production controls.

Some Important Distinctions

Accepting that attention is a multidimensional construct, it is useful to understand some key distinctions between facets of attention. Such understanding enables the clinician or educator to distinguish between specific attention controls and pinpoint strategies for the student's learning plan. Just as important, making distinctions between attention controls supports demystification with students and parents.

Let's turn first to the processing controls and their collective role in taking in information. *Saliency determination* is the mind's capacity to efficiently recognize relevance. Because the senses are constantly bombarded with information, it is critical for the mind to filter out what requires additional focus from what does not. This control is like a spotlight that zeroes in on targets for illumination. Distractibility is a major sign of weak saliency determination, because if your mind has trouble identifying that the teacher's voice is more important than traffic noise on the street, you are more likely to be distracted by the traffic noise. Weak saliency determination can take other forms in academic work as well, such as trouble sifting out important details from less important information (as when solving math word problems and studying large amounts of material).

Once saliency has been established, information requires the right amount of concentration in order for it to sink in for understanding and storage in memory. This is where *processing depth* does its work as the mind's wax for imprinting. A shallow level of processing depth (or hard wax) leads to excessive glossing over of details—information goes in one ear and out the other, as the saying goes. On the other hand, overly deep processing depth can lead to problems in terms of grinding down on a piece of material, often resulting in getting mentally stuck and working inefficiently. Many pieces of incoming information need to be linked with existing information already stored in memory, and this is the role of *cognitive activation*. This particular control allows for identifying connections within and between pieces of material. Too much cognitive activation, though, causes tangential thinking (like surfing the Internet and straying far from the home page of the site you meant to visit), while too little cognitive activation leads to passive thinking and trouble seeing the big picture. Finally, it is important to pay attention for appropriate intervals of time; *focal maintenance* sustains attention for the other controls (and other constructs) to do their work.

> ☞ Weak *focal maintenance* is about focus drifting away from the task at hand, whereas weak *saliency determination* is about focus being lured away from the task at hand by a distracting stimulus.

Flipping over to the production controls, one of the most important things they accomplish is putting the brakes on all the myriad potential things that occur to us to say or do. This is primarily the domain of *facilitation and inhibition.* In any given day we could undertake numerous actions that, upon reflection, would be inadvisable. For a fifth grader that might be throwing an eraser at a classmate, or responding before hearing the entire question. Facilitation and inhibition is bolstered by the capacity to think ahead and anticipate potential outcomes, or *previewing*. Academic work is replete with tasks that require a student to first develop a plan of attack, such as when writing an essay or balancing an equation, which is why previewing is such an important attention control.

Both facilitation and inhibition and previewing primarily come into play just before one starts working. In contrast, pacing and self-monitoring kick into gear once the work begins. *Pacing* is how attention exerts control over how quickly one works. Weak pacing is like slippage in an engine clutch, a device that should help keep speed appropriate for the situation. *Self-monitoring* is attention's quality control system; akin to a surveillance camera hovering over one's shoulder, it catches errors and provides feedback during work. Without good self-monitoring, one is more likely to make avoidable mistakes, such as in writing, math, or in the social arena (for example, by failing to check how one is relating to peers during a group activity). Pacing and self-monitoring operate in tandem, and a weakness in one often coincides with a weakness in another. For instance, rushing through math homework often leaves scant opportunity to check over answers, whereas carefully editing a written assignment inherently leads to a slower and more methodical work rate.

As mentioned earlier, the production controls are similar to executive functions, especially when the latter are defined coherently around control of thought and output. Executive functions, though, have been written about by so many researchers and clinicians that their definitions have evolved and expanded to (according to some) include input functions and higher-order cognition functions such as how to use logic and solve problems. The neurodevelopmental framework presented in this book makes a cleaner break between attention's regulation of input, which is important but not necessarily sophisticated cognition, and the mind's higher thought processes.

It is also useful to look at how executive functions have been distinguished from attention itself, as this helps to understand how the processing controls differ from the production controls. Barkley (1996) described attention in terms of connecting the mind to the environment (or stimuli from the environment), which happens in the present (that is, data stream into the mind through the senses). In contrast, he defined executive functions in terms of

Table 8.1   Distinguishing Features, Attention Versus
Executive Functions

Attention	Executive Functions
Connects response to environment	Connects response to response
Set in the present	Related to future actions
Acts on environment	Acts on another response

connecting responses to responses (thoughts or actions), and as having a future orientation. (Table 8.1 summarizes the contrasts set forth in Barkley's work.) Regardless of the terminology, the bottom line is that a difference exists between mental functions that process input and those that are internally focused on thought processes, potential courses of action, and working speed.

General Assessment Considerations

Perhaps more than any other neurodevelopmental construct, attention needs to be assessed instead of merely tested. Weak attention controls can be easily overlooked in their subtle varieties. Though some tests are designed to examine facets of attention, as discussed in the next section, viewing multiple angles is critical in terms of using history and qualitative findings. A similar case has been made about executive functions: deficits are rarely reflected in test scores, meaning that qualitative observation and informed judgment must be used (Anderson, 1998). In addition, subscribing to the multi-factorial model of attention described in the previous section necessitates assessing a profile of attention controls, as opposed to looking at the functionality of attention as a whole.

The mental energy control system, in particular, requires an assessment approach rather than a testing approach. No formal tests address mental energy, meaning that it is assessed only through observation and history. Reports from home are critical in getting a read on the student's sleep/arousal balance: How many hours of sleep does the student get each night? What is the general quality of the sleep (for example, waking in the middle of night, tossing and turning)? How easily does the student fall asleep? Wake in the morning? Parents may need to complete a sleep log to record such observations over time. Significant problems with sleep may need medical assessment in terms of a sleep study.

Both parents and teachers can report on the student's mental energy. Everyone experiences cognitive fatigue to some degree when working on something that is challenging. The question, though, is whether the student experiences excessive fatigue. Put simply, is doing work too much work? Also, how consistent is the student's mental energy? Are there days or times of the day where tiredness is a particular problem?

Observing the student over the course of an assessment session also provides information about mental energy. Assessments are apt to be rather demanding of students, involving numerous academic and neurodevelopmental tasks that are often quite challenging. Though practically everybody would feel drained after a couple of hours of testing and interviewing, does the student seem excessively tired, or impressively resilient? Also, did the level of cognitive fuel seem to fluctuate over the sessions?

Obviously, personal norms play a pivotal role in interpreting observations about mental energy (as well as other aspects of attention). It takes experience with students of various ages to be able to perceive how an individual student is faring during an assessment session. Less experienced professionals need to rely on supervisors, mentors, or colleagues to help them interpret observations until they have built up their own personal norms.

A consideration when assessing the mental energy control system is the effect of the student's emotional status. A student experiencing depression, for example, may appear lethargic and subdued. So all observations about the student's cognitive fuel need to be interpreted along with available information about the student's emotional functioning. (Chapter Eleven includes a discussion on screening for emotional difficulty.)

History reports are also critical for assessing attention's processing and production controls. Specific signs of weak processing and production controls, as well as weak mental energy controls, are listed later in this chapter, in Table 8.3. The overarching goal, however, is to get multiple perspectives on how the student takes in information and how well the student regulates different aspects of output and thinking. As mentioned in Chapter Six, history reports may vary from setting to setting, which may reflect varying demands on the student. For example, some parents report few concerns about attention at home (where the student has relatively fewer work demands) while the student's teacher reports significant concerns. Sometimes the opposite pattern is reported, perhaps because the student has relatively more structure in the classroom than at home. Such clinical contrasts can be very revealing when the different learning and working environments in question are task-analyzed to determine the reasons for the differences between the reports.

An important source of history is the individual student. When asked the right questions, all students (even young ones) can provide information about their attention. An approach I have employed involves first mentioning how I've talked to a lot students about their learning and how they've each described unique things about their minds; this is intended to destigmatize learning problems. I usually then ask an open-ended question to try to get the student to start talking about attention (or another construct, for that matter), such as, "Before you started that task, what were you thinking about how you were going to do it?" or "I noticed that you missed some details in your summary of the passage I just read to you. Why do you think that was?" Interviewing about strategies (for example, "Tell about how you came up with that answer") is very important for assessing production controls such as previewing. Sometimes the questions need to be phrased in a multiple-choice format, especially with younger students or students with weak expressive language. For example, "Some kids who've missed details in that passage have told me that they had a hard time focusing while I read it, others that they didn't really understand it, and still others had trouble remembering it. What about you?" Engaging the student in this kind of interview is an example of how the actual assessment can also be part of the demystification process.

Again, attention interfaces with all constructs. However, there are particularly close connections between processing controls and certain other neurodevelopmental functions. These include short-term and active working memory; in order to retain information for brief periods, the information must first be filtered (saliency determination) and absorbed with sufficient intensity (processing depth). Memory is bolstered when attention is sustained for adequate intervals (focal maintenance) and if the right amount of connections are made with previous knowledge (cognitive activation). Receptive language is another critical interface, as information must first come in through the processing controls (via reading or listening) before it can be comprehended. Similarly, making sense of visual material (spatial ordering) and serial information (sequential ordering) can be compromised by problematic processing controls. It is important to point out, though, that weaknesses in memory, language, or other constructs can create the appearance of dysfunctional processing controls. I discuss such secondary attention deficits later in this chapter.

There are also close connections between the production controls and other functions. Expressive language takes ideas and converts them to words for communication (via writing or speaking), and is facilitated by good impulse control (facilitation and inhibition) and planning (previewing). In addition, the quality of communication is improved by proper speed (pacing) and a sense of how well one is conveying ideas (self-monitoring). Creating visual material (spatial ordering) and serial information (sequential ordering) is also bolstered by properly functioning production controls. Again, weaknesses in language or other constructs can lead to secondary attention deficits.

To summarize, here are some general considerations when assessing attention:

- Bear in mind that students have a profile of attention controls (weak, intact, or strong).
- Consider multiple angles, including history and qualitative findings in addition to testing.
- Collect history from the student.
- Watch for discrepancies in history reports—they can be useful clinical contrasts, and can help form learning plans.
- Closely examine interfaces between attention and other constructs, including memory and language.
- Take into account that signs of weak attention may actually be secondary attention deficits, or dysfunctions in other areas that appear to be weak attention.

Tasks Designed to Assess Aspects of Attention

Direct testing of some of the attention controls is possible and can be very revealing, but consideration of the context is always warranted; a testing environment is much different from a classroom, for example. Also, testing results should always be taken for what they are, which is merely one of the multiple angles that need to be considered when generating a student's profile. This section describes some of the tasks that are available for assessing aspects of attention. Task descriptions are summarized in Table 8.2, along with

Table 8.2   Assessment Task Types for Attention

Task Type	Description	Primarily Assesses[1]	Examples[2]
Visual vigilance	Searching through an array of pictures, symbols, numbers, and letters, and marking only those that are identical to one or more targets; often has time limit (for example, one to three minutes); also known as target tag	Attention (processing controls, production controls)	Cancellation, Symbol Search (WISC-IV Integrated); Pair Cancellation, Visual Matching (WJ-III Cognitive); Visual Attention (NEPSY); Receptive Attention (CAS)
Target tag	See visual vigilance	Attention (processing controls, production controls)	See visual vigilance
Continuous performance task (CPT)	Pushing button or clicking trigger when a target is heard or seen (usually on computer screen); inhibiting impulse to respond to non-targets; usually lasts several minutes	Attention (processing controls, production controls)	TOVA; Auditory Attention and Response Set (NEPSY); CCPT; Auditory Attention (WJ-III Cognitive)
Complex figure copy	Copying a large, complex, and abstract figure; sometimes linked with drawing recall	Attention (production controls), spatial ordering, graphomotor function	RCFT; Complex Form Copying (PEERAMID-2)
Stroop task	Identifying the color in which displayed words are printed, resisting the urge to read to words themselves (even though the words spell various colors)	Attention (facilitation and inhibition)	Color-Word Interference Test (D-KEFS)
Tower	Shifting balls or disks from peg to peg (three total) in specific number of moves to match picture displayed on an easel; multiple rules must be followed (for example, cannot put ball or disk on table)	Attention (production controls), higher-order cognition (reasoning and logic)	Tower (NEPSY); Tower Test (D-KEFS)

[1]The neurodevelopmental functions and constructs listed here are those that are primarily assessed by the given task; other functions and constructs may be tapped as well.
[2]Full test and battery citations are listed in Appendix D.

Figure 8.2   Mock Visual Vigilance Task, Searching for Single Target

	Target:	nunmb		
nunmb	nuumb	nunmd	nunwb	nuumb
nunwb	nunmd	unumb	nunmb	nnumb
nunmd	nunmb	nunwb	nunmd	nunmb
nnumb	unumb	Nuumb	nunmb	unumb

names of batteries and subtests. (Appendix D includes full battery names for acronyms, along with test publishers.)

For the processing control system, *visual vigilance* (or target tag) tasks tap a student's ability to discriminate between important and unimportant information and to maintain focus over time. The idea behind visual vigilance is that the student is presented with a specific visual target (for example, a set of letters or shapes) and then must scan through an array and quickly circle or mark only the targets, avoiding non-targets that look similar to the target. The target is the salient information, and focus must be maintained over the allotted time interval (say, three minutes). This kind of task requires saliency determination, processing depth, and focal maintenance.

The targets are typically devoid of meaning, although they could be real words or pictures of real objects (such as animals). Figure 8.2 shows an example of a visual vigilance task featuring non-words, which factors out the student's decoding skill; this particular example involves a single target that must be found several times in the array. Note that many of the non-targets are nearly identical to the target, requiring good processing depth in order to detect.

Visual vigilance tasks can vary in complexity. The example in Figure 8.3 includes two targets for which the student would search in the array. This example also uses abstract shapes or figures which, for some students, make the task more difficult since they do not hold any inherent meaning or context. However, students with excessive cognitive activation sometimes perform better with abstract material than with contextualized information, which can lead to more connections with personal experience and thus be distracting; for example, a student would have a hard time navigating through an

Figure 8.3   Mock Visual Vigilance Task, Searching for Multiple Targets

Targets: ●■O   X◇▼

●■O	O■●	X◇▼	X◇▲	●■O
X◇▼	●■O	●□O	X▼◇	+◇▼
●□O	●■O	X◇▼	●■O	O□●
X◇▼	+◇▲	X◇▲	◇▼X	●■O

array of animal pictures if they kept calling up images of a recent trip to the zoo or of favorite books about jungles and ocean reefs.

Another type of visual vigilance task introduces a basic rule for the student to follow when working through the array. The rule for the example in Figure 8.4 is that the lowest number in each row must be circled. Regardless of the format of the visual vigilance task, obviously two types of errors are possible:

- Not marking a target
- Marking a non-target

The first kind of error is often referred to as an *omission,* or false negative, and can be a sign of weak saliency determination, shallow processing depth, or insufficient focal maintenance. The second kind of error is often referred to as a *commission,* or false positive, and can result from impulsive responding or

Figure 8.4   Mock Visual Vigilance Task, Searching for Multiple Rule-Based Targets

Circle the Lowest Number in Each Row

3	6	2	7
4	5	8	6
78	45	51	63
32	61	49	31
212	272	834	440
791	778	801	770

Figure 8.5   Target and Non-Target for a Mock Visual Continuous
Performance Task

from weak facilitation and inhibition. In the example in Figure 8.4, a student
may impulsively circle the number 3 in the first row because 3 is lower than
the 6 right next to it without looking ahead and seeing the 2 right after the 6.
Also, students who work too quickly (weak pacing) may make commission
errors.

The continuous performance task (CPT) is another category of attention
test for processing and production controls. Such tasks require the student
to perform some simple action, such as hitting the space bar on a keyboard,
when presented with a target. CPTs usually last several minutes (sometimes
more than twenty minutes) and can be either visual or auditory. Visual CPTs
often involve a computer screen on which targets and non-targets are displayed (see Figure 8.5). As with visual vigilance tasks, the student needs to respond only to targets and resist the impulse to respond to non-targets. Hence,
both omissions and commissions are possible and can be signs of weak processing and production controls, respectively.

Auditory CPTs involve an extended recording to which the student listens, only responding to a target sound and resisting the impulse to respond
to non-target sounds. Many CPTs, visual and auditory, make use of decontextualized information. Visual examples would be abstract designs or symbols, such as those in Figure 8.5. Auditory examples include a basic tone of
a specific pitch. By using decontextualized material, CPTs can factor out the
effect of meaning on the student's performance (such as decoding a word or
interpreting a picture). However, some CPTs do incorporate contextualized
information, such as spoken words or pictures of real objects; the advantage
of this kind of CPT is that it more closely approximates the attention demands faced by the student (for example, listening for specific instructions
in the classroom).

☞ Various tests designed to assess the same area, such as attention, often have different features. Selecting a particular test for a battery is a bit like shopping for a car: although any car will get you from point A to point B, the choice you make depends on the features you want. For CPTs and target tags, for example, situations may arise when contextualized information is needed, and others when decontextualized material might be better (and using both for comparison is also an option).

Several tasks put a premium on planning and methodical work, consequently assessing the production controls. I have discussed use of the complex figure copy (illustrated again in Figure 8.6) several times already, and it can be a very useful test of previewing, especially when the student's copying process is closely observed. A good strategy, for example, would be to first construct the large center rectangle, using the horizontal midline to extend the cross out to the right and the partial vertical midline to determine where the two triangles converge at the top; smaller details can then be added once the basic structure is in place. This is not the only good way to go about the copy, but it reveals a planned approach. In contrast, a student with weak previewing might simply start from the left and work to the right, which could result in poor alignment of the figure's elements. I have even seen some students run out of room at the edge of the paper because they did not plan how much space they would need! Facilitation and inhibition also come into play, as some students may have trouble resisting the urge to start the copy with certain intriguing elements, such as the small concentric circles in the

Figure 8.6   Mock Complex Figure

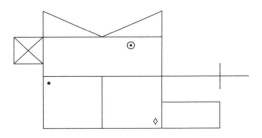

middle, without regard to first organizing the drawing. A student with weak pacing might rush through the task, while another with weak self-monitoring might not check the copy against the original.

Although the final product of a complex figure copy can inform attention functioning, the copying process is probably more important. It is not uncommon for a final product to look quite good (suggesting intact or strong spatial ordering), even though the approach was haphazard. Processing depth is also tapped by this task, as the student has to pick up small details, such as the little diamond at the center bottom in Figure 8.6.

An interesting test of facilitation and inhibition is the Stroop task, in which the student is asked to name the color in which displayed words are printed, even though the words spell out colors (for example, the word *red* might be printed in blue). This task is much harder than it appears to be, as the impulse to read the word (instead of naming the color in which it is printed) can be powerful.

An attractive feature of many attention tests is that they can seem a lot like games to students. This is especially true of tower tasks, which usually involve three narrow posts on a platform and a set of rings or pegs. The student moves rings or pegs from post to post in order to recreate a displayed design. The catch is that the student needs to use a certain number of moves and must also follow specific rules, both of which put a premium on previewing and facilitation and inhibition. In the mock tower task in Figure 8.7, the goal is to move different sized disks from peg to peg to build a designated tower design in as few moves as possible. Two rules need to be followed: only one disk can be moved at a time and a larger disk can never be placed over a smaller disk. Impulsivity leads to breaking one or both of the rules. Poor planning leads to false starts and an inefficient approach to moving the disks from the starting position to the ending position.

Other tests that emphasize the production controls include navigating mazes and strategic tracing. As with tower tasks, rules or parameters force the student to plan and resist impulses in order to succeed. A maze task, for instance, may require movement in only certain directions (for example, no backtracking allowed) or to reach points in the maze in a particular sequence. Strategic tracing asks the student to trace over a design, but without backtracking or crossing over previously traced lines (which is why previewing is necessary).

Figure 8.7   Mock Tower Task

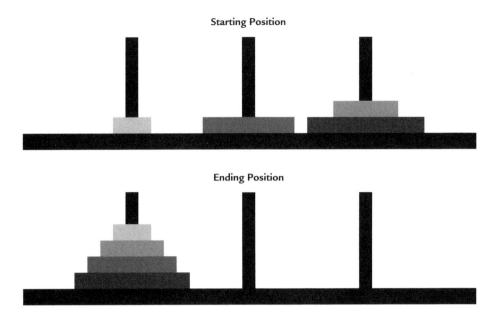

Beal (1993) described some qualitative procedures that assess self-monitoring on applied tasks. In an error detection task the student is shown a brief written passage that is deliberately confusing, and is then asked to review the passage and identify the problems (for example, incongruent details or unclear terms). A scribe procedure asks the student to read a passage and then suggest changes that would make it easier for another reader to understand. Such tasks are qualitative in nature (requiring personal norms for interpretation of observations) and can be invented for the individual assessment (for example, drawn from material similar to what the student might be working on).

Task-Analysis for Attention

Since attention permeates all aspects of thinking and working, any task is actually an opportunity to observe attention in action. One facet of personal norms is awareness of the particular attention demands of a given assessment task. This section will discuss some of the main considerations in the task-analysis for attention.

As mentioned earlier in this chapter, receptive language is an area that has particularly strong interfaces with the processing controls. Processing depth, for instance, can be assessed during language tasks. For example, a student may make errors on a listening test (such as following multistep instructions) but correct them easily if the item is repeated; in contrast, a student with weak receptive language (for example, sentence comprehension) would not benefit as much from repetition of items. Similarly, verbal tests of short-term memory (such as repeating series of orally presented digits) can be derailed by superficial processing depth, and repeating items can help determine the real issue (attending versus recalling). Some memory tests involve multiple learning trials (that is, a list is presented each time, and the student recites as much of the list as possible after each trial), which reveals a learning curve. A student may have trouble recalling list items after the initial learning trial, but then show a good learning curve; this would suggest that the initial trial was undermined by shallow processing depth, but that the information burned through the weak attention and was appropriately embedded in short-term memory.

The accuracy pattern of tasks can reveal difficulties with focal maintenance. On a multiple learning trial task (such as a word list read to a student several times for memorization), for instance, a student may recall little from the middle or end of the list, suggesting an inability to maintain focus for the entire presentation of the material. A student may show inconsistent responding on a test (say, of receptive language or math operations) where the items get progressively more difficult (that is, easy problems are at the beginning, and harder ones are at the end). In the example in Figure 8.8, an

Figure 8.8   Inconsistent Response Pattern Indicative of Weak Attention

Inconsistent Accuracy		Consistent Accuracy	
1	Correct	1	Correct
0	Incorrect	1	Correct
1	Correct	1	Correct
0	Incorrect	1	Correct
1	Correct	1	Correct
1	Correct	1	Correct
0	Incorrect	0	Incorrect
1	Correct	1	Correct
1	Correct	0	Incorrect
1	Correct	0	Incorrect
Total	**7**	**Total**	**7**

inconsistent accuracy pattern is shown on the left, with the student missing some of the easier items but then getting harder ones correct. On the right is a consistent accuracy pattern, with the student missing only some of the harder items. Note that each student earned the same total score of 7, but the inconsistent accuracy pattern on the left suggests that processing depth and focal maintenance were the real culprits.

A student who is asked to recall information from memory (for example, on a multiple learning trial or word retrieval task) may make different kinds of errors. For instance, reciting non-list words that are in the same category as correct responses (say, the list included several vegetables but the student named other vegetables, a type of error referred to as an *intrusion*) can be indicative of excessive cognitive activation (list words triggered tangential responses within the category). Intrusions outside the list categories altogether can stem from weak facilitation and inhibition, or impulsive responding. Also, on a recall task the student ideally will avoid repeating pieces of information. That is, when asked to quickly list vegetables, the student will say each one that comes to mind only once, not give you something like this: "carrots, broccoli, zucchini, carrots, mushrooms, green beans, carrots, celery, carrots." Such repetition errors, or *perseverations,* suggest weak self-monitoring, as the student is not doing well with tracking past responses (perseverations can also be a sign of weak active working memory, or of not being able to mentally juggle past and potential responses).

Academic tasks are important opportunities to observe attention in an applied mode. Any time the student is taking in information, the processing controls are in play: decoding words, reading passages, looking over math problems, listening to instructions. The extent to which a student identifies important information (say, in a reading passage or in a math word problem) relates to saliency determination. Picking up details sufficiently (for example, correctly identifying math function signs, or correctly decoding words with similar beginning letters) speaks to processing depth. Whenever the student is generating work, the production controls are in play: solving a math problem, spelling words, writing a passage. A rushed, haphazard approach (as opposed to planning or using strategies) suggests weaknesses in previewing, facilitation and inhibition, and pacing; a useful experiment during testing is to explicitly request that the student work at a slower rate, which will allow you to assess the student's capacity to restrain working speed when prompted. Also, the degree to which the student detects and corrects errors in the work relates to self-monitoring.

> ☞ A student assessed by the Student Success Program was asked about several homework errors he made on math problems related to misreading "+" and "−" signs. His explanation was that when he worked on the problems at school they were addition, but that magic had transformed them to subtraction by the time he got home.

As mentioned earlier, interviewing students about their approach ("How are you organizing the writing?") and use of strategies ("What's your plan for solving that math problem?") provides a window into previewing. Another reason that personal norms are so important is that they give you an experience base to assess how students typically approach tasks and solve problems. As you work with students it is important to compare the strategy or plan that a student employs with those of similar-age students on the same task. In essence, you need a rubric or checklist (even if only in memory) on strategy usage for just about every task.

Attention Signs and Symptoms

Obviously, the discussion up to this point has already touched on many potential signs of weak attention.

> ☞ Some clinicians differentiate *signs,* which are observed by others, from *symptoms,* which are reported by the student (or patient or client). This distinction may not be important except to underscore the need to include the student's perspective (for example, via interview) when assessing to understand.

Table 8.3 presents typical findings to consider for specific attention controls. The table includes different types of findings, asset indicators, and signs of dysfunction. Similar information is also found in Appendix C, along with

Table 8.3 Signs and Symptoms of Attention

Attention Control	*General Findings*
Mental energy control system	Asset Indicators • *Appearing to have ample energy when working* • *Easily starts and completes tasks* • *Appropriate and consistent working speed* Signs of Dysfunction • *Cognitive effort and academic work seem excessively draining* • *Irregular sleep/wake cycles (for example, trouble falling or staying asleep, waking in morning)* • *Inconsistent levels of alertness and mental fuel* • *Student describing feeling overwhelmed and drained by work*
Cognitive activation	Asset Indicators • *Making innovative connections from the topic at hand to other information* • *Extensive elaboration* • *Student citing prior knowledge in connection to reading passage* Signs of Dysfunction • *Comments that are tangential to the discussion topic* • *Student describing thoughts that race from topic to topic* • *Forming few relevant associations, passive thinking, trouble seeing the big picture* • *Being excessively reminded of prior knowledge when working with decontextualized material* • *Disorganized train of thought in written or oral expression, or both*
Focal maintenance	Asset Indicators • *Maintaining concentration for extended periods* Signs of Dysfunction • *Concentration fading during lessons or academic work* • *Excessive daydreaming* • *Inconsistent accuracy pattern (for example, missing easy items or words and getting harder ones)* • *Student describing focus as drifting (for example, "zoning in and out")*
Processing depth	Asset Indicators • *Detecting small details in a copy of a complex figure or picture* • *Picking up subtle pieces of information when reading or listening*

Table 8.3   Signs and Symptoms of Attention (*Continued*)

Attention Control	General Findings
	Signs of Dysfunction • *Asking for repetitions of oral instructions* • *Errors in listening comprehension that are readily corrected after repetition* • *Inconsistent accuracy pattern (for example, missing easy items or words and getting harder ones)* • *Getting stuck on little details encountered in reading and other assignments* • *Student describing tendency to skim over material* • *Decoding errors that are visually close with some phonics (*inside *for* insist)* • *Math errors stemming from misread signs and details in problems*
Saliency determination	Asset Indicators • *Identifying main points in reading text* • *Selecting the most important information to study for a test* Signs of Dysfunction • *Distractibility* • *Focusing on irrelevant details in math word problems* • *Student describing tendency for focus to be lured away from the topic or material at hand* • *Disorganization with materials, trouble filtering and prioritizing what to keep and what to discard*
Facilitation and inhibition	Asset Indicators • *Well-controlled behavior (for example, not giving in to urges)* • *Pausing before starting a task to survey it* • *Taking a moment to think before answering a question* Signs of Dysfunction • *Jumping too quickly into work or tasks* • *Impulsive behaviors in the classroom or in social situations* • *Student describing urge to act too quickly* • *Decoding errors that are visually close with some phonics (*inside *for* insist)*
Pacing	Asset Indicators • *Copying a complex figure at an appropriate pace* • *Spatially organized math work (for example, aligned columns)* Signs of Dysfunction • *Rushing through homework or other assignments* • *Student describing tendency to work too quickly*

(continued)

Table 8.3   (*Continued*)

Attention Control	General Findings
Previewing	Asset Indicators • *Planning and outlining an essay, report, or term paper* • *Forming a good plan for copying a complex figure* • *Estimating what the solution to a math problem will be prior to solving it* Signs of Dysfunction • *Starting to solve a math problem without first thinking through the best approach* • *Student describing a tendency to work on assignments without initially planning them*
Self-monitoring	Asset Indicators • *Editing and revising written work* • *Catching errors in math problems* • *Checking on comprehension when reading* • *Comparing the copy of a complex figure with the model* • *Detecting how one is affecting peers in social situations* Signs of Dysfunction • *Making errors that the student can readily correct when they are pointed out* • *Inconsistent accuracy pattern (for example, missing easy items or words and getting harder ones)* • *Student describing trouble with detecting errors in own work or with sensing how an exercise is going*

typical findings for other neurodevelopmental constructs. As I've mentioned, personal norms are extremely important for gathering findings and then interpreting them. In particular, personal norms help with developmental considerations, or knowing what to expect of students at different ages. For example, the length of time a typical seven-year-old student can attend (focal maintenance) is definitely shorter than that of a seventeen-year-old. Developmental distinctions can be difficult to quantify, but professional experience helps a great deal.

Again, we all have a profile of attention functions, with some controls operating reliably and some that are not as reliable. An attention problem can often stem from a mismatch between a brain and the demands of the environment. For example, cognitive activation has two extreme forms: *underactivation* or passive processing and *overactivation* or excessive processing.

Although overactivation can lead to tangential thinking and a sort of internal distractibility (being engrossed in one's own ideas), this form of cognitive activation can reap benefits in terms of innovative thinking. So the fifth grader whose comments are off-task may become a successful inventor or artist as an adult. Similarly, processing depth can swing from being shallow or superficial (skimming over material and missing details) to being overly deep (transfixed by a piece of information). Though both extremes of processing depth can pose problems in eighth grade (leading students to make little mistakes or work too slowly, respectively), the world has situations and roles that call for each; we need some people who work quickly and focus on the forest, as well as others who are more particular about the trees. The point is that we need to describe weak or strong functions in the context of the demands of the moment, which could be junior high school English class.

Secondary Attention Deficits

Imagine (or recall from personal experience) what it would be like to live in a country where you are not fluent in the native language. Your understanding of what you hear and read is limited, and your capacity to communicate your ideas and needs is spotty and laborious. As you struggle to comprehend, you may drift off and appear inattentive. You would be likely to miss details. You would probably experience frustration and might even respond impulsively in situations in an effort to get your needs met. In short, you might seem like a person with attention weaknesses.

This example is a metaphor for secondary attention deficits, or the appearance of attention weaknesses that are actually due to other neurodevelopment dysfunctions. When reviewing findings related to attention, it is important to consider that observed or reported symptoms could stem from several different constructs. Language problems can create the appearance of weak attention. Specifically, weak receptive language, or trouble comprehending written and oral communication, can lead to a limited attention span, distractibility, and trouble picking up details. Trouble with expressive language, or difficulty putting thoughts into oral or written words, can lead to frustration and inappropriate decision making in efforts to get needs met (which can look like impulsivity). Also, Barkley (1996) described how internalized language served in a regulatory role for inhibiting or delaying responses. So language can act as brakes as the mind talks through potential courses of action.

Dysfunctions in other constructs can cause secondary attention deficits. Active working memory is discussed more in the next chapter, but having a limited amount of mental counter space for juggling information can create a need to have things repeated and even a rushed approach to work (that is, to an effort to get a task accomplished before important information evaporates from memory). Poor graphomotor function can create a number of difficulties (for example, rushed or sloppy work, task avoidance) that could look like signs of weak attention whenever output demands involve handwriting.

So why is it important to differentiate secondary attention deficits from primary attention dysfunction? The two main reasons both echo the rationale behind assessing to understand. First, demystification needs to pinpoint breakdown points so that students (and their parents and teachers) understand why they are struggling with learning. The fact that a student is having trouble with school should be readily apparent to all involved, but the underlying factors usually need to be illuminated. An attention problem is often raised as a possibility with struggling students, and if the observed and reported signs can be attributed to other weaknesses (for example, receptive language), then that needs to be illuminated too. Second, the learning plan will differ depending on whether or not attention controls are weak, and not just in terms of medication. A receptive language weakness, for example, would need to be addressed with approaches to improve the student's fundamental capacity to comprehend oral and written communication.

How can secondary and primary attention problems be distinguished? The various thought processes I've been describing can help make these differentiations. Viewing the student from multiple angles will bring in a range of findings and types of data. If only a single piece of data (say, the student is impulsive during math class) is used, then it would be virtually impossible to appraise attention. But looking across settings and considering several reporters enables a more holistic view. Recurring themes then come into play, as evidence mounts in support of attention being a primary or secondary concern. Clinical contrasts can tease apart and illuminate possible breakdowns; a student who misses details when reading but not when solving math operations problems is less likely to have superficial processing depth (as opposed to dysfunctions that undermine reading comprehension).

CASE STUDY

Jorge is seventeen years old and a high school junior. A film buff, he aspires to be a movie director, but he also is fascinated by architecture and technology. His favorite subjects include art, math, and physics, and he dislikes history, English, and reading. Referral concerns include trouble completing homework on time and appearing scattered and unfocused in class and while reading. He seems to become overwhelmed when faced with lengthy reading assignments and takes inordinate amounts of time to read material, often rereading pages several times. Finally, he is disorganized in terms of time and materials.

Several strengths were identified for Jorge in the assessment. Good higher-order cognition emerged through teacher descriptions of his critical thinking, understanding of concepts, and creativity; he also showed excellent use of logic when solving physics problems. All describe him as being able to get along very well with people of different ages, suggesting strong social cognition. He showed good memory by doing mental math, accessing procedures, and recalling details from a passage. In terms of language he displayed a good vocabulary when reading, understood various meanings of ambiguous sentences, drew proper inferences, and could expound on his ideas and different topics when conversing. Finally, his spatial ordering was evident in his excellent copies of geometric designs, and his parents reported that he is adept at fixing and building things.

Despite Jorge's impressive collection of assets, his academic performance is undermined by the attention processing control saliency determination. His parents note that he has difficulty deciding what is important to study; when interviewed about this, he said that he does better with the kind of "black-and-white" issues found in math and physics, but had much more trouble deciding how important information was when the material was more subjective (as in history or English). As a result, his studying often is not systematic and he gets inundated by facts that he has not first prioritized. When reading subjective material he gets bogged down in the details, which slows his reading rate. During the assessment he was asked to summarize a passage and he produced an avalanche of information, indicating good memory but weak saliency determination. His disorganization also relates to this aspect of attention, as he has a hard time filtering out unnecessary materials and distractions.

CASE STUDY

Elvia is a ten-year-old who has experienced learning problems since kindergarten but has really hit the wall in fifth grade. Her teacher describes Elvia as "bouncy," meaning that she has a hard time staying in her seat, resisting the temptation to call out in class, and working slowly enough to keep her accuracy from suffering. Though she has several friends and is generally liked by her classmates, she is sometimes rejected by her peers because of her boisterous demeanor. Academically, she makes a lot of careless mistakes in math and spelling, and her writing is quite disorganized.

During the assessment Elvia showed similar traits, which were identified as symptoms of an unreliable production control system. For instance, she was asked to recreate abstract patterns with colored blocks and she used a hurried, trial-and-error approach (suggesting weak facilitation and inhibition and previewing). Across tasks she tended to work quickly (weak pacing) and rarely caught her mistakes (weak self-monitoring), even on problems that were clearly in her skill range.

Reluctant to put Elvia on medication, her father asked for instructional and behavioral strategies to help her attention. First, she was demystified about her production control system, including how it affects her schoolwork, behavior in class, and relations with peers. Second, she was enlisted to help create prompts designed to remind her about planning before starting, not rushing, and checking over her work when finished. Third, a behavior system was set up to provide positive reinforcement for appropriate use of her production controls.

Attention was a natural starting point for discussing specific assessment approaches for neurodevelopmental constructs. Information needs to enter the gateway of attention before it can be understood (by language, spatial ordering, temporal-sequential ordering, or higher order cognition). Attention is also the bridge into memory, which is the subject of the next chapter.

9

Assessing Memory

SCHOOLING INVOLVES A HUGE AMOUNT of memorization starting at the elementary grades and continuing past high school. We ask students to commit a wide range of information to memory, including math facts and procedures, word definitions, grammar rules, spelling rules, historical events and dates, and science terms. To navigate this deluge of information, students need organized approaches to memorizing. Some students come to such approaches naturally and some require explicit coaching to store information in their memory banks. Being a student also requires holding on to information for brief periods, such as when hearing a teacher's instructions or when moving from one task (say, reading a textbook passage) to a related task (creating notes on that passage). In addition, students frequently have to mentally suspend material as they are manipulating it or working with it in some way, such as when combining what the teacher is saying about a chemical reaction with what is happening in a lab demonstration.

Accordingly, memory is a construct that needs to be assessed when a student is experiencing learning problems. Several things can go awry with memory and impair academic performance. Also, students may have assets in memory (possibly hidden or previously unknown to parents and teachers) that need to be illuminated and used to advantage in learning plans.

This chapter follows a structure like the one I used in discussing attention, beginning with the concept and theory of memory as a construct and a discussion of important distinctions related to it. Then I'll present some general assessment considerations, followed by specific types of tasks that are designed to test memory. Then I'll go into some task-analysis approaches for memory and present potential signs of weak memory.

As with attention (and all of the constructs) memory needs to be assessed and not just tested. Gathering multiple points of evidence from multiple sources is critical in getting an accurate view of how the student's memory systems are operating. Although tests are available for many aspects of memory, you will still need history and qualitative observation, especially for areas that are not directly testable, such as recalling procedures and experiences.

The Construct of Memory

Memory . . . is the diary that we all carry about with us.

—Oscar Wilde

Unlike attention and some other aspects of the neurodevelopmental framework, experts generally agree about how memory is organized. In fact, components of memory seem to have worked their way into the language everyone uses, both inside and outside the learning field. For example, most experts identify an initial memory process, or *short-term memory*, that briefly registers new information that is subsequently used, stored, or discarded. Further, a two-part system operates with delayed recall of information: *long-term memory storage* and *long-term memory access*. Again, even students are likely to have a basic awareness and understanding of short-term and long-term memory. Working between these two systems is an important function that has been studied extensively in recent years: active working memory has been defined as the capacity to mentally suspend information while using or manipulating it. Figure 9.1 depicts the three-system model for memory, and Appendix A presents more detail.

Clearly, memory systems are interrelated (Wagner, 1996). Memory and the relationships between its component systems can be explained to students and families (during demystification sessions or in written reports) metaphorically.

For instance, memory can be likened to a library. Short-term memory would be the library's book return bin; everything enters through the bin, but material stays there only briefly, and the bin can hold only a small number of items. Active working memory is the librarian's counter space; material is transferred here from short-term memory and processed for storage into long-term memory. Students can easily see that organizing the space (rather

Figure 9.1 Three-System Model of Memory

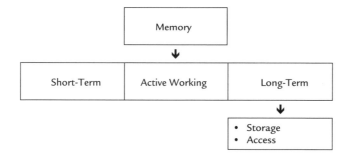

than piling things up haphazardly) allows it to handle more material. Long-term memory storage is the process of putting books on the shelves; placing the books systematically and filing multiple copies in different categories (for example, putting a book on race cars under both transportation and sport sections) make retrieving them later much easier. Long-term memory access is the process of locating and pulling books from the shelves; again, finding books is facilitated by systematic placement.

A computer can also serve as a symbol for memory. For instance, random access memory (RAM) would represent active working memory and the hard drive would represent long-term memory.

The capacity of active working memory will vary depending on how efficiently the person is at the specific processes demanded by the task (Daneman & Green, 1986; Siegal & Ryan, 1989). For example, language breakdowns have been shown to interfere with verbal mediation, a function that facilitates holding and manipulating information, thus weighing down active working memory (Crain, Shankweiler, Macaruso, & Bar Shalom, 1990). Extending the library analogy, the counter space can accommodate more material if the librarian is an efficient reader. Also, memory is intimately tied with attention (Sergeant, 1996), meaning that weaknesses in the attention controls will probably lead to memory difficulty.

Some Important Distinctions

As was the case with attention, understanding some distinctions within memory will help you not only with assessment but also with explaining memory to students and their parents in the demystification session and the written report. First, though some theorists (such as Lezak, 1995) have argued that short-term and working memory may actually be the same construct, it may be more useful to regard these two memory systems as points on a continuum, with some distinguishing features but no firm boundary between them.

One such distinguishing feature is the time element. Short-term memory is the retention of information over a very short interval (only a few seconds), whereas active working memory could hold on to information for an extended, continuous period (say, for a few minutes while the information is being used or manipulated). Another distinction is what happens to the information. Short-term memory is a holding station for information that remains relatively intact. On the other hand, active working memory is where information may qualitatively change as it is mentally manipulated or employed in some way. Finally, while the gateway into short-term memory is generally attention (specifically, the processing controls), active working memory can mentally suspend incoming information as well as material accessed from long-term memory (Denckla, 1996a). To illustrate, you would be using your working memory by recalling your social security number and putting it in reverse order in your head.

Second, the complementary processes of storage and access need to be distinguished within long-term memory (see Figure 9.2). Information needs to be stored, obviously, if it is to be accessed at a later time. So a storage weakness can have major implications for memorizing and studying. But it is also possible to store information but then have trouble accessing it later. This can be illustrated by the difference between *recall* and *recognition*. You might be stumped by an open-ended question like "What was the name of your first-grade teacher?" but be successful with a forced-choice question like "Was the

Figure 9.2   Long-Term Memory: Storage Versus Access

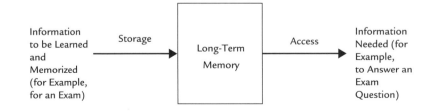

name of your first-grade teacher Ms. Cox, Mrs. Anderson, or Mrs. Felts?" Open-ended questions employ free recall and tap both long-term memory storage and access. On the other hand, forced-choice questions employ recognition and, because they provide a prompt of some kind, bypass access and tap into storage. So if you could answer a multiple-choice question about your first-grade teacher's name, you clearly stored the information even though you had trouble accessing it.

Third, it is important to consider the different types of material that can be committed to memory. Two major types are visual material and verbal or language-based information. Some theorists actually divide active working memory into two systems, *phonological* and *spatial* (Denckla, 1996a). What they call a "phonological loop" manipulates and briefly stores speech-based information. In contrast, a "visuospatial sketchpad" generates and momentarily stores visual images. Long-term memory also accommodates different memory types (Torgesen, 1996). Other examples include sequences (the order of steps, events, or other linear information), procedures (such as math algorithms), and orthographic patterns (specific configurations of printed letters).

Fourth, understanding and remembering clearly differ. It is possible to comprehend something but not recall it later; you probably understand what you hear on the radio or read in the newspaper but do not remember everything you've heard or read. Conversely, it is possible to have weak or tenuous comprehension of something that you can recall later. Memory, in and of itself, is distinct from the constructs that handle the understanding of information, such as higher-order cognition, language (for verbal ideas), and spatial ordering (for visual material). Memory is usually bolstered, though, by good understanding of the material, since it can then be placed in context and a wider array of prompts can be used to trigger access.

General Assessment Considerations

To remember something, you first need to attend to it. Put differently, information needs to come through attention's processing control system before it enters into short-term, active working, and long-term memory. Consequently, assessing memory is practically impossible without jointly assessing attention (particularly the processing controls). So when a student exhibits problems on a memory task (such as recalling series of orally presented digits), it can be tough to figure out whether the issue is really memory or attention (or some other factor).

One tactic is to repeat the material. A student with superficial processing depth may miss things the first time, but perform better after a second pass. Many tests of memory involve multiple learning trials, and comparing performance across trials can provide hints about the effect of attention. (For example, poor performance across trials suggests weak memory, as opposed to attention.)

Active working memory can be assessed separately from processing depth by asking the student to mentally juggle material already committed to long-term memory (for example, reversing the months of the year or simultaneously counting by letters and numbers, such as "A1-B2-C3"). Finally, interviewing the student can be revealing, such as asking, "When you had trouble remembering those numbers, was it because you hadn't paid good attention when I read them to you, or because you just couldn't remember them very well?" Even students in elementary school can answer questions like this during an assessment.

Remembering something that you understand is much easier than re-membering something that you do not understand. To illustrate, try memorizing the details in a technical manual for an appliance or piece of computer hardware. Unless you have expertise with such devices, it would be much easier to memorize the details from a newspaper story or from one of your favorite authors. As a result, receptive language, spatial ordering, temporal-sequential ordering, and higher-order cognition weaknesses can really derail memory. Fortunately, we have several techniques for teasing out the effect of understanding on memory.

First, as with attention, interviewing the student can be fruitful. For example, the student could be asked, "Do you think you had a hard time with that because you couldn't remember the stuff or because you had a hard time understanding the info in the first place?" Second, consider how the student performed on different tasks that called upon other constructs that have minimal memory demands; this kind of contrast can help to factor out possible reasons for a student's struggles. Third, compare the student's performance on various memory tasks, including those that require less understanding of the material (like a series of digits or shopping list words) and in various modalities (such as spatial and sequential).

Another consideration in memory testing is the degree of context or meaning of the material to be memorized. Material can be relatively *contextualized* (that is, it has meaning to the student) or relatively *decontextualized* (that is, it has little or no meaning to the student). The degree of context exists on a continuum and material that has a lot of meaning for one student may have less meaning for another; consequently, it is necessary to determine the student's exposure to and experience with material. (For example, you can ask, "Have you heard of these words before?")

Important contrasts can emerge regarding these two general types of material. A student may have an easier time recalling contextualized material (say, a narrative) than decontextualized information with less meaning (such as a string of digits or a list of unrelated words). Visual material can also vary along this dimension—a picture of a classroom as opposed to an abstract geometric figure—contextualized visual material may be easier to memorize because it can more readily be converted to a verbal format, using words to describe the components of the classroom picture or creating a story about the picture. On the other hand, context can be a distracting factor, especially for students with high levels of cognitive activation, who may make too many connections between the information and their prior knowledge and experience, leading to distracting tangents. Close analysis of specific items is often warranted to determine any pattern in student performance with contextualized and decontextualized material.

Active working memory is enormously important for academic work and should be considered under most circumstances when a student has learning problems. Any task where the student has to mentally suspend and manipulate information requires active working memory: decoding multisyllable words, making connections within extended pieces of reading text, juggling all the various things involved in writing (forming ideas, spelling, punctuation, grammar, organization), performing mental math calculations, executing multistep math procedures. Therefore, limited working memory can undermine several academic areas at once.

Concerning long-term memory storage, it is important to assess both how much a student can memorize as well as how the student memorizes. For many students, long-term memory problems can be traced back to their approach to memorizing, or use of mnemonic strategies. Interviewing the student about the typical process of preparing for an upcoming test can give you a lot of insight into study skills. Students should be carefully observed during long-term memory tasks for clues about how they are memorizing information. Again, students should be interviewed about their approaches to tasks. (For example, you can say, "Tell me how you went about learning that list of words?") Some students may perform adequately on recall tasks because they have good rote memory.

> ☞ *Rote memory* is akin to an analog recording (like a VHS tape) in that the information is not sortable and is therefore harder to access. In contrast, *strategic memory* is akin to a digital recording (like a CD) in that the information is tagged, sorted, inherently organized, and therefore easier to access.

In other words, students who rely on rote memory have minds like tape recorders that can take in and store information, but do not transform or categorize it in a way that would make it easy to recall. This is another example of why it is important to look beyond a score and take into account qualitative findings such as method of learning.

Here is an overview of things to think about when assessing memory:

- The attention processing control system and memory work together and influence each other.
- Weak understanding can lead to shaky memory.
- The degree of context has an effect on a student's memory.
- Active working memory can affect numerous academic skills.
- The student's study skills and use of mnemonic strategies can affect the efficiency of memory.

Tasks Designed to Assess Types of Memory

Numerous tasks are available for assessing memory. (Typical task descriptions are summarized in Table 9.1, along with examples of actual tests

Table 9.1   Assessment Task Types for Memory

Task Type	Description	Primarily Assesses[1]	Examples[2]
Digit span	Repeating series of orally presented numbers in same order (for short-term memory) or in reverse order (for active working memory)	Memory (short-term and active working)	Digit Span (WISC-IV Integrated); Digit Span (WAIS-III); Memory for Digits (CTOPP); Recall of Digits (DAS); Numbers (CMS)
Hand movements	Replicating series of hand movements, usually involving a prop such as a block set in same order (for short-term memory) or in manipulated order (for active working memory)	Memory (short-term and active working)	Nonverbal Working Memory (SB5); Finger Windows (WRAML 2); Spatial Span (WISC-IV Integrated); Geometric Form Tapping (PEERAMID-2)
Letter or number reordering	Reordering orally presented numbers (in serial order) and letters (in alphabetical order)	Memory (active working)	Letter-Number Sequencing (WISC-IV Integrated); Symbolic Working Memory (WRAML 2)
Competing language	Answering basic questions in sets, then recalling the last word from each question in the set	Memory (active working)	Verbal Working Memory (SB5)
Drawing recall	Drawing one or more figures after a brief (for short-term memory) or extended delay (for long-term memory); may also have a recognition trial; often linked with basic or complex figure copy	Memory (short-term and long-term)	Immediate Recall Trial, Delayed Recall Trial (RCFT); Design Memory (WRAML 2); Recall of Designs (DAS)
Picture recall	Naming details or identifying altered elements in drawings of real-life scenarios	Memory (short-term and long-term)	Picture Memory (WRAML 2); Family Pictures (CMS)
List recall	Recalling list of words (or pairs) after initial learning trials (for short-term memory) or extended delay (for long-term memory); may include a delayed recognition trial	Memory (short-term and long-term)	CVLT-C; Verbal Learning (WRAML 2); Word Pairs, Word Lists (CMS); List Learning (NEPSY); Memory for Words; (WJ-III Cognitive)

(continued)

Table 9.1   Assessment Task Types for Memory (*Continued*)

Task Type	Description	Primarily Assesses[1]	Examples[2]
Sentence repetition	Recalling orally presented sentences after a brief delay	Memory (short-term)	Sentence Repetition (CAS); Sentence Repetition (NEPSY); Recalling Sentences (CELF-IV); Sentence Memory (WRAML 2)
Passage recall	Recalling and summarizing information from an orally presented passage after a brief (for short-term memory) or extended delay (for long-term memory); may include a delayed recognition trial	Memory (short-term and long-term)	Story Memory (WRAML 2); Stories (CMS); Narrative Memory (NEPSY)
Sound-symbol recall	Recalling the name for a symbol or picture after initial learning trials (for short-term memory) or extended delay (for long-term memory)	Memory (short-term and long-term)	Visual-Auditory Learning (WJ-III Cognitive); Sound Symbol (WRAML 2); Memory for Names (NEPSY)
Factual recall	Answering general knowledge questions, either free recall (tapping both storage and access) or recognition and multiple choice (isolating storage)	Memory (long-term)	Information, Information Multiple Choice (WISC-IV Integrated); General Information (WJ-III Cognitive)

[1]The neurodevelopmental functions and constructs listed here are those that are primarily assessed by the given task; other functions and constructs may be tapped as well.
[2]Full test and battery citations are listed in Appendix D.

and subtests; Appendix D includes full battery names for acronyms and test publishers.) In fact, publishers offer far more tests of memory than could ever be used with a single student. Hence, you need to make some informed decisions about which tests will complement other sources of information (such as history).

A prime consideration is the particular memory system tapped by the task. When the student is asked to repeat back information after a very brief interval (say, a few seconds), the task is aimed at short-term memory. Examples include reciting series of numbers or letters, repeating sentences, summarizing a paragraph (read or heard), drawing a figure, or recreating a series of hand movements (for example, when tapping blocks). Recall after a brief delay, coupled with some sort of mental manipulation or transformation of the information, employs active working memory. Examples include reversing or reordering series of numbers or letters, following multistep instructions with challenging sequences, or simultaneously responding to questions while memorizing information.

Obviously, remembering after a delay of, say, twenty or thirty minutes involves long-term memory. Tasks can be structured, though, to differentiate between long-term memory storage and long-term memory access. Specifically, comparing performance on recall and recognition tasks can help separate storage from access (as mentioned in Chapter Six). Recall tasks provide no cues or prompts to support retrieval; an example is an open-ended question such as, "Who invented the electric light bulb?" To answer such a recall question, the key information (Thomas Edison) has to have been stored and then accessed. Recognition tasks, in contrast, provide some sort of cue or prompt to support retrieval; a multiple-choice question is a classic example, such as "Was the inventor of the electric light bulb Alexander Graham Bell, Thomas Edison, or George Washington Carver?" Answering such a recognition question requires the information to have been stored, but the access is facilitated by the response options.

As with the Thomas Edison example, the same piece of information can be the centerpiece of both recall and recognition questions. A student who struggles with recall but performs better with recognition trials has probably stored the information but has trouble accessing it. In contrast, difficulty with recognition suggests that the student did not store the material in the first place. So recall tasks tap both long-term memory access and long-term memory storage, while recognition tasks isolate long-term memory storage. Figure 9.3 displays examples of recognition and recall questions for different types of information, a memory assessment consideration to be discussed next.

As Figure 9.3 illustrates, many kinds of information can be committed to memory. For some information types, no direct memory tests exist. For example, memory for rules and procedures must be assessed qualitatively in the context of academic work, such as during spelling, writing, or math. Teachers

Figure 9.3   Assessing Long-Term Memory Storage and Access

[1] Such as multiple-choice and matching.

[2] Also referred to as *open-ended questions*.

[3] Decoding involves recognizing *orthographic patterns*, especially for irregularly spelled words.

[4] Remembering a rule is different from understanding a rule (an aspect of higher-order cognition).

[5] Memory is usually stronger for information related to affinities.

	Long-Term Memory	
	↑ Storage	↓ Access
Type of Information	Can be Assessed with *Recognition* Questions[1]	Can be Assessed with *Recall* Questions[2]
Verbal	"Is the *capital of Ohio* Raleigh, Springfield, or Columbus?"	"What is the *capital of Ohio?*"
Visual	"Which of these 4 shapes is a *hexagon?*"	"Draw a *hexagon.*"
Orthographic Patterns (Letter Combinations)	"Pick the correct spelling of *fountain*: Fowntane, Fountain, or Fountinn."[3]	"How do you spell *fountain?*"
Paired Associate	"Does 7 times 6 equal 35, 76, or 42?"	"What is 7 times 6?"
Procedural	"Does *perimeter* equal total of side lengths or width multiplied by height?"	"How do you calculate *perimeter?*"
Rule[4]	"When adding 'ly' to a word ending in 'i,' do you keep or drop the 'i'?"	"What do you do when adding 'ly' to a word that ends in 'i'?"
Topic Specific[5] (for Example, Airplanes)	"Is the *fuselage* part of the plane's wing, a type of landing gear, or the body?"	"What is a *fuselage?*"

also can provide insight into memory for these information types by answering questions such as "How much does Lee benefit from a little reminder or prompt about a rule or procedure?"

Orthographic patterns are common letter patterns found in alphabetic languages such as English and Spanish. English examples include *-tion* and *pre-*. Orthographic memory is the capacity to store and recall letter patterns. Spelling requires recall of orthographic patterns, and therefore involves long-term memory both for storage and access. To spell irregularly spelled words, in particular, letter sets need to be stored and accessed. In contrast, recognition of correct spellings (in multiple-choice format or with a spelling checker) isolates the storage of orthographic patterns. Figure 9.3 includes an example of a multiple-choice spelling task involving the word *fountain*. Also, decoding involves recognition of orthographic patterns; *-tion* needs to be identified as a unit that can then be matched up with a set of sounds.

CASE STUDY

Courtney is an eight-year-old second grader who is showing some perplexing un-evenness in her decoding and spelling skills. She is able to sound out many words, including long words and even nonsense words. She also can decode an expected number of sight words for her grade. Her spelling, though, is delayed. She can correctly spell most words that follow regular patterns, such as *bake* and *gum*, but irregularly spelled words (such as *light*) give her a lot of trouble (in such instances she often falls back, erroneously, to regular patterns like *lite*). Interestingly, Courtney's recognition of irregularly spelled words, as in a multiple-choice format, is highly accurate. She also has no trouble with tasks involving oral blending, segmenting, and re-blending.

Based on all the findings, Courtney appears to have appropriate phonological processing, which allows her to re-blend, for example, as well as to decode lengthy words and nonsense words; put differently, she has an intact sense of the sound structure of spoken words. Her difficulty, though, lies in her recall of orthographic patterns. She can recognize orthographic patterns, during decoding and multiple-choice spelling, suggesting that she has stored common letter patterns in her memory banks. However, she has trouble accessing these patterns without prompts or cues, which is the case when she has to spell words for a test or a composition. With words that follow regular patterns she can apply her good phonology, though she sometimes overuses this strategy (as when spelling *light* as *lite*). Courtney's learning plan centered around efforts to bolster her recall of commonly encountered letter patterns (that is, word chunks) and coaching in the use of a spelling checker (which requires recognizing correct spellings).

Orthographic patterns are a specific type of visual material, and memory assessment can look more broadly at how a student handles information that comes in visually. A major category of visual memory tasks involves drawing from recall. The student is shown a design, often geometric and abstract, and then has to draw it from memory (after a brief or long delay). Performance on drawing recall tasks can suffer from a few obvious neurodevelopmental functions aside from memory. Without accurate spatial perception, it can be very difficult to commit designs to memory (akin to having weak receptive language when memorizing verbal information). Also, unreliable graphomotor or fine motor function can create problems in terms of manipulating the pencil for accurate drawing. Therefore, drawing recall performance should be interpreted alongside findings from tasks that are more targeted for these other neurodevelopmental functions (for example, a visual matching task like the ones described in Chapters Six and Eleven). Several visual memory tasks require the student to replicate (short-term memory) or transform (active working memory) series of hand movements demonstrated by the clinician, such as tapping blocks in sequence, which eliminates potential difficulty with using a pencil. Some tasks briefly present students with contextualized pictures and then ask them to identify elements after short or extended delays; these can take the form of "What's missing or different?" games in that a slightly different version of the picture may be presented after the delay.

So why worry about assessing visual memory? Answering that question requires looking at how visual memory plays into academic skills. Obviously, orthographic memory is important for decoding and spelling. Math and science involve visual material in terms of geometric shapes and diagrams. Maps are often encountered in social studies. Many procedures and rules can be memorized visually, such as those for long division, dividing fractions, and punctuating a sentence. If a student is experiencing difficulty with these skills and subjects, visual memory may need to be examined via testing. In the classroom students receive information visually, such as on a board or screen; problems with short-term or active working memory can cause students to lose information between seeing it and recording it (writing it down) or using it.

For better or worse, verbal memory is even more important for school than visual memory; students take in much information via listening and reading. Therefore, it is extremely useful to assess memory for verbal information. Verbal memory tasks present information to students that they either hear or read, though listening tasks are often preferable because they eliminate the potential for trouble caused by weak reading. Verbal memory tasks can vary in the amount of context the information has. On the decontextualized end of the spectrum are digit and letter span tasks in which the student recites orally presented series or manipulates them in some way, such as reordering, reversing, or alphabetizing (all of which involve active working memory). One way to force the student to use active working memory is to call for things to be done simultaneously. For instance, competing language tasks ask the student to first answer "true" or "false" to sets of short sentences while memorizing the last word from each sentence in the set.

More contextualized verbal material includes sentences, which usually need to be repeated back verbatim, and passages, which usually need to be summarized. Multiple learning trial list recall tasks present the student with information several times, asking for recall of list items after each presentation. Then, following an extended delay (for example, twenty to thirty minutes), the student is asked to recall list items again. An example would be a list of ten to fifteen words, which could be unrelated (that is, decontextualized) or members of categories (that is, contextualized). The degree to which the student can identify categories and use them to facilitate storage and recall is an important observation about strategies and study skills. Figure 9.4 contains a sample list of words in random order (as they would be read to the student), and the same words reorganized by categories: sports, drinks, and things to read. Reordering words into meaningful categories obviously can boost recall, whereas sticking with the original order means relying on rote memory.

Multiple learning trial tasks allow you to teach as well as test, and to observe how the student responds to instruction; a learning curve can be observed across the trials, and standard scores for each trial are often available for comparison with same-age peers. As I mentioned in connection with attention, students with shallow processing depth often retain very little after initial exposure to the information, but then improve after additional learning trials. Many word list learning trial tasks also include an interference task, such as a different list of words following the learning trials with the original list; the interference list may have items belonging to the same groups (say,

Figure 9.4   Memory Task Word List, Illustrating Strategic Use of Categories

Words Listed Randomly	Words Listed Categorically	
Soccer	Hockey	
Milk	Golf	Sports
Juice	Soccer	
Newspaper	Tennis	
Tennis		
Magazine	Milk	
Web Site	Soda	Drinks
Golf	Water	
Water	Juice	
Hockey		
Soda	Magazine	
Book	Web Site	Things to Read
	Book	
	Newspaper	

sports and drinks). Following exposure to the interference list, the student is then asked to recall words from the original list. Ideally, the learning of the new words will not interfere with the recall of the original words, but for some students this is problematic.

In addition to a recall trial after an extended delay, many multiple learning trial tasks include cued recall or recognition trials. Using the list in Figure 9.4 as an example, a cued recall task might involve asking the student, "What were the sports in the list? The drinks? The things to read?" A recognition trial would include a long list of words that are read to the student, who answers yes or no after each to indicate their presence on the original list. Cued recall and recognition tasks isolate the storage aspect of long-term memory. Students who struggle with recall of the material but then improve with cues and prompts have stored the information but demonstrated weakness with access. Students who also perform poorly with cues and prompts have not adequately stored the material in the first place.

Tasks are available that tap paired associate memory, which is involved when two pieces of linked information have to be stored and accessed. The learning of math facts, for example, requires this kind of long-term memory in that facts are really two connected bits of information: "5 × 7" = "35." A

Figure 9.5   Mock Sound-Symbol Paired Associate Memory Task

multiple learning trial task that can offer insight into the learning of verbal information pairs would be a word-word task in which the student is taught words in pairs (such as "grass-desk"), and then must name one word (for example, "desk") when in response to its partner ("grass").

Paired associate memory is also important for learning verbal-visual pairs, such as a sound with a symbol. Phonics is the pairing of speech sounds (phonemes) with printed letters (graphemes). One way to test this kind of paired associate memory is to teach students sounds partnered with specific symbols. Figure 9.5 displays three such sound-symbol pairings; these kinds of pairings would be taught over several learning trials, and then reassessed after a long delay.

Another consideration is the amount of information the student is asked to memorize. Regardless of the modality of the material (visual, verbal, combination), the chunk size can vary from very small to relatively large. Examples of small verbal chunks include series of digits and individual words, medium chunks include sentences and word lists, whereas large chunks are paragraphs or passages. Visual chunks range from small, basic figures to large, complex pictures or diagrams. Chunk size is important to bear in mind, because students who perform well on memory tasks when the chunk is small may falter when it is large.

Task-Analysis for Memory

Again, schooling places huge demands on memory. Although this means that students with unreliable memory are at a distinct disadvantage, it also means that history from teachers and a careful review of academic work can provide important insights into memory systems. As mentioned earlier, some information types (such as procedures and rules) cannot be assessed via direct testing. Academic tasks, therefore, need to be task-analyzed to uncover their specific memory demands. (Table 9.2 includes signs of weak memory

Table 9.2   Signs and Symptoms of Memory

Memory System	General Findings
Short-term	Asset Indicators • Minimal recall that significantly improves after repetition Signs of Dysfunction • Student describing trouble remembering recently heard or seen material • Recalling information predominantly from the end of an orally presented passage
Active working	Asset Indicators • Mentally juggling various task components when writing (punctuation, ideation, grammar, spelling) • Segmenting and re-blending long and unfamiliar words • Making connections within extended text • Accurate mental math calculations Signs of Dysfunction • Errors within multistep math procedures • Minimal recall that does not improve much after repetition • Difficulty following multistep instructions, especially when steps are given in different order from how they should be executed • Needing to refer back to text to answer comprehension questions • Student describing trouble manipulating information mentally
Long-term storage	Asset Indicators • Identifying sight words and irregularly spelled words Signs of Dysfunction • Student describing weak recognition (for example, on true/false tests) • Decoding errors that are visually close but with poor phonics (siege for sieve or fat for first) • Weak sight word recognition and laborious sounding out of basic words
Long-term access	Asset Indicators • Recalling math procedures (such as long division, finding least common denominator, factoring an equation) • Recalling math facts • Recalling factual information for quizzes and exams • Retrieving phonemes that are matched with certain graphemes • Citing prior knowledge in connection to reading passage Signs of Dysfunction • Student describing trouble recalling information on tests and quizzes, and during class discussions • Trouble recalling academic rules (for example, for spelling, punctuation, math) • Hesitancy when called on in class • Misspellings that are phonetically logical, but err in terms of letter patterns (for example, enuf for enough)

in the context of academic work.) Writing involves numerous rules, such as for spelling and grammar. Weak spellers often know spelling rules but may not apply rules when writing, necessitating the assessment of both *competence*, or knowledge of spelling under sampling conditions, and *performance*, or use of spelling knowledge in spontaneous writing (Moats, 1994a).

Math is loaded with procedures. Storage versus access can be assessed for math algorithms and rules by looking at how students perform when freely recalling procedures or rules and when all they need to do is recognize them. Teachers can observe a great deal about memory, including recall and recognition of orthographic patterns (for example, spelling without supports versus spelling recognition and use of a spelling checker). Teachers typically employ different kinds of questions in their classroom tests, and reviewing how students perform on recall items (open-ended or essay) and recognition items (multiple-choice, true-false, matching) can inform differences in functioning between storage and access. When calling on students in class, teachers also make use of various question types.

☞ Here are some examples of the difference between being able to commit a rule or procedure to memory (and later recall it) and understanding that rule or procedure. One could add -*ly* to the word *bad* because it "sounds right," without understanding that -*ly* converts *bad* from an adjective to an adverb (and the implications of the conversion). One could accurately execute an algorithm for simplifying fractions without understanding what numerators and denominators represent or how they relate to each other.

Even assessment tasks that are designed to tap other neurodevelopmental constructs and academic skills can inform memory functioning. Most tasks initially involve giving the student instructions. How well does the student remember those instructions while working? Does the need to remember multiple instructions simultaneously cause particular difficulty? The complexity of a task can be a gauge of how much active working memory is needed to complete it. For instance, a student who has access to the needed information on an easel and can work with paper and pencil probably requires little active working memory. In contrast, an oral question that will not be repeated, allows no pencil or paper, and asks the student to compute or reason probably requires a fair amount of active working memory. Also, how much does the task require the student to use previously stored information (facts, rules, procedures)? Does the student have to use recall or recognition?

Obviously the way questions are phrased makes a difference regarding whether long-term memory access plays a pivotal role. Tasks and questions can also differ in terms of *convergent* and *divergent* recall. Questions with one or very few correct responses (for example, a specific factual question) employ convergent recall. Naming the sixteenth president of the United States (Abraham Lincoln, in case you are wondering) is a convergent recall task. On the other hand, questions with multiple correct responses (that is, open-ended questions) use divergent recall. Listing factors leading to the U.S. Civil War is a divergent task.

Memory Signs and Symptoms

As with attention in Chapter Eight, I've already described many potential signs of memory; these and others are listed in Table 9.2, divided by memory system. You will find similar information in Appendix C. Standard scores can be useful in comparing the student's performance on specific tasks with those of same-age peers, but such scores should always be interpreted within a pattern of findings from multiple angles; in other words, look for recurring themes about aspects of memory. Personal norms are helpful with developmental considerations, such as how much mental math a fifth grader should be able to do.

CASE STUDY

Sayid is twelve years old and attends seventh grade. Though he demonstrated good oral expression (for example, defining words, forming sentences from prompts), his writing is not elaborative, particularly well-organized, or consistently accurate in terms of spelling and mechanics. He showed excellent reasoning and logic during math, but was stumped several times by mental math problems and made some calculation errors when he had to work through multiple steps. Sayid has a wide and deep factual knowledge base, but he was stymied when asked to manipulate common sequences (for example, reversing the months of the year) and when alphabetizing or reordering letter or number series simultaneously.

Sayid's neurodevelopmental vulnerability is his active working memory. Because of his limited capacity to mentally suspend information, the multiple aspects of writing overwhelm him and what he gets down on paper does not match up with the sophistication of his speech. Mental math and multistep problems also involve active working memory. Though his long-term memory is good, he has trouble manipulating information he pulls from his memory. Demystification will be an important ingredient of Sayid's learning plan, as he needs to understand that his ideas, thinking, and language are all top-notch, but that his active working memory gums up the works.

CASE STUDY

Zhen is fourteen years old and is experiencing frustration about school tests. She and her parents agree that she puts in considerable time studying but has trouble scoring well on quizzes and exams; other aspects of her academic work (homework assignments, papers) go much better for her. Her teachers note that she seems a bit hesitant to participate in class discussions, rarely volunteering to answer questions.

During the assessment she performed poorly on long-term memory tasks, such as recalling details of a passage that had been read to her or answering factual knowledge questions. (For example, "On what continent is Austria?") However, Zhen actually was highly accurate when she had the opportunity to recognize items. For example, she could answer almost all of the multiple-choice questions about the oral passage or about her factual knowledge. ("Is Austria in Asia, Europe, or Africa?") She also could spot altered details in pictures she had been shown before a delay.

Zhen's weakness pertains to her long-term memory access. She stores information, which allows her to recognize correct responses and items when they are presented to her. However, free recall is a major barrier. When this pattern was described to Zhen and her parents during demystification, they realized that on school tests she does indeed perform better with multiple-choice, matching, and true/false items; open-ended items, especially essay questions, are quite formidable to her. Zhen's teachers will be asked to balance question types for her (including during class discussions) as much as possible to accommodate her memory profile. At the same time, Zhen's use of memory strategies will be reviewed so that her study time can be put to the best use in terms of filing information for easier access.

CASE STUDY

Gavin is a first grader who is having a tough time learning how to read. Though he seems to understand stories when he is read to, sounding out words is not coming easily to him. His mother reports that he did not show problems with preschool language-sound activities like rhyming. During the assessment he was able to count syllables in spoken words, as well as drop out phonemes to create new words (for example, say "bland" without the /l/ sound). In contrast, he struggled with a memory task in which he was shown several symbols and taught a different sound for each; after a delay he recalled very few of the sounds in conjunction with the symbols.

Taken together, Gavin's decoding seems to be undermined by his paired associate memory, despite age-appropriate phonology. He can handle oral word sounds (for example, when manipulating phonemes to create different words), but he has a hard time linking word sounds with symbols. Therefore, improving his phonics will depend on strengthening his memory connections for phoneme-grapheme pairs so that he can take better advantage of his good phonology.

CASE STUDY

Afryea is an eleven-year-old who is delayed in math skills and some aspects of writing. During the assessment she performed well on various tasks of higher-order cognition. For example, she was accurate and fast with matrix analogies, in which she had to identify subtle relationships between abstract figures and apply those relationships to other figures. She was observed carefully and interviewed when solving some math problems. She frequently was stumped by problems and actually said, "I can't remember how to do very many of these." However, when given just a little prompting she was able to retrieve procedures and could even explain the logic behind the procedures (for example, for calculating volume) when she reached her answers. Similarly, her writing contains rule-based errors (such as subject-verb agreement), but when her mistakes were pointed out to her she could express the rationale for the corrections. Though Afryea understands procedures and rules (related to good higher-order cognition), she has unreliable procedural memory. A strategy that might help her is development of a personal database of procedures (perhaps a journal she maintains with common procedures, situations for using them, and examples).

Having discussed both attention and memory, I can turn to the construct of language. It is possible to make use of attention and memory with relatively little understanding or meaning. Language, though, is critical for comprehending meaning and for communicating information in meaningful ways.

10

Assessing Language

ONE OF THE FASCINATING aspects of the human brain is its predisposition for language. Our capacity for expressing ourselves and communicating with one another was a crucial outcome of the evolutionary process. Listening and speaking have been natural processes for the human brain for ages. Reading and writing, though, are tasks that human civilization developed in the last few thousand years. So although language needs to be strongly considered whenever a student has reading or writing problems, it is common for other neurodevelopmental functions to interfere with these outgrowths of human society.

Language is often a very interesting construct to assess. Parents and teachers can provide a plethora of information, and multiple points of evidence should be reviewed for recurring themes. Numerous tests address different aspects of language, though some features do remain outside the reach of testing (but can still be assessed).

For this chapter, I follow a similar structure to the discussions of attention and memory. That is, I describe language conceptually and theoretically, and then outline important distinctions related to the construct of language. Next I discuss language assessment in general, as well as specific types of tasks designed to test language and task-analysis considerations, then outline potential signs of weak language and provide some case studies.

The Construct of Language

High thoughts must have high language.

—Aristophanes

Language is the dress of thought.

—Samuel Johnson

Figure 10.1   Two-System Model of Language

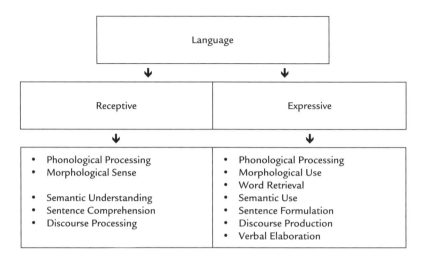

Language can be grossly divided into receptive language and expressive language (a division outlined in Figure 10.1 and discussed in more detail in Appendix A). *Receptive language* is about comprehending incoming information (listening, reading, observing hand signs). *Expressive language* is about communicating or attaching meaning to outgoing information (speaking, writing, making hand signs). In general, expressive language development lags behind receptive language. For instance, think about toddlers and young children, who can understand language at a higher level than they can speak it. Auditory receptive language development begins at about nine months, followed by expressive language development, which begins to emerge at about twelve months; not all receptive language precedes oral expressive language, but one must comprehend in order to use language meaningfully (Johnson, 1993). As another example, consider the experience of learning a foreign language; the capacity to understand what you hear usually comes earlier than the ability to communicate via words and sentences. Students with learning problems can show discrepancies (that is, useful clinical contrasts) between their receptive and expressive language.

Within both sides of language, specific levels differ in terms of the size of the language unit (for example, word or sentence) and the amount of meaning (see Figure 10.2). At the smallest and most basic level is phonological

Figure 10.2   Levels of Language

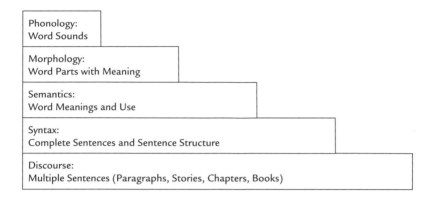

processing, which handles and manipulates the individual sounds that make up spoken words. The English language contains forty-four basic sounds, or *phonemes*. Phonological processing (also referred to as *phonology*), which has been widely studied, has both a receptive component (used when listening and decoding) and an expressive component (used when generating words and spelling). The next level down from word sounds would be meaningful word parts, or *morphemes*. Morphemes are not syllables (which are sound divisions in words) or simply letters; the smallest unit in a word that contributes to the meaning of the word is a morpheme. Some words (like *it*) contain only one morpheme, while others contain several (like *postmodernism*, which has *post*, *mod*, *ern*, and *ism*). Morphemes include root and base words, as well as suffixes and prefixes (Cooper, 2000). Having a deep understanding of a language and the etymology of words is closely related to *morphological sense* (comprehending morphemes when listening and reading) and *morphological use* (applying morphemes when spelling and writing).

Morphology leads to *semantics*, or the understanding and use of whole words. Aspects of semantics include being able to identify or recognize word meanings (*semantic understanding*), define words and use them in sentences and discourse (*semantic use*), and appreciate connections between related words. On the expressive side of language, *word retrieval* is the capacity to access words from memory efficiently when they are needed.

> ☞ Word retrieval, like other language functions, is closely related to long-term memory access. In a way, word retrieval is a narrow slice of more general memory retrieval. It is important to remember that theoretical frameworks help you organize findings, but they are not the be-all-and-end-all in terms of how the brain is wired.

Most communication involves putting several words together into phrases and sentences. *Syntax* is the understanding (*sentence comprehension*) and construction (*sentence formulation*) of language at the sentence level. *Discourse* is the largest size of language, and is made up of multiple sentences (sometimes thousands, as is the case with this book). As with other language levels, discourse has a receptive side (*discourse processing*) and an expressive side (*discourse production*).

Within each of these five levels of language is an additional hierarchy of functions. For example, awareness of individual phonemes is the most advanced component of phonological processing; children tend to become aware of larger linguistic units (such as words and syllables) before becoming aware of smaller linguistic units like phonemes (Snider, 1995). Also, some experts distinguish *phoneme awareness* (analyzing and isolating different sound units in a word) and *phoneme discrimination* (determining whether two phonemes sound alike or not); phoneme awareness has been found to be a better correlate of reading skill than simple phoneme discrimination (Joshi, 1995). Experts also have posited an intermediate unit between the phoneme and the whole word called the *onset-rime*; the onset is the initial consonant or consonant cluster (for example, /d/ in *door*) and the rime is the vowel and the remainder of the syllable (the /-oor/ part of the word) (Foorman, 1995). Morphemes and whole words can vary in terms of size, complexity, and degree of abstractness. Sentences can have basic structures or be more challenging in terms of word order and deployment of conventions (for example, clauses, commas, semicolons). Discourse also varies along similar lines, such as a paragraph in a newspaper article versus a poem by e. e. cummings. Using language to extend and develop ideas is at the apex of discourse production, and is referred to here as *verbal elaboration*.

> ☞ Two major processes of phonemic awareness are *segmenting* (hearing a spoken word and identifying its phonemes) and *blending* (hearing individual phonemes and putting them together to form a word); segmenting and blending can occur without letter knowledge (Cooper, 2000).

Language functioning relates to other neurodevelopmental constructs, including attention and memory. As I point out in Chapter Eight, language development enhances regulation of output, making it easier to avoid acting on impulse (Anderson, 1998). Difficulty with sustaining attention to ideas and thinking could explain weak listening comprehension and language production in students with attention deficits (Zentall, 1993). In addition, Johnson (1993) pointed out that all oral language requires memory, particularly sequential memory.

Some Important Distinctions

As mentioned in the preceding section, an important distinction in language is between *receptive* (incoming) and *expressive* (outgoing) functions. Because students can have understanding and communication at very different levels, it is important to be aware of this distinction when task-analyzing assessment methods and academic skills. Other general distinctions involve the terms *auditory*, *oral*, and *verbal*. *Auditory* refers to the processes of hearing any and all sounds, including both linguistic sounds and nonlinguistic sounds (such as a train whistle). *Verbal* refers to use of language in either written or spoken form, though many use it to describe information that is printed. Finally, *oral* refers narrowly to spoken language (not writing).

Again, *phonemes* are individual word sounds (as I said, English has forty-four of them), whereas *graphemes* are printed letters. Common letter sequences are known as *orthographic patterns*, and usually do not have any associated meaning (Keene & Zimmermann, 1997); in contrast, *morphemes* are word parts that do convey some meaning. The word "microscopic" contains eleven letters but fewer orthographic patterns (*cr*, for example) that are commonly found in other words (see Figure 10.3). However, its morphemes (such as *micro-*) arguably are orthographic patterns as well. Though

Figure 10.3   Components of a Printed Word

	Microscopic									
Phonemes	m	i	c	r	o	s	c	o	p	i	c
Graphemes	/m/	/ĭ/	/k/	/r/	/o/	/s/	/k/	/ä/	/p/	/i/	/k/
Orthographic Patterns			cr			sc			pic		
Morphemes		micro-					scop-			-ic	
Base or Root Word						scope					
Prefix and Suffix		micro-								-ic	

orthographic patterns may not be morphemes (that is, have meaning), most morphemes are also orthographic patterns. In terms of tactics for spelling, words can fall into three general orthographic patterns: those with regular and simple patterns (such as *boot*); words with more complex patterns that can be deciphered using phonology, semantics, syntax, and etymology (such as *extravagant*); and challenging words that just have to be learned by rote (like *Wednesday*) (Aaron, 1995). Finally, the base word or *root word* is the core component in terms of meaning, to which prefixes or suffixes may be added to modify meaning in some way.

The difference between phonemes and graphemes leads to the important distinction between phonological processing and phonics. Let's return to *microscopic*, as a spoken word, made up of a series of sounds, or phonemes (see Figure 10.4). Phonological processing (or phonology) enables distinguishing the eleven distinct sounds within the word, such as between the sounds /r/ and /ō/. The printed word *microscopic* comprises eleven letters, or graphemes, some of which also constitute orthographic patterns. Phonics is the system of the connections between phonemes and graphemes, such as the sound /k/ with the letter "c." So while phonological processing is based in sound, phonics is based on the connecting of sound to print (Foorman, 1995; Snider, 1995).

Weak phonological processing can lead to difficulty with phonics; if one has trouble distinguishing word sounds (for example, /t/ from /d/), then

Figure 10.4   Phonics Versus Phonology

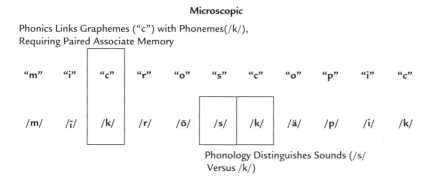

connecting them to printed symbols is also going to be hard. On the other hand, difficulty with phonics does not necessarily mean that phonology is weak, because phonics is a skill that requires not just phonology but other neurodevelopmental functions as well (such as paired associate memory). Another clinical contrast, then, is weak decoding (specifically word attack) but intact or strong performance on pure phonological processing tasks (without print), which would isolate the memory component of phonics as the possible culprit.

> ☞ A *consonant digraph* is two consecutive consonants that represent one sound; a *consonant blend* is two or three grouped consonant sounds in which each individual sound is heard. Similarly, a *vowel digraph* is two consecutive vowels that represent one sound; a *diphthong* (sometimes referred to as "vowel blend") is two grouped vowel sounds in which two sounds are heard (Cooper, 2000).

Discourse production refers to language beyond the sentence level (for example, summarizing paragraph or telling a story) and involves the rules of language (such as grammar, punctuation, basic organization) and organizing and sequencing of ideas to convey meaning or make an argument. In contrast, *verbal elaboration* is expansion of ideas through language and involves extended thinking and the quality of ideas. To assess discourse production, lengthy pieces such as passage summaries and book reports would be examined for organization and for how well the various rules of language were followed (that is, how well the sentences are connected and paragraphs constructed). To assess verbal elaboration, the same pieces used to assess discourse production could be considered in terms of quality of thought, or how extended the ideas in the piece are for conveying good thinking. An instruction manual for a DVD player, for example, may be written cleanly with good discourse production, but because it is just conveying basic information it would be sparse in the way of verbal elaboration. In contrast, discourse can be quite elaborate in terms of idea density and meaning (for example, a poem, a song, an improvised speech) while not following traditional language conventions.

> ☞ If forced to choose, I would rather have good verbal elaboration and weak discourse production than vice versa. Verbal elaboration is about the quality of thought that can be developed through language, and this is harder to teach and remediate. Discourse production is more coachable (for example, by providing rules and examples to follow).

Narrative discourse tells a story or relates events and characters. Narratives are often fictional, but not always (they can relate a personal anecdote or historical event). Expository discourse is intended to convey information and is often nonfiction and more detail-laden (textbooks, lectures, manuals). This is an important distinction because some students show better comprehension for narrative material, perhaps because it tends to be more contextualized than expository language. On the other hand, a student with excessive cognitive activation may get distracted by the details and connections in a narrative passage (being reminded of experiences similar to those of characters in a story).

As described in Chapter Six, *oral expression* is communication through speaking and *written expression* is communication on paper (or via word processing software). While expressive language is a central ingredient to both oral and written expression, each involves a slightly different set of neurodevelopmental ingredients. What is perhaps most important, writing requires neuromotor function in terms of either graphomotor (handwriting) or fine motor (keyboarding); motor difficulties in these areas will usually restrict speed and volume of written output. In addition, the process of writing

Figure 10.5   Oral Expression Versus Written Expression: Constrictions on Writing

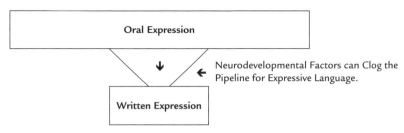

involves numerous rules and conventions that need to be recalled from long-term memory, mentally suspended in active working memory, and executed with the help of the attention production control system. Finally, the complexity of writing (relative to speaking) means that it is more draining in terms of the mental energy control system.

Because of the different sets of neurodevelopmental ingredients for writing and speaking, students may display clinical contrasts in their oral and written expression, depending on their profiles. If, for example, a student has intact or strong expressive language but a weakness in some aspect of memory or attention, then you are likely to observe longer and more sophisticated speaking than writing from this student, whose expressive language would be mired by weaknesses in other areas. It would be as though a pipeline (between brain and page) was clogged up (see Figure 10.5).

Finally, a student's language can differ dramatically in terms of what is comprehended and generated between social situations and academic work. Most students naturally engage in large amounts of automatic or social language, which is their informal, less structured conversational language (or lingo). For the most part, a person can dictate the topic of discussion during social language. On the other hand, in the classroom students are required to employ literate language, which is more formal and analytic. Also, the topics for literate language are usually imposed on the student.

General Assessment Considerations

Because of language's prevalence in school, an enormous amount can be learned about a student's comprehension and communication from teacher reports and a review of academic work. Although product observations, such as reviewing a student's writing sample or piece of math homework, can be revealing, process observations may be even more important for language assessment. For instance, listening to a student read a list of words or a passage is extremely informative about decoding, as is observing the writing process and interviewing about plans for a written assignment.

However, language assessment usually also requires isolating language from reading and writing skills. Though receptive and expressive language are critical components of reading and writing, respectively, many other neurodevelopmental functions are involved in these skills. Assessment of oral formulation involves tasks such as telling stories, giving summaries of what has been read, or telling how to make or do something (Johnson, 1993). Also, language should be assessed in relation to other functions, including attention, memory, and neuromotor function (Moats, 1994b). As I mentioned earlier, when a student has difficulty understanding after a presentation of information (a set of oral directions, for example) but readily improves after a repetition, the culprit is often attention (superficial processing depth), as opposed to language; when repetition does not help, language is more likely to be the undermining factor.

Finally, language and behavior have significant interactions. The co-occurrence of social-emotional and behavioral problems and language weaknesses ranges between 50 percent and 70 percent. Research on this relationship has been conducted in both directions. First, children with primary language weaknesses have been tracked over time and found to have elevated rates of social, emotional, and behavioral problems. Second, children with primary diagnoses in the emotional-behavioral realm have been found to have moderate to severe language difficulties. The interaction may be a downward spiral in which students with communication difficulties resort to inappropriate means to meet their needs (such as aggression), leading to repeated failures (for example, peer rejection) and consequent feelings of inadequacy and potential psychopathology (McCabe, 2005). Therefore, assessments of students with language difficulty should also consider the possible connection with behavior problems (and vice versa).

Here are some steps that are generally useful to take when assessing language:

- Make use of both product and process observations within academic work.

- Isolate language functions with specialized tasks (for example, oral expression, listening comprehension).

- Assess language in the context of a student's overall neuro-developmental profile, considering other areas such as attention and memory.

- Be aware that language difficulty and behavior problems can go hand in hand.

Tasks Designed to Assess Components of Language

This section provides descriptions of some of the most useful tasks for isolating particular language functions. Most do not involve reading or writing because, as has been pointed out, these academic skills involve so many other functions that deciphering specific breakdown points can be very difficult without specialized methods. Task descriptions are summarized in Table 10.1, along with examples of available tests and subtests. (And Appendix D includes full battery names for acronyms and test publishers.)

Starting at the most basic level of language, several kinds of tasks assess phonological processing at increasing levels of complexity: appreciating sounds, comparing and contrasting sounds, blending and splitting syllables, segmenting phonemes, and manipulating phonemes (Snider, 1995). An example of a sound comparison task is matching words that start with the same sound (for example, which word starts with the same sound as *cook: book*, *dog*, and *cat*); often sound comparison tasks include pictures of the words to be compared, which is particularly useful for younger students or those with extreme decoding weaknesses. Segmenting words (for example, breaking the word *bug* into the three phonemes /b/, /u/, and /g/) is a phoneme analysis task, while blending sounds (putting the sounds /k/, /a/, and /t/ into the word *cat*) is a phoneme synthesis task (Snider, 1995). One of the more challenging phonology tasks is elision, in which the student transforms orally presented words by omitting specific phonemes. (For example, "Say *trap* without the /r/ sound.") A similarly difficult task involves replacing a specific phoneme to create a different word. (For example, "If you change the /s/ in *sail* to /t/, what word do you create?")

Table 10.1 Assessment Task Types for Language

Task Type	Description	Primarily Assesses[1]	Examples[2]
Sound matching	Matching pictures of objects with similar initial word sound or final word sound (response can be speaking or pointing)	Language (phonological processing)	Sound Matching (CTOPP); Test of Phonological Awareness (TOPA)
Blending	After hearing segmented words (for example, played at slow speed on audiotape) blending the word sounds by stating the words at normal pace	Language (phonological processing)	Blending Words, Blending Non-words (CTOPP); Phonological Awareness (CELF-IV); Sound Blending (WJ-III Cognitive)
Elision	Transforming words by deleting phonemes from orally presented words	Language (phonological processing)	Elision (CTOPP); Phonemes (PAL); Phonological Awareness (CELF-IV); Phonological Processing (NEPSY)
Rapid automatic naming	Quickly naming visually displayed letters, numbers, and objects; taps convergent retrieval because of the required specificity of responses	Language (word retrieval)	Rapid Digit Naming, Rapid Letter Naming, Rapid Object Naming (CTOPP); Rapid Picture Naming (WJ-III Cognitive); Speeded Naming (NEPSY)
Category naming	Quickly naming words belonging to a semantic (such as vegetables) or phonemic (such as words that start with "t") category; taps divergent retrieval because of multiple potential responses	Language (word retrieval)	Verbal Fluency (NEPSY); Verbal Fluency Test (D-KEFS); Word Associations, Rapid Automatic Naming (CELF-IV); RAN-Digits, RAN-Letters, (PAL); Retrieval Fluency (WJ-III Cognitive)
Receptive vocabulary	Pointing to picture of orally presented word in a multiple-choice array; selecting the correct definition of a word in a multiple-choice format	Language (semantic understanding)	Picture Vocabulary Multiple-Choice, Vocabulary Multiple-Choice (WISC-IV Integrated); PPVT-III
Expressive vocabulary	Orally defining words	Language (semantic use)	Verbal Knowledge (SB5); Vocabulary (WISC-IV Integrated); Vocabulary (WAIS-III); Word Definitions (DAS); Word Definitions (CELF-IV)

Direction following	Following orally presented directions, usually by pointing to objects on an easel or in a booklet, sometimes by drawing	Language (sentence comprehension)	Concepts and Following Directions (CELF-IV); Verbal Instructions (PEERAMID-2); Verbal Instructions (PEEX-2); Comprehension of Instructions (NEPSY)
Complex sentences	Answering questions that are challenging in terms of sentence structure or vocabulary, or both; response may be oral (using expressive language) or multiple-choice (no expressive language)	Language (sentence comprehension)	Comprehension of Basic Concepts, Inferences (CASL); Yes, No, Maybe (PEERAMID-2); Complex Sentences (PEEX-2); Figurative Language (TLC); Sentence Questions
Ambiguous sentences	Identifying and explaining at least two of the multiple possible meanings of a sentence; can be in multiple-choice format, which isolates the receptive demand	Language (sentence comprehension)	Ambiguous Sentences (TLC); Ambiguous Sentences (CASL); Sentence Ambiguity (PEERAMID-2)
Sentence construction	Generating oral sentences that include provided sets of words (usually two to four); words are usually displayed on a page or easel, sometimes with an accompanying picture	Language (sentence formulation)	Oral Expression: Recreating Sentences (TLC); Formulated Sentences; Sentence Assembly (CELF-IV); Sentence Formulation (PEERAMID-2); Sentence Formulation (PEEX-2)
Passage listening comprehension	Answering questions about orally presented passages; response may be oral (using expressive language) or multiple-choice (no expressive language)	Language (discourse comprehension)	Missing Information (PEERAMID-2); Paragraph Summarization and Comprehension (PEEX-2); Understanding Spoken Paragraphs (CELF-IV)

[1]The neurodevelopmental functions and constructs listed here are those that are primarily assessed by the given task; other functions and constructs may be tapped as well.

[2]Full test and battery citations are listed in Appendix D.

All the tasks described thus far are sound-based, in that the words are presented orally and not in print. This is an important feature of most phonological processing tasks because it minimizes the effects of the various other functions that can undermine decoding. However, having the student read pronounceable non-words, or nonsense words, can provide a window into the student's relatively pure use of phonics (Aaron, 1995; Joshi, 1995). Examples of nonsense words are *hune*, *jepfar*, and *lomun*. Decoding such words requires word attack skills, because their unfamiliarity precludes using sight word recognition and recall of common orthographic patterns. Consequently, decoding demands are focused on sound-symbol connections (paired associate memory) and phonological processing, both needed for phonics.

Few available tasks assess morphology specifically. Those that do exist generally ask the student to alter a word in some way, such as converting from singular to plural (for example, *goat* to *goats*, *mouse to mice*, *stimulus* to *stimuli*) or changing a verb tense (such as *bake* to *bakes* or *baked*). For such tasks, the focus is on suffixes, which are a particular type of morpheme. A great deal can be learned about morphology, though, through informal techniques and limit testing, such as asking the student to name some words that are related to a word in a reading task (for example, going from *capture* to *captive*, *captivity*, and perhaps even *caption*), which would assess the student's understanding of base and root words, as well as other morphemes. Another tactic is to ask the student to define a morpheme (for example, "What does 'civil' mean?") and then interview about how it can be altered (for example, "How does the meaning of 'civil' change if we add '-ity'?").

☞ Exploring the student's morphology probably is not necessary unless a problem is first detected at the semantic level. But when the student has trouble with word meanings, it can be very useful to isolate any difficulty understanding or using morphemes.

By contrast, many kinds of tasks can help you assess word retrieval. Most are timed, and students are often engaged in them by describing them as a sort of "brain race." (For example, "Let's find out how fast you can pull words out of your brain when you need to.") Word retrieval tasks fall into one of two general categories: convergent and divergent. *Convergent tasks* require the student to quickly retrieve a specific word, such as naming something displayed visually (pictures of objects, letters, numbers, colors). *Divergent tasks* ask the student to quickly retrieve words that belong to a defined category, which could be a semantic category (such as plants) or a phonemic category (such as words that start with "m"). Students can differ in their performance across convergent and divergent word retrieval tasks. Some students benefit from the visual prompting and structure of convergent tasks, whereas others perform better with the degree of freedom afforded by divergent tasks.

Practically all language tasks have receptive demands of some kind, which could be simply understanding instructions for the task. The major differentiation, though, between tests of receptive language and tests of expressive language is the kind of output the student is required to generate. In a nutshell, if the student has to respond in some way with language (using words, sentences, or discourse), then the task assesses both receptive and expressive functions. On the other hand, if the student can respond in a way that uses minimal language (by pointing, drawing, or selecting from multiple-choice options), then the task is targeted more on receptive function than on expressive function.

At the semantic level, any task that has the student provide definitions of words assesses semantic use (expressive). However, a multiple-choice vocabulary task, such as selecting a definition or pointing to a picture that illustrates a word, assesses semantic understanding (receptive). When a student struggles with an expressive task, it is usually important to follow up with an analogous receptive task to assess the extent of the language difficulty (see Figures 10.6 and 10.7), since some students actually have good understanding of words, sentences, and discourse despite having a hard time using them to communicate. For instance, maybe the student knows what a tree is, but has a hard time putting that knowledge into words. Converting any open-ended question into a multiple-choice question is an example of limit testing.

Sentence comprehension tasks vary in the complexity of language. The capacity to understand basic sentence structures (for example, subject, object) can be assessed via direction-following activities. For instance, the student may be asked to follow orally presented instructions using printed shapes and symbols. A more advanced task would be to answer comprehension questions about orally presented complex sentences (that is, challenging in terms of sentence structure or vocabulary, or both); the questions themselves can

Figure 10.6   Expressive Versus Receptive Vocabulary Tasks: Basic Examples

Expressive Task:	What is a *tree*?	
Receptive Task:	Which is the definition of *tree*?	
A.	B.	C.
Plant with one main stem or trunk, which develops branches	Structure that is relatively higher than its length and width	Part of a plant that produces a seed; usually has petals and pollen

Receptive Task:	Point to the picture of a *tree*:	

also be challenging for students. Still more advanced is understanding the multiple meanings of ambiguous sentences (such as "We've got to get to the bottom of this"). Sentence ambiguity tasks can combine receptive and expressive demands; identifying subtle double meanings of sentences obviously is receptive, but explaining those possible meanings is expressive and can be just as challenging. One student may not decipher the multiple meanings (suggesting weak sentence comprehension), while a second student might understand the different meanings but be unable to explain them clearly. A multiple-choice format can help you differentiate between these two levels of

Figure 10.7   Expressive Versus Receptive Vocabulary Tasks: Advanced Examples

Expressive Task:	What is an *arch*?	
Receptive Task:	Which is the definition of *arch*?	
A.	B.	C.
Segment of a curve or circle	Curved structure that supports weight of material over open space	Structure over open space that provides passage for pedestrians or vehicles

Receptive Task:	Point to the picture of an *arch*:	

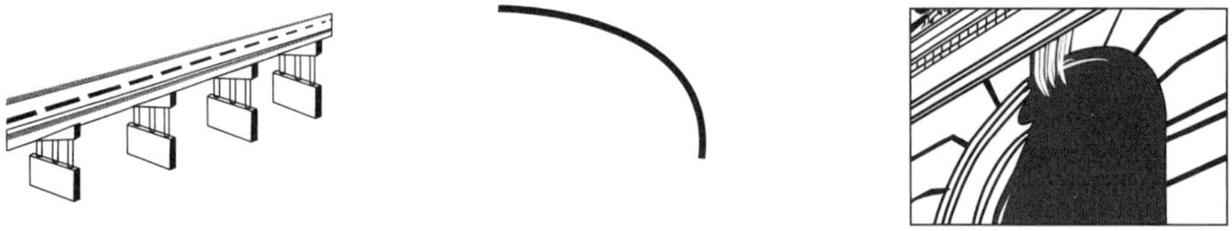

Figure 10.8   Mock Sentence Comprehension Tasks

Basic: "Point to the black square after you point to the white square and the triangle."

□   ∩   ▼   ■

Complex: "If they hadn't arrived early, nobody would have had a chance to see it. *Would anybody have seen it if they had arrived late?*"

Ambiguous: "What are different things that this sentence could mean? *That's really up in the air.*"

task performance, since the second student would probably be able to select correct meanings from displayed options. Figure 10.8 includes examples of sentence comprehension tasks.

Again, neurodevelopmental tasks of receptive language usually avoid reading and tasks of expressive language usually avoid writing, the rationale being to isolate specific functions that might be causing a learning or skill breakdown. Sentence formulation tasks exemplify this principle, as they are generally designed so that the student creates sentences orally. One such task displays two or three words, sometimes with an accompanying picture, and then asks the student to create a meaningful sentence that includes all the words in their given form (for example, no tense changes to verbs). Figure 10.9 gives you another look at a mock sentence generation task originally presented in Chapter Six, which presents a set of words that the student must order so as to construct at least one meaningful sentence. In one version of this task, the words are displayed on an easel and the student responds orally. In a second version of this task, the words are displayed on individual cards and the student responds by sequencing the cards on the table. Both versions of this task assess sentence comprehension without mixing it with

Figure 10.9   Mock Sentence Generation Task

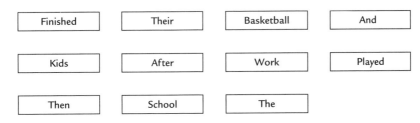

graphomotor function, but the second version requires less active working memory since the reordering of the words can take place on the table instead of on mental counter space.

Assessing discourse processing via listening comprehension generally involves simply reading a passage to the student and then asking questions to determine the level of understanding. It is usually advisable to use both narrative and expository discourse, since students encounter both in their academic work. Comprehension questions should also vary in type, including factual recall, inference drawing, and predicting. In addition, multiple-choice questions can be used to factor out expressive language difficulty.

Royer, Greene, and Sinatra (1987) described an interesting method called the Sentence Verification Technique (SVT), which could be used to assess discourse processing and sentence comprehension (as well as processing depth). SVT, which was used successfully with students in Grade 3 and higher, first involves developing an equal number of four types of test sentences derived from sentences in a text passage. The four test sentence types are *originals*, or exact copies of passage sentences; *paraphrases*, which have the same meaning as passage sentences but with most of the words changed; *meaning changes*, which are sentences with altered meanings that contain several of the same words as passage sentences; and *distracters*, which relate to the same passage topic but differ in meaning and wording from passage sentences. With the four types of test sentences developed in advance, the student then reads or listens to the passage and, without having the text for reference, judges each of the test sentences to be *old* (originals or paraphrases) or *new* (meaning changes and distracters). Students who are overly focused on decoding (to the point of missing the meaning of the passage) may perform well on originals and distracters but have difficulty with paraphrases and meaning changes; in contrast, students who are overly focused on meaning might accurately identify originals, paraphrases, and meaning changes, but display difficulty with distracters.

To assess discourse production as separate from written expression (that is, through oral expression), the student needs to be given a prompt or topic and asked to discuss it. One tactic is to have the student read or listen to a passage and then summarize it, although insufficient understanding or lack of memory will interfere with the task and keep it from providing a clear window into expressive functioning. As an alternative, the student could be asked to describe a personal experience (for example, something that happened last vacation), a hobby or favorite activity, or the adult job that seems most appealing.

> ☞ As a movie buff, I am biased toward asking students to summarize movies they have recently seen. This can put students at ease since the topic is nonacademic and fun.

Personal norms are needed when appraising the student's summaries and descriptions. How well is the information organized? Are the references (for example, the pronouns) clear? Do sentences link together in logical ways? Does the student check in to see that the listener is following? As mentioned earlier in this chapter, assessing verbal elaboration involves going beyond how well the student's discourse is organized and based on the rules. What is the quality of thought in the student's language? How extended or well-formulated are the ideas? Does the student communicate the bare minimum or provide a complete picture of the thought process?

Task-Analysis for Language

Practically any assessment task is an opportunity to look at a student's language functioning. To take advantage of the opportunity, however, you need to be aware of the specific language demands of a task, regardless of whether it is designed to assess language. Table 10.2 lists some considerations for language task-analysis.

Again, academic tasks can be very revealing windows into language functioning, especially when used in conjunction with specific language tasks that isolate particular functions. Although math has many nonverbal aspects, language (especially semantics) is also a factor for success in math. The student's understanding of word problems relates to sentence comprehension and discourse processing. Thus you can assess a student's expressive language and

Table 10.2   Considerations for Language Task-Analysis

Question About Task	Analysis of Language Demands
• How much language is presented to the student (including task instructions)?	• Extent of receptive language
• How much visual support (such as pictures) is provided along with language?	• Complexity of receptive language
• How complicated is the language presented to the student?	• Complexity of receptive language
• How much language is the student required to generate?	• Extent of expressive language
• Can the student respond without having to use language, or with very little language?	• Complexity of expressive language
• How sophisticated or elaborated do the student's responses need to be?	• Complexity of expressive language
• Does the task involve word sounds, word parts, whole words, sentences, or discourse?	• Levels of language

verbal elaboration during an interview that focuses on procedures the student used for solving various math problems.

Reading, writing, and spelling obviously are loaded with language demands. Passage reading can be modified into a *cloze task* (one in which words are removed and the student needs to identify missing words using the remaining information); such a task requires understanding of context clues and receptive language at several levels. Cloze tasks can also be based on individual words with letters removed. Reading decoding tasks can be used to assess phonological processing, especially when nonsense words are employed (weak decoding, though, may be caused by factors other than language). Nonsense words can also be used for spelling tasks to assess phonics, as well as knowledge and application of spelling rules (Moats, 1994a). Spelling is a multifaceted task that requires several constructs, including memory (such as recall of rules, orthographic memory, and paired associate memory) and language (such as phonological processing, morphological use, and semantic use). When a student spells well, it suggests intact or strong functioning across these neurodevelopmental areas. Weak spelling, though, needs to be closely examined (in conjunction with neurodevelopmental tasks) to determine

Table 10.3   Considerations for Spelling Assessment

Element	Examples
Predictable Phoneme-Grapheme Correspondences	
Blends	flat, dragon
Digraphs	chip, fish
Unpredictable Phoneme-Grapheme Correspondences	
Single consonants	dress, edge, result
Tense vowels	grown, fight, explain
R-controlled vowels	fear, port, bird
Diphthongs	boil, power, bout
Consonant blends	blink, square, scary
Consonant digraphs	which, kitchen
Syllable Patterns	
VCCV	sister, September
Open VCV	behind, nobody
Closed VCV	damage, management
C-le	bugle, treatable
R-controlled vowel	porter, curdle
Idiosyncratic	action, atomic
Orthographic Rules and Syllable Juncture	
-ve	hive, give, glove
Doubling	jogging, flopped
y to i	studious, beautiful
Drop silent e	caked, coming
Inflections	walked, logs, fishes
Silent Letters	sign, bomb
Irregular (Odd) Spellings	of, enough, said
Homophones	their, there; to, two, too

Source: Based on Moats (1994a).

the specific breakdown points. Spelling assessment should include words that sample a range of orthographic patterns, sound-symbol relationships, and morphemes. Dynamic assessment of spelling incorporates instructional elements such as talking about base words and their derived words, pronouncing by syllables, and segmenting phonemes (that is, orally breaking down words by sounds) (Moats, 1994a). Table 10.3 includes detailed information about elements of a spelling sample.

A writing sample can be an important tool for appraising a student's expressive language. Providing a standard prompt (for example, "What are some steps our society can take to reduce pollution?") helps the student get started, and also makes it easier to compare across students and better use personal norms to identify typical and atypical errors, patterns, and overall quality. Writing prompts can be pictures, and guidelines for developing such prompts include using a picture that depicts an interesting scene or event, contains at least two characters, and displays potential conflict between characters requiring resolution (Hooper et al., 1994). Since writing also requires other constructs besides expressive language, it is important to compare the student's written and oral expression (Chapter Six describes these and other useful clinical contrasts). To make full use of writing as an assessment task, it is important to have the student describe the thought process that accompanies writing (sometimes referred to as a "think-aloud protocol"). In addition, semi-structured interviews can be used to probe the student's thinking after the writing task (Hooper et al., 1994). Sample questions: What was your main idea? What were your supporting ideas? Why did you put the information in this order? How clear was your summary? Would you make any changes to the paper now?

Language Signs and Symptoms

The preceding discussion about tactics and tasks for assessing language has already illuminated numerous indicators of language functioning. Table 10.4 summarizes these and other potential signs of language. (Note: Similar information is provided in Appendix C, which also lists typical findings for other neurodevelopmental constructs.) It is important to remember that a student's language may seem different depending on the setting or social context. For instance, a student may sound fluent during casual conversation or with peers but fall apart on more challenging or decontextualized tasks. Academic tasks involve literate language that places specific demands on the student. Put differently, language weaknesses are harder to conceal in academic work than in social interactions. In some cases, though, a student may have better literate and academic language than social language, perhaps having a hard time with the speed and lingo of peer conversation. (For further discussion of social cognition, see Chapter Eleven.)

Table 10.4   Signs and Symptoms of Language

Language Level	General Findings
Phonological processing	Asset Indicators • *Decoding words (including nonsense words) through phonics-based word attack strategies such as segmenting and re-blending (rather than recognizing sight words)* • *Rhyming words and syllables* • *Misspellings that are phonetically logical (such as* enuf *for* enough) Signs of Dysfunction • *Reading with little fluency or rhythm* • *Misspellings that are not phonetically logical (such as* alpel *for* apple) • *Decoding errors that are visually close but with poor phonics (*siege *for* sieve *or* fat *for* first)
Morphological sense	Asset Indicators • *Identifying words that are related via root or base* Signs of Dysfunction • *Trouble determining meaning of a word by looking at its component parts* • *Decoding errors involving omissions of prefixes or suffixes (for example,* distribute *for* distributed)
Morphological use	Asset Indicators • *Figuring out how to spell words based on morphemes (for example, "idio-syn-crat-ic")* Signs of Dysfunction • *Spelling errors that reveal limited understanding of morphemes (such as* carsik *for* carsick)
Word retrieval	Asset Indicators • *Good automaticity and fluency with decoding* Signs of Dysfunction • *Overreliance on nondescript words such as* stuff *and* things *in speech and writing*

(Continued)

Table 10.4   Signs and Symptoms of Language (*Continued*)

Language Level	General Findings
Semantic understanding	Asset Indicators • *Understanding words encountered in reading* • *Grasping math and science terminology* • *Correctly spelling homophones (such as* piece *and* peace*) based on context* Signs of Dysfunction • *Student describing trouble understanding words teachers use* • *Trouble understanding social lingo* • *Decoding errors involving stress on wrong syllable ("dom-IN-ate" for "dominate")*
Semantic use	Asset Indicators • *Accurately defining terms on tests and quizzes* • *Explaining meanings of words encountered when reading* • *Forming clear answers to comprehension questions* Signs of Dysfunction • *Erroneous, vague, or limited word use in speech and writing* • *Difficulty using social lingo*
Sentence comprehension	Asset Indicators • *Understanding task instructions* • *Reading math word problems and identifying the procedure needed to solve the problem* • *Self-correcting decoding errors based on context* Signs of Dysfunction • *Errors in listening comprehension that are not readily corrected after repetition* • *Trouble answering comprehension questions about reading* • *Difficulty determining word meanings based on sentence context*
Sentence formulation	Asset Indicators • *Adroitly rephrasing ambiguous sentences into other versions that convey multiple meanings* • *Forming clear answers to comprehension questions* Signs of Dysfunction • *Repetitive or frequent use of simplistic sentence structures in written work* • *Trouble with grammar (for example, unclear pronouns or noun-verb disagreements)*

Table 10.4   Signs and Symptoms of Language (*Continued*)

Language Level	General Findings
Discourse processing	Asset Indicators • Comprehending lectures and class discussions • Reading math word problems and identifying the procedure needed to solve the problem • Self-correcting decoding errors based on context Signs of Dysfunction • Errors in listening comprehension that are not readily corrected after repetition • Trouble answering comprehension questions about reading (such as drawing inferences) • Difficulty determining word meanings based on passage context
Discourse production	Asset Indicators • Providing good summaries of listening or reading passages • Forming clear answers to comprehension questions Signs of Dysfunction • Disorganized ideas in written work, sentences not connected cohesively • Trouble describing personal experiences in a clear fashion
Verbal elaboration	Asset Indicators • Sharing developed thinking during class discussions • Ideas extended through oral and written expression Signs of Dysfunction • Frequent use of very brief responses to questions • Having a hard time explaining how problems were solved or tasks approached • Minimal written and oral output

CASE STUDY

Nate is ten years old and in the fifth grade. Although he can decode effectively, throughout his schooling he has experienced reading comprehension problems that have gotten more severe. His grades on quizzes and tests have also been poor. He does not enjoy reading at all, but his parents note that he likes movies; in fact, he tends to watch some of his favorite animated movies over and over on DVD.

Nate is quite social and can be seen interacting with his circle of buddies during recess, P.E. class, and lunch.

The assessment confirmed that Nate has weak receptive language, from the whole word level through understanding of discourse. He has thin vocabulary knowledge, is easily confused by different sentence structures, has trouble with ambiguous language, and struggles with inference drawing. His language weaknesses certainly affect his reading comprehension, and that poses more of a problem now that he is "reading to learn," but they also affect his listening comprehension; as a result, his knowledge base is not developing as it should and his test performances have suffered. (He also may have a hard time understanding some test questions.)

Nate's receptive language is particularly weak with the literate material that abounds in schoolwork. When interacting with peers he has a better time understanding their more casual, social language (their lingo). Also, he has soaked in animated movies through repeated viewings, and such movies also provide a great deal of visual support for the language. Nate's learning plan may need to prioritize his language weaknesses, as it is unlikely that he can tackle everything at once. It might make sense to start with his semantic understanding (for example, bolstering his lexicon through word families) and then move to sentences and discourse.

CASE STUDY

Shawn is a ten-year-old fifth grader. Socially, he is described by his teachers as shy and relatively quiet in class. He has a very good friend with whom he spends the majority of his free time at school. Academically, writing has emerged as a major issue; his output is typically brief, nondescriptive, and general, and also lacking good structure and organization. However, he is an accomplished reader and seems to be focused in class. Shawn's parents report that he reached his early childhood developmental milestones on time, with the exception of putting words together to form short sentences (delayed by about six months).

During the assessment Shawn showed a significant discrepancy between his receptive language and his expressive language. He demonstrated a good grasp of word meanings through multiple-choice items, but struggled to define words on his own. He comprehended various orally presented sentences and passages, but had trouble constructing sentences from word and picture prompts. In general, he seemed to understand task directions and questions, but expressed himself slowly, briefly, and with noticeable effort; for instance, he had a hard time describing a book he recently read.

In short, Shawn has weak expressive language but good receptive language. This clinical contrast plays out in his academics in terms of much better reading skill than writing ability. He also takes in material when listening, but his class participation is limited because he struggles with putting his ideas into words. His somewhat withdrawn nature probably also stems from his weak expressive language, as he may be uncomfortable communicating with peers unless he is very comfortable (as with his good friend).

Shawn may require language therapy to improve, but much can be done in the classroom and at home to help him. He needs regular opportunities to practice using language, such as during family meals and when riding in the car; affinity topics may engage him better, and over time he can be pushed to elaborate on other material. At school, small group work (perhaps including his friend) may elicit more oral participation than whole-class discussions. Also, his receptive language and reading skill need to be acknowledged, celebrated, and nurtured.

CASE STUDY

Maya is fifteen years old. She is off to a rocky start in high school in her freshman year. Her father reports that she has generally been a "solid B student," but only by "working her tail off." Her teachers similarly describe her as a very determined worker, but she is having real trouble in English, science, and history classes. She says that the reading and writing assignments are very difficult for her. Her best subjects are math and art. She is also a fine athlete, but her parents are considering pulling her out of sports so that she can spend more time on her studies.

The assessment determined that Maya has appropriate decoding skills, but that her receptive language varies. At the lower levels (that is, sound and word), she has pretty good functioning, but she has more difficulty with the higher levels (sentence and discourse). In particular, she has trouble with abstract and complex language that comes in extended pieces (such as that found in novels and textbooks). Maya's expressive language shows a similar pattern. She can provide word definitions, for example, and construct basic sentences and paragraphs, but she really struggles with composing complicated sentences and writing essays. By working very hard, Maya was able to maintain fairly good grades through middle school, but high school hit her with a great deal of extended, complex language demands that have overwhelmed her.

One approach to Maya's learning plan is providing her alternative means of accessing information. For example, she would probably do better with history information that has been condensed into notes, rather than having to read through lengthy chapters. Her writing process may need to be explicitly staged, so that she does not feel so overwhelmed. Also, she might be allowed to substitute some writing assignments with other formats, such as completing detailed graphic organizers or constructing a diagram (for science, for example). Finally, her assets in math and art (which, incidentally, involve relatively little language) need to be highlighted. Taking away athletics should be an absolute last resort, as sports are probably making her feel better about herself.

This and the two chapters that precede it have covered the big three constructs of attention, memory, and language that play such huge roles in academic work. The neurodevelopmental framework contains other constructs, though, which should be considered when assessing to understand. The next chapter is devoted to assessment considerations for these other factors.

11

Other Neurodevelopmental Factors to Consider

THIS CHAPTER IS DEVOTED TO THE ASSESSMENT methods for the remaining constructs in the neurodevelopmental framework (see shaded portions of Figure 11.1). I won't go as deep as I did with attention, memory, and language in the past three chapters, but the same thought processes (understanding theory, making important distinctions, considering general assessment principles, conducting task-analysis, knowing typical signs of weak and strong functioning) can and should be applied to all neurodevelopmental areas (and to the elements of any other framework). Descriptions of major assessment tasks are summarized in Table 11.1, along with examples of real tests and subtests you can use. Appendix D includes full battery names for acronyms and test publishers. Appendix A contains additional information about supporting research for these constructs, while Appendix C lists general findings, clinical contrasts, and assessment tasks for each.

Spatial Ordering

The concept of *spatial ordering* appears in many theoretical frameworks, often as visual processing or visual-spatial processing. In a sense, spatial ordering is the opposite of language, in that it deals with material that is nonverbal in nature (pictures, diagrams, drawings, geometric shapes, maps, sculptures). Like language, spatial ordering has input and output sides, with input having to do with interpreting and comprehending visual-spatial information and output relating to the generation of visual-spatial material (for example, making a drawing, constructing a device). It is also possible to view spatial ordering as

Figure 11.1   A Neurodevelopmental Framework

Attention	Memory	Language	Spatial Ordering	Temporal-Sequential Ordering	Neuromotor Function	Higher-Order Cognition	Social Cognition
Cross-Construct Phenomena (Rate, Chunk Size, Metacognition, Strategy Use)							

the opposite of temporal-sequential ordering in that spatial information exists in gestalts or simultaneously interpreted sets, whereas sequential information is interpreted in linear fashion, piece by piece. Both ordering constructs, spatial and temporal-sequential, can be viewed as interfaces with other neurodevelopmental constructs; for instance, both spatial and sequential information must be recalled (memory) and comprehended (higher-order cognition).

> ☞ Spatial ordering is very important at the early grade levels (for example, in learning shape names), but decreases in importance. In contrast, temporal-sequential ordering is used increasingly in school (in stepwise procedures). However, many adult pursuits, such as graphic design, require good spatial ordering.

Although it is linked to some of the core academic skills such as math (see Chapter Four), two other reasons can be offered for assessing spatial ordering. First, this particular area may represent an unidentified or untapped asset for a student that could be nurtured or built into a learning plan. Second, spatial tasks can be used to look for certain clinical contrasts (as discussed in Chapter Six.) Thorough assessment of spatial ordering would consider both input and output, as well as recall and higher thinking. Also, spatial tasks can differ in their degree of contextualization (for example, by presenting an abstract figure or a drawing of a real-life object).

Figure matching and identification, basic figure copying, and complex figure copying were jointly discussed in Chapter Six in terms of potential clinical contrasts between them. Figure matching tasks require the student to examine a target figure and then to select from among a set of potential responses a figure that is the exact match. Such tasks tap spatial perception

Table 11.1   Assessment Task Types for Other Constructs

Task Type	Description	Primarily Assesses[1]	Examples[2]
Figure matching	Selecting from a set the figure or shape that matches a target; mental manipulation of the figure is sometimes required; sometimes linked with basic figure copy	Spatial ordering	Visual Perception (VMI); Block Design Multiple Choice (WISC-IV Integrated); Lock and Key (PEERAMID-2); Visual Whole:Part Analysis (PEEX-2); Spatial Relations (WJ-III Cognitive)
Basic figure copy	Copying relatively small, simple, and abstract figures; sometimes linked with drawing recall	Spatial ordering, graphomotor function	Visual-Motor Integration (VMI); Bender Visual-Motor Gestalt Test (Bender); Design Copying (NEPSY); Geometric Form Copying (PEEX-2)
Complex figure copy	Copying a large, complex, and abstract figure; sometimes linked with drawing recall	Spatial ordering, attention (production controls), graphomotor function	RCFT; Complex Form Copying (PEERAMID-2)
Block construction	Replicating patterns (modeled or displayed in a booklet) with colored blocks; usually has time limit or bonus points for speed; task variant provides pictures of blocks in multiple-choice format	Spatial ordering	Block Design, Block Design Multiple Choice (WISC-IV Integrated); Block Construction (NEPSY); Pattern Construction (DAS)
Sequence completion	Completing sequences involving pictures, symbols, numbers, and so on; response can be verbal, nonverbal (pointing), or written	Temporal-sequential ordering	Pictorial Sequences, Geometric Sequences (CTONI); Sequential & Quantitative Reasoning (DAS)
Finger localization	Making specific finger movements without visual support; usually involves imitating movements demonstrated by the examiner	Fine motor function	Imitative Finger Movement, Motor Sequential Imitation (PEERAMID-2); Imitative Finger Movement, Motor Sequential Imitation (PEEX-2); Finger Sense (PAL); Imitating Hand Positions (NEPSY)

(continued)

Table 11.1   Assessment Task Types for Other Constructs (*Continued*)

Task Type	Description	Primarily Assesses[1]	Examples[2]
Finger tapping	Tapping fingers rapidly; can be a repetitive movement (for example, index finger on table) or as a more complex sequence (such as thumb and each finger tip)	Fine motor function	Finger Tapping (PEEX-2); Sequential Finger Opposition (PEERAMID-2); Finger Sense (PAL); Fingertip Tapping (NEPSY)
Maze tracing	Drawing a line along a narrow winding path without touching the sides; usually has time limit or bonus points for speed, and penalty for touching sides of path	Graphomotor function	Pencil Control, Pencil Speed (PEEX-2); Pencil Speed (PEERAMID-2); Visuomotor Precision (NEPSY)
Similarities	Describing how two or three words are related or similar; format may be open-ended (using expressive language) or multiple-choice (no expressive language)	Higher-order cognition (conceptualization)	Similarities, Similarities Multiple-Choice (WISC-IV Integrated); Word Classes-Expressive (CELF-IV); Similarities (DAS)
Visual concepts	Selecting the two or three pictures or symbols that are related or similar	Higher-order cognition (conceptualization)	Picture Concepts (WISC-IV Integrated); Pictorial Categories, Geometric Categories (CTONI)
Matrix reasoning	Completing an analogy (such as "This picture goes with this picture just as this picture goes with which one of these?") with pictures or symbols displayed on an easel; multiple-choice format	Higher-order cognition (reasoning and logic)	Geometric Analogies (CTONI); Nonverbal (KBIT-2); Matrices (DAS); Matrix Reasoning (WISC-IV Integrated); Matrix Reasoning (WAIS-III); Nonverbal Fluid Reasoning (SB5)
Tower	Shifting balls or disks from peg to peg (three total) in specific number of moves to match picture displayed on an easel; multiple rules must be followed (for example, cannot put ball or disk on table)	Higher-order cognition (reasoning and logic), attention (production controls)	Tower (NEPSY); Tower Test (D-KEFS)

Table 11.1   (*Continued*)

Task Type	Description	Primarily Assesses[1]	Examples[2]
Use of feedback	Using only feedback (from examiner or computer) about accuracy of preceding responses to figure out a rule to guide subsequent responses (for example, sort cards, pick category members)	Higher-order cognition (reasoning and logic)	CCT; WCST; Analysis-Synthesis, Concept Formation (WJ-III Cognitive)
Social vignettes	Describing appropriate responses for social scenarios, presented orally or through a picture, or both	Social cognition	Pragmatic Judgment (CASL); Roberts-2; TEMAS

[1]The neurodevelopmental functions and constructs listed here are those that are primarily assessed by the given task; other functions and constructs may be tapped as well.
[2]Full test and battery citations are listed in Appendix D.

(input), because the student does not have to generate anything; processing depth (attention) is also involved in terms of detecting the subtle differences between response options. Figure 11.2 contains a sample of a figure matching item, including a target and three response options. Other types of spatial perception tasks include identifying shapes (such as two triangles) that, if combined, would form another shape (in this example, a square), and detecting a small shape (such as a rectangle) embedded somewhere within a larger design.

Figure 11.2   Mock Basic Geometric Figure Matching

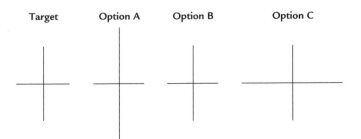

Target   Option A   Option B   Option C

Figure 11.3   Mock Basic Geometric Figures

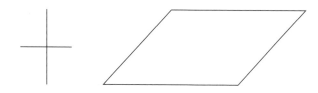

Basic figure copy tasks also tap spatial perception because the student has to adequately process the visual information from the figures, but such tasks add a spatial output demand in that the student needs to draw copies of the figures as well. Poor pencil control, obviously, can undermine performance on such a task, in addition to weak spatial ordering. Figure 11.3 contains two examples of basic figures that would be copied by the student.

Copying a complex figure (like the one in Figure 11.4) requires all the functions involved in copying basic figures, but planning is also important because of the size and intricacy of the design. Finding the source of weak performance on a complex figure copy usually requires looking at basic figure copies and figure matching to determine just where the breakdown is occurring: pencil control, perception, output, planning, or whatever else may be interfering with the task.

Block construction tasks eliminate the potential *confound* of pencil control while still tapping both spatial perception and spatial output. In such tasks the student is typically shown a design on an easel (see Figure 11.5) and is asked to replicate it by assembling multicolored blocks (the tops of the blocks would need to match the displayed design). The example in

Figure 11.4   Mock Complex Figure

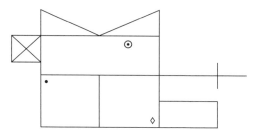

Figure 11.5   Mock Block Construction Design

Figure 11.5 could be made even more complicated by removing the grid lines (which are useful clues in the perception of the design's organization) or by displaying it as a three-dimensional figure. Careful observation of the student's work process during block construction (for example, watching for signs that the student is taking a moment to think about how to recreate the design or just start using trial and error) can provide more insight into not only spatial ordering but also previewing (attention) and strategy use. Also, block construction tasks can be converted into pure spatial perception tasks by offering them in a multiple-choice format. As with the example in Figure 11.2, the student would be shown a target design on an easel along with response options showing different response configurations—in this case consisting of separated squares or triangles, only one set of which could form the target if the elements were brought together.

Another aspect of spatial ordering is the organization of space, including materials like books, paper, pencils, and other academic resources. Such spatial organization cannot be tested, but it can be assessed via history, direct observation of student's work and storage spaces, and interviewing to get the student's own view of handling various materials. Does the student keep good track of notebooks? How ordered or disheveled are the student's backpack, locker, and desk? Spatial ordering also includes reasoning and conceptualizing without language, such as understanding principles of geometry and solving problems involving space (such as perimeter or area). Higher spatial thinking can be assessed, in part, through testing (see "Conceptualization" and "Reasoning and Logic" later in this chapter), but history and reviewing academic work, such as mathematics, is usually necessary as well.

Temporal-Sequential Ordering

The concept of sequencing appears in several theoretical frameworks. For example, it's "successive" in the PASS model (Das, Naglieri, & Kirby, 1994). Sequential information is pervasive in school; students encounter multistep instructions, number lines, math procedures, narratives, historical time lines, and so on and on. In addition to collecting and reviewing history about the student's capacity to work with sequences in school, several types of tasks are available for assessing sequencing. Any task in which the student needs to process or generate information that has to preserve its linear order involves sequencing to some degree. As with spatial tasks, some sequencing tasks involve highly contextualized data, such as the days of the week, and some more decontextualized data, such as a string of numbers.

Short-term recall for sequences can be assessed with many of the same tasks described for memory in Chapter Nine, especially the digit or letter span tasks or movement imitation tasks. A pattern of errors on memory tasks may reveal that the student could accurately recall the individual elements presented, but could not preserve the serial order (for example, recalling "7–1–5–8" as "7–5–8–1"). Asking the student to follow multistep instructions in a specified order also involves sequencing. When the student is summarizing a passage (either read or heard), it is useful to observe how close the summary comes to the original sequence of the information. Long-term recall for sequences can be tested by asking the student to recite things like the months of the year in correct order.

Reasoning with sequences can be assessed through sequence completion tasks, which present the student with sequences (visual or verbal) that are missing elements; the student needs to decipher the sequential pattern and determine what element would complete the sequence in a logical way. In the example in Figure 11.6, the student needs to use the three elements in the top row to determine a sequential pattern and select one element from the bottom row that would conclude the pattern.

Figure 11.6   Sequential Completion Reasoning Task

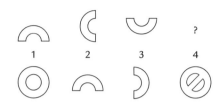

Temporal organization refers to how systematic and ordered one is with time. Academic work, particularly in the middle and upper grades, requires a fair amount of *stepwisdom*—a sense of how to stage and plan complicated and extended tasks (for example, researching and writing a term paper). Being able to schedule study time so that sufficient time is allotted to various pieces of work is another application of temporal organization. Put simply, it is important to have a good sense of time. Assessing this aspect of sequencing requires history and interviewing, as it cannot really be tested.

Neuromotor Function

Neuromotor function refers to the brain's coordination of muscle movements, particularly voluntary movement. Neuromotor functions can be divided into several categories, according to the body parts coordinated:

- Gross motor
- Fine motor
- Oromotor
- Graphomotor

Gross motor function is probably the least critical for direct academic work, since it would be used only for classes like physical education or dance. It is important to note, however, that athletics and other physical activities are often important self-esteem boosters for students with learning problems. Conversely, students who are physically awkward and struggle athletically can feel humiliated in front of their peers.

Few test batteries include any gross motor tasks (such as demonstrating balance or hopping in sequence). Observing the student run, throw, and catch can provide a quick screening for motor control. History is an important source of information about gross motor functioning, including questions about how adept the student is at sports and other activities involving large muscle control (such as dancing or playing). Some sports, such as gymnastics, are relatively pure when it comes to gross motor functioning, whereas others, such as tennis, also require hand-eye coordination and spatial perception. Sports like swimming and golf have an element of sequencing in that particular motions or strokes include elements that need to be executed in the proper order to be effective. Team sports, obviously, involve collaborating with peers and so require social cognition and language (many sports have unique lingoes that need to be learned). Attention is used for any activity, but any sport with severe fluctuations between downtime and action, such as baseball, puts particular stress on the processing control system. So by using task-analysis, information can be gleaned not only about the student's gross motor function, but about other constructs as well.

> ☞ When task-analyzing team sports, considering the position can be revealing. In baseball, for example, playing in the outfield is very taxing on attention because of the extremes of downtime and action, whereas the pitcher and catcher are always involved. The catcher is also in a leadership position. The point is to look carefully at any activity in which the student participates, watch for recurring themes, and make linkages with specific functions.

Fine motor function is used in the early grades when utensils like scissors are prominent and when basic life skills, such as using clothing buttons, are learned (traditionally, tying shoelaces was a life skill requiring fine motor function, but slip-on shoes and Velcro straps have been replacing laces). Playing many musical instruments (such as the woodwinds or piano) requires good control over hands and fingers. A critical academic linkage involving fine motor function is keyboarding. To use a keyboard effectively, one has to have smooth coordination of finger movements and be aware of finger positioning without visual information (also important for playing many musical instruments). Finger localization tasks ask the student to make specific hand and finger movements (usually first demonstrated by the examiner) without looking. Finger tapping simply has the student make tapping motions (for example, finger tip to thumb tip, finger tip to table) that might be basic (repeated motion with one finger) or more complex (a series of motions with several fingers). Both localization and tapping tasks are analogs for fine motor activities such as keyboarding. Tasks designed to tap other areas (for example, the ones that use block construction for spatial output) may also involve fine motor function.

> ☞ For many clinicians, assessment of neuromotor function will be at a screening level, with significant problems or concerns referred to specialists such as physical therapists (for gross motor), occupational therapists (for fine motor and graphomotor), and speech pathologists (for articulation and language).

Oromotor function, obviously, is needed for clear articulation of oral language; listening to the student's speech is a window into enunciation and general fluency. Finally, *graphomotor function* links to the coordination of hand and finger movements for handwriting. Whenever the student uses a pen or pencil to write, you have an opportunity to assess graphomotor function; observations should be made about the quality of the student's grip (see Figure 11.7), the amount of pressure (excessive pressure can be a sign that the student gets insufficient feedback on hand and finger positioning and therefore compensates by pressing harder), and eye positioning (staring intently at the letters being written can also be a sign of insufficient feedback on hand and finger positioning).

Writing letters and numbers involves not only pencil control but also memory for the movements involved in forming the letter or number and for what the final product should look like. Therefore, several graphomotor tasks factor out the memory component by having the student simply copy small and basic symbols or trace through a maze of some sort. Maze tracing tasks involve narrow tracks on the page through which the student must navigate as quickly as possible without touching the lines (some tasks are untimed to focus on precision rather than efficiency). Mazes typically are either square-edged (see Figure 11.8) or curved (see Figure 11.9), to mimic the small, precise movements involved in printing or handwriting.

Figure 11.7 Handwriting Grips
Source: Photography by Patti Donnelly.

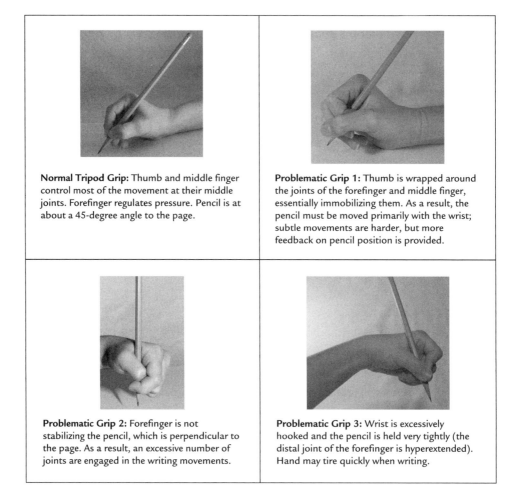

Normal Tripod Grip: Thumb and middle finger control most of the movement at their middle joints. Forefinger regulates pressure. Pencil is at about a 45-degree angle to the page.

Problematic Grip 1: Thumb is wrapped around the joints of the forefinger and middle finger, essentially immobilizing them. As a result, the pencil must be moved primarily with the wrist; subtle movements are harder, but more feedback on pencil position is provided.

Problematic Grip 2: Forefinger is not stabilizing the pencil, which is perpendicular to the page. As a result, an excessive number of joints are engaged in the writing movements.

Problematic Grip 3: Wrist is excessively hooked and the pencil is held very tightly (the distal joint of the forefinger is hyperextended). Hand may tire quickly when writing.

Weak fine motor, oromotor, or graphomotor functioning can have a funneling effect on a student's output. Imagine three students with age-appropriate expressive language (that is, all can convert their ideas into words, sentences, and discourse effectively and efficiently) but weaknesses with a

Figure 11.8 Graphomotor Maze Tracing Task, Square-Edged Track

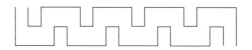

Figure 11.9   Graphomotor Maze Tracing Task, Curved Track

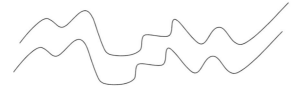

different kind of neuromotor functioning. The first, Becky, has weak fine motor function, which leads to struggles with keyboarding; her oral speech is much more fluent and sophisticated than what she can type. The second, Dontrelle, has weak oromotor function leading to significant enunciation problems; he generates ideas and language in his head, but struggles mightily to articulate what he wants to communicate (his written output would probably be of higher quality than his speech). The third, Karl, has weak graphomotor function leading to inefficient and illegible handwriting; his written expression is far less elaborated and sophisticated than his oral expression. The respective neuromotor dysfunctions of these students act as funnels on their expressive language; their output (whether it be through keyboarding, speech, or handwriting) is significantly less than their oral language shows them to be capable of. It is as if they have functioning computers (expressive language), but are stuck with faulty printers (fingers, mouth muscles). Such neuromotor dysfunctions can be very frustrating for students.

Conceptualization

A concept is stronger than a fact.

—Charlotte Perkins Gilman

I have used the term *concept* several times in this book, but what exactly is a concept, anyway? A concept is, in essence, a set of essential features that together define a category of ideas or objects (Levine, 1998). *Tree* designates a concept whose defining features include being a plant with roots, a trunk, branches, leaves, use of photosynthesis, and relatively large size. Some features help differentiate a tree from other concepts that share some features (tower, light pole, bush). There are offshoots of the *tree* concept, such as a schematic decision tree, which share only some features (trunk, branches) with the core concept. Concepts are often abstract (in contrast to a tree, which is tangible) and can take many forms or modalities, including verbal (for example, due process, foreshadowing) and nonverbal (place value, geometric shapes). Process concepts explain mechanisms or how something works or progresses; examples include the water cycle, photosynthesis, chains of historical events, metamorphosis, and digestion (Levine, 1998).

Conceptualization, then, is an aspect of the higher-order cognition function involved with integrating sets of features that jointly define categories of ideas or objects. The capacity to conceptualize can really spare memory because once the essential features of a concept have been learned, it is then possible to identify examples of the concept without having to memorize every member of that category. For example, by knowing the critical features of an abstract verbal concept like democracy (say, voting rights, representational and open government, free press), it is possible to classify countries as democratic or nondemocratic; the alternative would be memorizing en masse all the world's democratic governments and nondemocratic governments.

Because concepts are integral in academic work, teachers can provide important insight into this component of higher thinking. Conceptualization can also be assessed with a few different kinds of tasks. During *category naming* tasks (used to assess word retrieval), the degree of clustering can inform verbal conceptualization. For instance, when naming modes of transportation, a student who groups responses into categories such as motorized, aerial, water, animal-powered, and so on is applying concepts to the task.

Knowledge of concepts can also be assessed with *similarities* tasks, in which the student is asked to describe (or select a response that describes) how two words are related or alike. An item may ask, for example, "How are an ant's antennae and a rabbit's ears alike?" An answer revealing a conceptual understanding would be a description of how both are used to sense the surrounding environment, whereas a surface or concrete response might be to say that both are long and stick out of the head. Similarities items may be structured as open-ended (requiring expressive language as well) or multiple-choice (eliminating expressive language demands).

Another way to assess concept knowledge is through visual tasks, which also factor out expressive language but provide insight into nonverbal conceptualization. Figure 11.10 contains two examples of visual concept items. Example A is abstract and nonverbal in that three geometric forms share the

Figure 11.10 Examples of Visual Concept Items

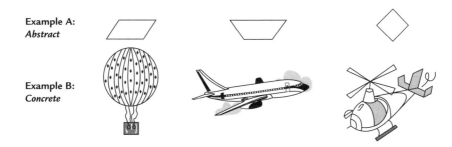

Example A:
Abstract

Example B:
Concrete

critical features of four straight sides or four corners; the student typically would need to select two or three of these related shapes from a larger set of unrelated shapes. Example B, though visual, is concrete and actually more verbal in that the three pictures depict means of flight or air transportation (for the student to convert to language); again, the student might be asked to pick out two or three of these pictures from a bigger set of unrelated pictures.

Another type of concept is a rule. Students are exposed to, and asked to follow, numerous rules in their academic work. Examples include math algorithms and rules of grammar. It is possible to merely memorize rules and then be able to use them fairly effectively. However, the ideal is to really understand or conceptualize a rule. For instance, it is possible to learn that the suffix "-ly" is added to words like "bad" when it seems to fit the situation (for example, "She sang badly after straining her voice") and be correct a majority of the time. A conceptual understanding, though, would involve knowing that "-ly" can change an adjective to an adverb (such as *bad* to *badly*); that adverbs modify verbs, adverbs, and adjectives; and what are the differences among those parts of speech.

CASE STUDY

Sun is a sixteen-year-old girl who is having a very hard time with math. Though never a stellar student in math, she didn't really have to struggle with it before high school. In working with Sun, it is clear that she can recall math algorithms, such as the procedure for simplifying fractions. When provided with basic math operations problems (those with numbers only), she can execute procedures accurately. Where she has trouble, though, is applying math procedures and rules to real-world situations. For instance, she has a tenuous sense of how to set up a word problem that boils down to the same fraction simplification that she can solve in isolation.

Interviewing Sun as she worked on various problems revealed that she does not really understand the conceptual logic behind the very procedures she has memorized. As a result, she can use algorithms rigidly—that is as long as she knows exactly what information to plug in and where. But she gets confused when she has to think flexibly about a scenario and adapt procedures to it. Whereas Sun used to be able to get by with a good memory, math in the upper grades really demands an understanding of algorithms and concepts. Sun's learning plan will need to provide her with support in this area, such as modeling the thought process behind setting up problems and having her talk through plenty of practice work. Diagramming problems may also help her to visualize the logic.

Determining whether students understand rules and concepts (as opposed to simply recalling them) requires looking closely at error patterns. It also takes interviewing. Does the student rigidly execute an algorithm or guideline, or adapt to different scenarios and flexibly select correct rules? How well can the student explain how or why a certain problem was solved in a certain way? Articulate the underlying meaning or rationale for the rule? A response like, "That's just the way you're supposed to do it" indicates an overly rigid approach. So—as with all other elements of the neurodevelopmental framework—testing alone will not suffice to assess conceptualization.

Reasoning and Logic

Reasoning and logic, another higher-order cognition function, refers to the application of systematic and stepwise approaches to complex questions or challenges. In academics, this function is hugely important for solving math problems. Determining how the student completes a math task and what portion of the task is actually based on understanding is critical when evaluating math skills, and having the student explain the thought processes followed during math work provides this insight (Vaughn & Wilson, 1994). Reasoning and logical thinking are also used during scientific inquiry and when problem-solving around social issues (for example, decreasing air pollution in a region where industry is critical to the local economies). In-ference drawing from incomplete information (that is, "reading between the lines") is another form of applied reasoning.

Many games and activities require logical thinking. For example, to be successful at Twenty Questions (that is, to succeed at guessing a person, place, or thing using no more than twenty yes-no questions), the players have to use questions in a logical way to rule out possibilities, identify the right category, and narrow down potential solutions. Several games require use of clues or context cues to identify a mystery word. In fact, reading a mystery story and trying to figure out whodunit is an application of reasoning and logic.

In terms of standardized assessment, matrix reasoning tasks can be found on numerous tests of intelligence. A matrix reasoning item is akin to a visual version of a verbal analogy (see Figure 11.11); the student first determines the relationship between two symbols or pictures (top row) and then applies that relationship to two other symbols or pictures. For the example item in the figure, the two symbols in the top row of the matrix are identical but inverted. Option #4 is the correct selection to go in the shaded box to complete the analogy (the pairs include identical but inverted symbols). This task does not require the student to use any language, other than understanding some ini-tial oral instructions. However, it can be useful to interview the student about the thought processes used for completing analogies. Did the student fully understand the relationship between the elements of the analogy? Or narrow the options down based on surface similarities and then guess? The quality of this explanation also informs expressive language, particularly verbal elab-oration. In addition, observe when the student might make errors based on

Figure 11.11   Mock Matrix Analogy Item

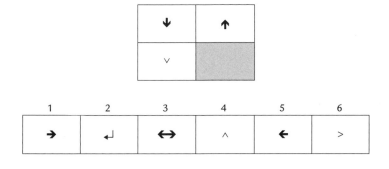

shallow processing depth, such as making an incorrect selection that is very similar in appearance to the correct response (such as option #6 in Figure 11.11).

Tower tasks, introduced in Chapter Eight as a method of testing the attention production control system, typically have three narrow posts attached to a platform and a set of rings or pegs (see Figure 11.12). The student moves rings or pegs from post to post to recreate a displayed configuration (for example, pictured on an easel). Because the student is required to use a limited number of moves and follow specific rules, previewing and facilitation and inhibition are needed. However, this kind of task also involves reasoning to think through how to solve the problem in the most efficient way.

A number of standardized tasks are designed around the use of accuracy feedback to test hypotheses and learn rules. For instance, a student may simply be told to start sorting or categorizing abstract figures. Each time the student makes a move, the examiner says whether it is correct or incorrect; the student then needs to use that feedback for subsequent responses, either sticking with a sorting or categorizing rule that seems to be working or shifting to

Figure 11.12   Mock Tower Task

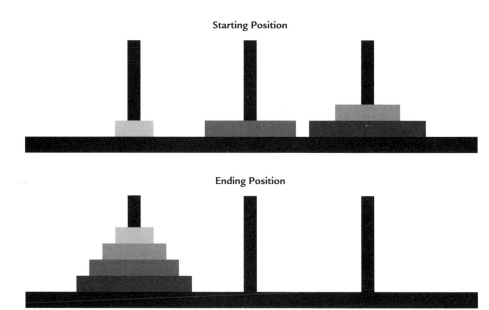

another potential rule. The task might be administered via software, with the feedback coming from the computer (perhaps with different tones) rather than the examiner. Another type of feedback task requires the student to determine (via accuracy feedback) and use rules for solving coded puzzles.

Creativity

Imagination is far more important than knowledge.

—Albert Einstein

An important facet of higher-order cognition is the capacity to generate innovative ideas. Creativity and imagination are critical in many endeavors, not just in the arts. Scientists, engineers, mental health professionals, educators, parents, cooks, civil servants—people in every walk of life all need fresh thinking. Some students have trouble with brainstorming, or rapidly producing ideas that can later be evaluated (for practicality or relative merit). Similarly, students may have a hard time coming up with unique ideas (for a short story, poem, or drawing).

Direct tests of creativity and brainstorming do not exist, but it is possible to assess these areas via history and qualitative observation. Parents and teachers, for example, can provide information about a student's imagination. It is usually necessary, though, to get specific examples. Do students write creatively, and, if so, about what topics? Do they show imagination in how they make comments about the world (for example, on field trips, family vacations, during class discussions)? What are their artistic creations or scientific forays like?

You can get a glimpse into creativity by reviewing student work such as writing samples. In response to a standard writing prompt (say, "What would you do if you were the principal of your school for one week?"), how innovative are the student's ideas relative to those of others of the same age? If written expression is problematic (for example, due to weak graphomotor function), then the student should also have the opportunity to share ideas through discussion. Category naming tasks, which assess word retrieval and can also reveal verbal conceptualization, can be an opportunity to see creativity in terms of how unique the student's responses are (for example, when naming modes of transportation, "car" would be a relatively ordinary response, whereas "escalator" would be more inventive).

Social Cognition

The last construct in the neurodevelopmental framework, but arguably the most important for lifelong success, is social cognition. Many studies have demonstrated that students with learning problems also tend to experience difficulty in the social domain (Haager & Vaughn, 1995; Nowicki, 2003; Sabornie, 1994). Specifically, students with learning problems have been found to have limited social information processing as well: difficulty understanding how complex emotions operate (Bauminger, Edelsztein, & Morash, 2005), problems regulating strong emotions and trouble recognizing emotions in themselves and others (Elias, 2004), reduced social adaptation in school and lower interpersonal understanding (Kravetz, Faust, & Lipshitz, 1999), and less acceptance and more rejection from peers than students without learning problems (Gresham & MacMillan, 1997). A meta-analysis of studies concerning social skills of students with learning problems, conducted by Swanson and Malone (1992), showed that such students were less liked and more likely to be rejected than normally achieving students and to be rated as aggressive.

A lingering question in the literature is causality: Do social difficulties stem from the same phenomena as those that produce learning problems (Kravetz et al., 1999)? It can be useful to differentiate socialization and social cognition. *Socialization* is the application of several neurodevelopmental functions, including social cognition, toward interacting with others in a positive manner. *Social cognition* is a more narrowly defined term for the ability to process social information and solve social problems. In a sense, socialization is like an academic skill in that it is applied in nature and requires multiple functions.

Socialization, then, is affected by social cognition as well as other constructs and functions (see Figure 11.13). A neurodevelopmental factor that may undermine socialization is language, which naturally is critical for communicating with peers, and research has found that language dysfunction leads to social skills deficits (Vallance, Cummings, & Humphries, 1998).

Figure 11.13 Major Linkages between Socialization and Neurodevelopmental Constructs

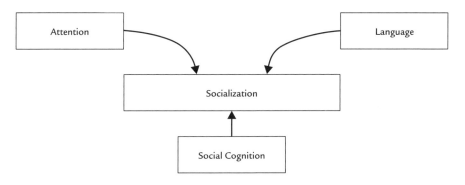

☞ *Language pragmatics* refers to the use and understanding of language for social purposes. Pragmatics can also be nonverbal, relating to the tactical selection of behaviors for fostering relationships.

Prutting and Kirchner (1987) identified numerous verbal pragmatics and nonverbal pragmatics (for example, selecting a topic for conversation, maintaining or changing the topic, turn-taking, vocal intensity, physical proximity, body posture, gestures, facial expression) that, if weak, could result in social difficulties. Expressive language needs to be gauged for the audience. For example, it can be inappropriate to speak with teachers with the same familiarity that one speaks with peers. Conversely, it can be socially problematic to speak with peers in the formal way that is expected when speaking with adults.

Attention can also undermine interactions with peers, as unpopularity has been shown to be prevalent for students with attention deficits (Gaub & Carson, 1997). In addition, students with attention deficits were rated as having significantly more difficulty with social perception and were perceived by their teachers as being more limited in prosocial behaviors, as compared to a control group of students without attention deficits (Hall, Peterson, Webster, Bolen, & Brown, 1999).

With a student who is experiencing social difficulty, then, it is important to also look at attention controls and language functions. Specific to social cognition, though, Eslinger (1996) described examples of social executors that can be considered: *self-regulation* (managing interactions in terms of initiation, rate, intensity, and duration), *self-awareness* (knowledge and insight about oneself in social settings, such as perceiving one's effect on others), and *sensitivity* (understanding another's perspective or emotions). Information about these aspects of social cognition need to be gained from teachers and others who regularly see the student in social settings. How easily does the student make friends? Keep friends? How does the student do with entering a game, conversation, or activity in process? What about conversational skills (for example, turn-taking, topic selection)? Capacity to resolve conflicts? How well does the student read others and respond with appropriate empathy? Respond to situations with the right kind of affect (such as not acting silly when the mood of the group needs to be serious)? In addition to asking informal questions about social cognition, you can use standardized ratings scales that tap areas such as cooperation, empathy, and general social skills. Also, certain writing samples can provide information about how well the student gets into the head of the reader, such as anticipating potential points of confusion and then providing necessary clarification.

Tests of social cognition are available. At their best, however, they can only show you how students read social information and solve social problems in a simulated way. Such tests typically involve a vignette (presented orally or displayed in a picture, or both), followed by questions and discussion that tap the student's perception of the social details (such as body language or other cues to a character's intentions or thinking) and problem solving (for example, "What should this character do to resolve this situation?"). In a nutshell, social vignettes assess the student's capacity to identify social problems and then to decide on appropriate action for solving those problems. Again, a student may do well in both regards with vignettes but struggle to apply social cognition in the real world (this is often where attention is a factor, particularly the production control system).

Cross-Construct Phenomena

Cross-construct phenomena interact with all the neurodevelopmental constructs and functions. In a sense, these phenomena provide the frame around the neurodevelopmental framework. Examples include rate of processing and production, chunk size, metacognition, and strategy use. For the most part, these phenomena need to be assessed in parallel with other functions, as opposed to direct testing. For instance, rate of processing and production can be observed during any timed task, whether the task is intended for attention, language, or some other area. Judgments of rate can be based on standard scores or personal norms (for example, a sense of how quickly most fifth graders solve a particular math problem). Identifying rate as an issue requires seeing a pattern of relatively slow work across a variety of tasks, not just on a single measure.

☞ Rate of processing and production and pacing are problematic extremes of working speed. *Rate* refers to working too slowly, and *pacing* refers to working too quickly.

Chunk size describes the volume or amount of material (for example, length of reading passage, number of math problems, required pages in a book report) that the student needs to process, comprehend, or generate or solve. So chunk size should be considered regarding all aspects of an assessment task. How much is presented to the student (length of the questions, size of the figure)? What is the student expected to generate (length of the response, size of the drawing)? Chunk size is a relative term. For verbal material, it can be delineated as small (even a single word), medium (a sentence), or large (a passage). As with rate, chunk size needs to be assessed by looking for a pattern, specifically consistent evidence of breakdowns when engaging with large pieces of information or material.

Talking with the student about learning is perhaps the best tactic for assessing *metacognition.* One way to start the discussion is to ask which academic skills are difficult and which are easy. The dialogue can be woven into a testing session by interviewing about the specific tasks, making sure to probe for specifics about why certain tasks were easy or enjoyable and why others seemed challenging. Assessing metacognition involves comparing the student's self-descriptions with other findings. Students whose descriptions of their own assets and weaknesses closely match those that emerge from history, testing, review of academic work, and the rest of the assessment have strong metacognition.

☞ Increasing metacognition is a critical goal of demystification, the notion being that self-knowledge of assets and weaknesses leads to more buy-in to learning plan strategies (that is, understanding their rationale) and improved self-esteem.

Strategy use is the capacity to solve problems and complete tasks in systematic ways. It can be assessed by closely observing how the student goes about completing tasks. Do the tactics increase efficiency and accuracy? Or is the work haphazard, reflecting simple trial and error? Interviewing the student about ways problems were solved is similarly informative. Some students, especially elementary students, may need support in explaining their strategy use. For instance, when interviewing about a digit span task, say, "Some students tell me that they remember the numbers by repeating them in their head like a tape recorder, and others tell me that they try to picture them in their mind like on a telephone number pad. What did you do?" Strategy use needs to be assessed by looking at a pattern of work, using personal norms to compare the student's tactics to those of same-age peers.

☞ *Strategy use* is using the right tactic or system for a given task or problem, whereas *previewing* refers to anticipating outcomes (predicting, estimating, planning). Previewing happens just before starting a task. Strategy use occurs throughout a task.

Degree of Context

I've discussed context as a way of sorting task-related information and material into two relative extremes: contextualized (familiar and often concrete) and decontextualized (unfamiliar and often abstract). The idea is to determine if the student has more or less success (for example, with understanding, memorizing, or generating) with information and material that is unfamiliar. Many students perform better with relatively contextualized tasks, since such tasks can more readily be connected with prior knowledge or meaningful experiences. Sequences, for example, are often easier to discern or recall if they have a context, such as a narrative chain of events. Also, contextualized visual material (say, a picture of a shoe) can more easily be translated to a verbal format than many kinds of decontextualized visual material (such as a Picasso painting). On the other hand, students with attention processing control weaknesses (for example, with saliency determination or cognitive activation) may perform better with decontextualized information because contextual details can distract them from the essential elements of the task or problem or lead them to tangential thinking. No tests address contextualized or decontextualized thinking directly, so what you need to do is task-analyze with context in mind, watching for a pattern across tasks or types of academic work.

Other Factors That Can Affect Learning

The focus of this book is assessment of neurodevelopmental factors related to learning. Beyond areas such as memory and language, though, other factors can affect learning and school success. This section will list some of these factors and describe tactics for screening them. When red flags emerge regarding such factors, a referral to another clinician or specialist for additional assessment or consultation is often warranted.

First, emotional-behavioral issues (such as anxiety) can take a toll on a student's academic performance. In contrast, research has found that increasing positive affect leads to more accurate performance on math, improved acquisition of vocabulary words, and better performance on new learning tasks (Yasutake & Bryan, 1995). Therefore, assessing a student with learning problems usually should include a screening for emotional difficulty. This kind of screen can be conducted with standardized questionnaires, some of which are designed to be completed by parents, teachers, or students themselves. If the results of the questionnaires indicate some difficulty (for example, an elevated number of anxiety symptoms, such as worrying about school tests), they can be followed up through a brief interview.

Second, it is important to consider the confounding factors of academic exposure and quality of instruction. When conceptualizing linkages it is easy to look in just one direction (that is, working from neurodevelopmental function to academic skill). But while functions contribute to skill development, the use of the developed skill in turn strengthens the functions that were employed to acquire it. This two-way effect can occur in a positive cycle (for example, experience in writing building up to expressive language) or in a negative cycle (for example, limited reading practice leading to weakening of receptive language) (Johnson, 1993). Another example involves phoneme awareness, which is highly correlated to reading achievement but apparently in a reciprocal fashion (Snider, 1995). Some posit that phonological processing begins as a unidirectional and prerequisite relation with reading and spelling, while others defend a two-way or reciprocal relation throughout the learning process (Foorman, 1995). In other words, "The rich get richer and the poor get poorer"—which is why some refer to this issue as the *Matthew Effect*. To get a handle on this phenomenon, it is sometimes necessary to ask questions about the quality of the learning environments at home and in school, especially if it seems likely that the student did not have an ideal learning experience (for example, frequent moves, teacher changes, lack of special support at school or via tutoring, mismatch between student and instructional style).

Third, a basic screening for medical factors should usually be conducted. If a medical professional is not directly involved in the assessment (as part of a multidisciplinary clinical team), it is still possible to ask some questions and make a referral if any concerns arise from the responses. For example, what is the quality of the student's sleep? Does the student have a regular nighttime routine and fall asleep at a fairly consistent time? Stay asleep throughout the night or toss and turn? What is the student's usual waking time and how easy is it to wake up? Sleep quality problems should be assessed by a physician, possibly by reviewing findings from a sleep log (a journal kept by parent and student to track sleep patterns) or with a formal sleep study (an overnight sleep in a laboratory where all phases of sleep can be assessed).

Signs of extreme weaknesses in the attention processing control system, such as severe swings of alertness or lapses of awareness, could stem from a seizure disorder. The circumstances of such signs should be investigated, including their frequency, intensity, and duration. Watch out for allergies or asthma, particularly if untreated, since they can encumber learning in terms of distraction and discomfort. A question about family history for learning problems should also be asked. Genetic factors account for about half the variability in the development of reading skills, with environmental factors accounting for the other half; for instance, parents with weak reading skill may read to their children less frequently (Lyon et al., 2001). And genetic or neurologic conditions can lead to learning problems, so be prepared to refer to medical professionals any student you suspect of having such conditions. Even if these issues are beyond the realm of your professional training, it is still critical to know about them, to know how to recognize the possibility of their existence in a student, and to know where to send the student for further help, if necessary.

Organization

For many students, difficulty with school does not stem from weaknesses in traditional academic areas such as reading or math, but rather from disorganization. Trouble with organizing can take many different forms, including disordered materials (messy backpack, notebook, desk, locker), unsystematic work habits (particularly around extended assignments and projects), and haphazard thinking (for example, when studying or writing). For a student to be organized, several neurodevelopmental factors need to be in place. First, spatial organization is needed to track various academic materials. Second, temporal organization is involved with tracking time, schedules, and staging extended work projects. Third, several attention controls play a part in organization, such as *saliency determination* (filtering out unnecessary details or materials), *pacing* (working at the right speed), and *self-monitoring* (tracking the quality of one's output and making necessary course corrections). Fourth, strategy use is important for organized thought (as opposed to unsystematic or haphazard work). The same assessment approaches described earlier for these functions can also be employed within the context of linkages to organization (Figure 11.14).

As with all learning issues, identifying the specific linkages to an organization problem paves the way to the specifics of the learning plan. A student who is disorganized due to weak attention, for instance, would need strategies different from those that would help a student with temporal disorganization (although their plans may overlap in some areas). Getting students to buy in to using organizing tactics can be very difficult in some instances, especially with adolescents. Two points can help students to give organizational improvement methods a try. First, though organizing may appear to be extra work (on top of what might already be a heavy load for a student),

Figure 11.14   Neurodevelopmental Factors for Organization

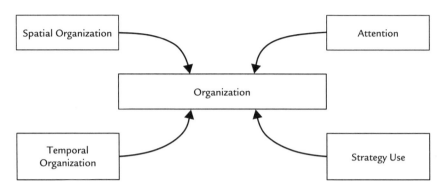

organizing actually makes work easier. It is an upfront investment that will pay dividends later in terms of increased efficiency. Personally, I am a very organized person and I like to tell students that I organize because I'm lazy. I don't like to waste time looking for things or having to redo projects because I didn't organize a plan. If I didn't organize, I would have much less time to do the things that I really enjoy (like spending time with my family or watching movies or photography).

Second, organization should be viewed as a continuum or spectrum, rather than as a yes-no proposition. In other words, avoid telling students that they are "not organized," since everybody (even the messiest individuals!) uses at least a small degree of organization. Thinking in terms of a continuum (such as a 1–10 scale, with 10 being the most organized) can help students see that improvements in this regard may not be so daunting after all. The goal of a learning plan should be for the student to reach a level of organization that is workable (for example, moving from a 4 on the 1–10 scale up to a 6). Incidentally, many parents of students with organization problems are highly organized themselves and have a hard time understanding why their children have such trouble in this regard. In those instances, it can be beneficial to acknowledge the differences in the family, even comparing scores on the scale, and negotiating achievable goals (for example, a parent who claims to be a 10 may agree to the student's goal of improving from a 4 to a 6). The bottom line is that disorganization is an issue to keep in mind, as it deserves thought regarding potential causes and potential solutions.

Turning the Corner

This and the preceding three chapters have focused on specific assessment considerations for aspects of the neurodevelopmental framework. The next two chapters pull the lens back to more general issues related to assessment. Once an assessment has uncovered the explanations for a student's learning struggles, the next step is to find effective tactics for communicating the findings to those who need to understand the student. In other words, the student's story needs to be told.

1 2

Telling the Story

IF ASSESSMENT IS ABOUT understanding the student, then it clearly fails if its findings are not conveyed in an understandable way. Parents need to be able to make sense of the findings. Educators and specialists need to understand the student's profile, how it links to academics, and its implications for the learning plan. Finally, the student needs to understand the profile too—that is a cornerstone of demystification. In short, those involved in assessment need to tell the student's story in a user-friendly way that bridges the understanding gap between professionals and stakeholders, including the student.

Importance of Demystification

Demystification is the process of taking the mystery out of learning. One of the goals is for students to have meaningful understanding of how their minds work with respect to academic work and to general life tasks. So many students with learning problems feel down on themselves or see schoolwork as a hopeless endeavor. Demystifying involves showing them that they have assets: skills or functions that are working well for them, applied activities (computer use, music, cooking, collecting postcards) they are good at, or content areas or topics (history, auto racing, movies) about which they have particularly deep or wide knowledge. Assets may be exceptional relative to same-age peers (that is, strong assets), merely intact or reliable (which still might be important to point out), or noteworthy relative to other, still weaker areas.

Students should hear specifics about their assets—that will make the assets feel more tangible and will dispel any harbored doubts about the existence of positive attributes among all the things to worry about. For example, if the student has solid receptive language, point out the tasks that revealed that finding along with what parents and teachers reported about it, and explain why it is important (for example, for reading and for listening). The student should learn about as many assets as emerged from the assessment. (No need to put a cap on the number of assets you discuss.)

☞ To appreciate the importance of hearing specifics about assets, think about how you would respond to two different compliments: "You are a good cook!" And, "You are a good cook, and your guacamole is excellent. I love how you use just the right amount of salt, garlic, and lemon to give it that zing." Details make the compliment seem more sincere.

Students do need to learn about their weaknesses too. As with assets, though, weak areas need to be described with specifics. Students with learning problems often have eroded self-esteem. They have attributed dreadful and invalid characteristics to themselves (such as general stupidity and laziness) or have lumped themselves into demeaning categories (calling themselves losers or dummies). Demystifying involves laying out weak areas, explaining how they were identified, and showing how they link to academic work. For example, if the student has weak previewing, describe how this attention control was assessed and how it affects the ability to think ahead, anticipate outcomes, and plan out work in advance.

Regardless of the theoretical framework you use, it is important to draw terms from that framework when describing profiles to students and parents. This may seem counterintuitive, since frameworks tend to contain jargon that may seem arcane to those outside the field. However, demystification is supported by using such terms because it underscores that the student's weaknesses are not unique. Using a term like *active working memory* demonstrates that the phenomenon is something that has been seen before in other students and even researched. The trick, obviously, is to pair framework terms with understandable explanations, as discussed under "Communicating Outside the Box" later in this chapter.

Another consideration when describing weaknesses is putting parameters around them (Levine, 2002). First, the weaknesses listed in a profile should be those of the highest priority for improving school success, at least for the immediate future. Prioritizing weaknesses involves knowledge not only of the student's profile but also of the academic demands the student is facing or soon will be facing. This kind of analysis leads to pushing some weaknesses to the back burner, so to speak. For example, a student with problematic expressive language may have weak semantic use, sentence formulation, and discourse production. If the student is in second grade, when writing tasks tend to be relatively brief, it might be warranted to target the word and sentence levels and set aside the discourse level for the time being. If the student is in high school, though, discourse production would probably need to be a focus. When a weakness does not have any pertinent linkages to the student's academic work (perhaps spatial ordering for a tenth grader), then it probably does not need to be listed in the profile.

Second, weaknesses should actually be numbered when listing and discussing them (for example, "There are three aspects of your learning that aren't as reliable as we would like them to be. First, ..."). Numbering weaknesses puts parameters around them by underscoring that the list of shortcomings is not endless. It shows the student what the priorities need to be and that specific areas will be addressed, not a total overhaul of mind and character. It confronts the student's misconceptions about overall abilities or self-worth with a confined list of objectives. Incidentally, prioritizing weaknesses also makes it much more straightforward to craft practical learning plans.

Demystification should also incorporate discussion of affinities. An *affinity* is a topic or activity that a student finds deeply or passionately interesting. Though an affinity might also be an asset, what we really enjoy and what we are good at do not always overlap. For example, someone may enjoy composing poetry, even though the resulting poems are not of particularly high quality. Nevertheless, affinities can be critical sources of gratification, especially for a struggling learner. For instance, being the class or family expert on space exploration (that is, the go-to person whenever a question arises about this topic) can help a student feel hopeful and self-confident despite a significant writing or math problem.

> ☞ The approach described in this book bears similarities to Hale and Fiorello's (2004) Cognitive Hypothesis Testing (CHT) model: cognitive processes are linked to academics; students have unique learning profiles of strengths and weaknesses, and academic deficits should be addressed with customized interventions based on the student's profile. Both approaches also emphasize initial hypotheses based on history and task-analysis to reveal underlying processes. However, the neurodevelopmental approach described in this book has several unique features, including the critical role of demystification and the highlighting and nurturing of assets (including applied strengths) and affinities. In addition, the neurodevelopmental approach often omits intelligence testing (as a screening procedure or otherwise), and it is not necessarily a structured and gated process (as CHT is described).

Affinities are identified through history (for example, asking parents and teachers about the student's strong interests) and discussion with the student. Some students may only have potential affinities, such as a passing interest in a topic that could be nurtured and expanded. Another reason to identify affinities is that they can be used in learning plan recommendations. For example, a student with expressive language weaknesses would probably be more motivated to practice speaking and writing about an affinity (say, the history of America's space program). Math and science problems can be invented around areas of interest (for example, calculating distance traveled to reach the moon given an Apollo spacecraft's velocity and travel time). Even strategies for improving organization can make use of an affinity (for example, researching how space shuttle crews keep their gear organized for easy access). Such use of affinities is limited only by one's imagination.

Demystification is a long-term process that may actually begin before you even meet the student. For instance, completing a history questionnaire prior to testing may begin to increase the student's own understanding of the learning process. After the assessment, a demystification session with the student and the student's parents is a crucial step. Though styles for presenting the information may differ, this session should have some core features in place (Levine, 2002):

- Extended discussion of the student's assets and affinities
- Description of a prioritized, numbered set of weaknesses
- Explanation of linkages between profile and academic work
- Destigmatization of learning problems and neurodevelopmental weaknesses—helping the student understand that everyone has weaknesses
- Infusion of optimism—emphasizing that learning can be made easier, and that life will get better
- Alliance formation—letting both student and parents know that they are not alone in their struggles, that they have a support system

☞ Most students hear a great many supportive comments from their parents. Demystification with a professional, though, can have a particularly powerful effect. It can demonstrate that positive messages are not just emanating from a parent's unconditional love; they are actually valid descriptions (Levine, 2002).

Demystification should be a recurring dialogue with the student about learning. In other words, it should not end when a demystification session ends. Whenever possible, deliver booster doses of demystification by revisiting the student's profile, its implications, and messages of optimism. Parents need to be equipped with the means to continue the process through ongoing discussions with the student, which is one of the reasons that the written report is so important.

☞ As part of an ongoing process, demystification does not have to always occur as an extended conversation. Brief moments in the classroom and at home can be opportunities to comment on a student's profile, linkages, and plan.

Guidelines for Written Reports

A clinical report is a means of communication. As such, the report should use all available means to communicate most effectively, so that the findings and recommendations have the best possible chance of being understood and used to advantage. The report supports demystification, as it is a reference point for parents and others regarding the student's profile, linkages, and learning plan.

So what are some means for effective communications in a clinical report? It should employ any technique that makes findings, linkages, and the learning plan accessible to the people who use it, regardless of their professional background. Constructing a report is an opportunity to employ creativity, so there's no need to feel constrained by any suggestions provided here.

As mentioned in the preceding section, technical terms should be included in reports because they help you demystify and destigmatize phenomena, and they also provide a common vocabulary for discussing the student's profile. However, specialized terms can be confusing and intimidating jargon unless they are coupled with clear definitions and explanations. A term could be followed in the report by a definition in parentheses. Although it may be challenging in terms of word processing, definitions could also be placed in margins alongside the relevant text (as in a textbook). A different approach is to include a glossary for commonly used terms.

Along with definitions, reports should include illustrative examples from the assessment findings. For instance, after stating that active working memory is a weakness for the student (and defining what active working memory is), cite moments during the assessment when the student displayed this weakness (for example, when spelling words in context or when re-ordering series of letters and numbers). Such examples facilitate understanding of the functions in the student's profile. Definitions are helpful, but associating a term with an experience can really deepen understanding. Examples also can help explain linkages, or how seemingly arcane terms (like *active working memory*) relate to the real world.

Use both quantitative and qualitative findings to illustrate your points; I've mentioned the importance of this several times in this book already, but it is worth restating. Standard scores have a place, but they need to be accompanied by qualitative findings such as observations, direct comments from the student or history reports, and work sample reviews. Not only does this balanced reporting reflect the range of data collected during the assessment, the qualitative findings also help to communicate the meaning of the findings overall. A standard score attached to a subtest name probably won't make much sense to most parents—or to anyone else who doesn't use the test regularly. But scores that are listed in parallel with qualitative information will be more readily understood.

As with demystification overall, clinical reports should identify and discuss assets and affinities, not just weaknesses. Parents and others who work with students do need to know about weak areas and how they link to academic problems, but positive news is too often given short shrift for students with learning problems. The same depth of discussion—including balanced data-types of illustrative examples—should be employed for assets, including linkages for assets. When discussing affinities, highlight any uniqueness (for example, it would be noteworthy for a middle-schooler to be a big fan of movie musicals), as well as any opportunities to make use of them for learning strategies.

The clinical report should reflect the larger demystification message about the student's weaknesses. Rather than a laundry list of shortcomings, the weaknesses listed should just be the priorities for the student (and parents) to work on. They also should be numbered, to underscore that the weaknesses are circumscribed.

Reports should be organized in a way that makes sense for the readers (usually parents) and not just for the author. One way to do this is to structure the report according to a theoretical framework or set of constructs rather than a series of tests. For instance, all the findings (both quantitative and qualitative) for memory could be collected into one section so that the reader sees all the evidence together, as opposed to having to skip back and forth from the discussion of one test to another. This will help the reader see the recurring themes (for example, the converging evidence for weak active working memory) that emerged from the data. The content in the various parts of the report should be consistent, with connecting threads. For example, referral concerns should be addressed through discussion of the profile and linkages (so that questions about the student's math work are answered in terms of linkages with weak active working memory). Also, learning plan strategies should include references to profile components in order to convey the rationale for their selection (say, diagramming math problems to address weak active working memory by taking advantage of good spatial ordering); students and those working with them should know these rationales, which also serve to reinforce understanding of the profile and linkages.

Finally, the learning plan itself should reflect the priorities set forth in the student's profile. It is impossible for a student to work on many weaknesses at once, and parents and teachers can easily feel overwhelmed by too many recommendations. Even worse, the entire assessment process, including demystification, may be dismissed if readers of the report see it as an impractical document. It's best to pick strategies very carefully. What are realistic explanations for new approaches to learning for this student? What can this family handle? What are the realities of this classroom environment? It can help to imagine being in a reader's position as a barometer for the quantity and quality of the recommendations.

Checklist for an Effective Report

- ☐ Definitions and explanations for technical terms
- ☐ Illustrative examples, such as anecdotes or direct quotes
- ☐ Balanced review of data types, including quantitative and qualitative
- ☐ Discussion of assets and affinities, not just weaknesses
- ☐ Circumscribed and prioritized set of weaknesses
- ☐ Organizational structure designed for the reader
- ☐ Connected and consistent elements: profile, findings, learning plan
- ☐ Answers to referral questions
- ☐ Description of linkages, for both weaknesses and assets
- ☐ Practical and prioritized learning plan

Communicating Outside the Box

The guidelines described in the preceding section relate to the ingredients of a clinical report. This section is about how to present those ingredients in ways that maximize communication. It is easy to fall into habits at work, and report writing is particularly habit-inducing. Clinical training programs typically present report templates and emphasize a rather formal style and use of language. In the workplace, clinicians usually are either explicitly provided with report templates from the clinic leadership or colleagues migrate toward consistent report layouts through mutual influence. Independent practitioners may develop their own way of writing reports, but they too can develop habits that may not be particularly reader-friendly.

So it's good to ask a basic question (though the answer may be complex). What is a report? Put differently, what objectives need to be met by the report? If you're writing assessment reports, stop and think about your report-writing habits. Are you meeting important objectives (namely clear communication to stakeholders) or merely meeting expectations that do not really matter to families? Despite what you may have learned in graduate school or an internship or the workplace or from colleagues, report writing does not have unbreakable ground rules. For example, most clinicians learn to write reports that are entirely in a text format, with the possible exception of a table or two with standard scores. But no etched-in-stone rule requires reports to be dominated by text. In fact, relying heavily on text (that is, monolithic paragraphs) is usually counterproductive in terms of reader-friendliness.

With a little imagination, diagrams and pictures could be used to convey important ideas in reports, either replacing or augmenting some of the text. As the saying goes, a picture is worth a thousand words. Figure 12.1 depicts an example of a diagram (based on one shown in Chapter Ten) that could be used in a clinical report to explain how weak graphomotor function is constricting the student's good oral expression, resulting in relatively less sophisticated written expression. Note that the diagram is personalized, not only by including the student's name but by mentioning the functions and skills. Such a diagram could be constructed with a word processing program.

Figure 12.1   Example of Diagram for a Written Report

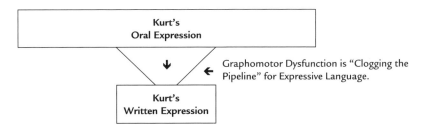

In addition to diagrams, digital photographs (for example, of a student's handwriting grip) or scanned images (for example, of a math work sample) can easily be inserted into report documents. There are other ways to use visual techniques to communicate in clinical reports. First, word processing tools such as differentiating fonts (bolding, italics, underlining, size) can place relative emphases on terms or phrases and help ideas pop off the page. Second, in lieu of an extended paragraph, a bulleted or numbered list of short sentences or phrases can be very effective and succinct. Third, tables can be used for other purposes besides reporting scores; just as tables in this book have been used to present text information in different ways, assessment findings can be conveyed via tables in reports. Fourth, headers and subheaders help break up the document and make searching for information easier.

It is unrealistic for a report to be entirely nonverbal, however, so you need to think in new ways regarding verbal techniques as well. As noted, illustrative examples and anecdotes with direct quotes can be effective augments to more formal terminology. For instance, Kurt (the fifth grader mentioned in Figure 12.1) may have commented during the assessment, "I would much rather talk about what I know than write about it." This quote, which really speaks to his writing problems, would be good to include in his report.

Metaphors and similes are other verbal tools for making arcane concepts more accessible to laypersons. In Figure 12.1, Kurt's graphomotor dysfunction is described as "clogging the pipeline" for his expressive language. Using metaphors and similes can be an enjoyable way to exercise creativity, and over time it is possible to develop a toolkit of available symbols (both visual and verbal). However, metaphors and similes should be adaptable, and some of the best symbolism incorporates the student's affinities. A student with a passion for computers, for example, may find analogies between human memory components and those of a computer (for example, active working memory and RAM, long-term memory and a hard drive) to be especially resonating.

Recurring themes have been a recurring theme in this book—and they're useful again here, offering a way to organize findings and identify connections. Including themes in reports is another innovative communication tool. For instance, a student may have particular trouble with the various output-related functions (for example, attention production controls, long-term memory access, expressive language), but have relatively good input functions (such as attention processing controls, long-term memory storage, and receptive language). It's not a good idea to force a theme upon the findings, but when a theme emerges it can really help readers of the report to pull everything together in a meaningful way.

Assessments are almost always initiated because someone—a parent, a teacher—has questions about the student's learning. As a result, an assessment is really an extended consultation, with one goal being to answer such questions. Reports can be made more understandable by being very explicit about the explanations for referral concerns, such as posing questions (for example, "Why is organizing so challenging for Edward?" or "Why is learning to decode words so hard for Kevyn?") and then answering them.

This section has focused on communication tactics for clinical reports. However, many of the same techniques can also be employed when speaking with students and others during demystification. Diagrams and figures can be drawn or constructed to support the dialogue. Anecdotes and quotes can be evoked to underscore points. Metaphors and similes and recurring themes can facilitate understanding just as well when presented orally as when written. The essential point is to be willing to use creativity and imagination when communicating with all stakeholders, whether through speaking or writing—even when this requires breaking away from your training, work expectations, and habits.

One final point should be made about communication, though, and that is to avoid bells and whistles. In other words, any and all innovations should meet the essential objective of improving understanding for the reader or listener. New tactics that merely festoon a presentation (for example, colored paper, images that are not content-related, tangential references) are not helpful and may even be a distraction from the critical ideas. Everything should support communication, in service of understanding the student.

1 3

Understanding to Assess

I shut my eyes in order to see.

—Paul Gauguin

THIS BOOK, ESPECIALLY IN THE LATER CHAPTERS, has included a great deal of practical information about assessing learning problems: questions to pose, signs to observe, clinical contrasts to interpret, tasks to select, findings to describe. But taking on this kind of assessment approach requires a whole new outlook for many professionals. This chapter is devoted to developing and reinforcing the worldview of assessing to understand.

So what do you need to understand to succeed at assessing to understand? Several important and overlapping qualities support that goal: acquiring a new perspective, being gratified by use of evidence to support hypotheses, learning to see splitting as preferable to lumping, an organized way of thinking, a prepared mind, and curiosity about learning.

Having New Eyes

The real voyage of discovery consists not in seeking new landscapes,
but in having new eyes.

—Marcel Proust

No matter how much data you collect, be it quantitative or qualitative, you will never absolutely prove that a particular function is weak or strong and you will never be absolutely certain about what is causing a learning problem. Therefore, those who assess learning problems need an openness to uncertainty. It is possible to support an argument, but any conclusions made or interpretations drawn should be in parallel with the acknowledgment that they may be wrong. Even when you see considerable evidence to support a conclusion, it is critical to be open to changing your mind when new findings emerge or different hypotheses are posed.

It can be very tempting to *reify* conclusions—to treat them as real things, as solid as chairs or houses—if standard scores appear to support them. That is never really possible, but if you use many different types of information, the variety of findings can help you *validate* conclusions, establishing them as real enough to go on with.

As an aside, it has intrigued me why soccer, a tremendously exciting sport with international appeal, is not more popular in the United States. One reason, I believe, is that soccer is not as quantifiable as baseball, football, or basketball. People in this country seem to love statistics, perhaps because the numbers seem tangible. To be a soccer fan, though, means appreciating it for its qualitative appeal. While you certainly should not forgo the use of scores in assessment, you may well find it useful to broaden your appreciation of nonquantifiable information when assessing learning problems.

Assessing to understand requires seeing kids in a certain way, and for many of us who work in assessment this is a new way. Whereas other assessment approaches (such as psychometric methods) culminate in the assignment of a diagnostic label or category, this approach is about describing the student's unique learning profile. So students really have to be viewed as originals with distinct combinations of assets, affinities, and weaknesses. In addition, the person doing the assessment needs to be attuned to original combinations of functions or even phenomena beyond the boundaries of the theoretical framework or experience base.

Making the Case

There is nothing as deceptive as an obvious fact.

—Sir Arthur Conan Doyle

One of the challenging aspects of this assessment approach is the way different kinds of findings are interpreted jointly to form conclusions. On the other hand, this is also an enjoyable and gratifying facet of the work. This type of assessment is not as simple (or boring) as adding and subtracting scores or lining up symptoms for a diagnosis. Once you embrace the challenge of using various pieces of evidence to build an argument about a student's strengths and weaknesses, while acknowledging that there is no absolute certainty in any assessment conclusions, you can come up with results far more practical than a simple diagnosis. The process is much like detective work, as it essentially involves making informed guesses about the student's learning based on available evidence, theory, research, and experience and personal norms. Clues are gathered, sorted, and organized. Then connections between clues are made and patterns emerge. Every student represents a mystery to be solved by asking and answering important questions about the way that student learns.

The Virtues of Splitting

A cornerstone of assessing to understand is the notion that *splitting* is a more useful tactic than *lumping*. That is, students should be viewed through the discrete phenomena they display and the profiles they demonstrate, rather than as members of a diagnostic category or classifying label (Levine, 2002). An implication of splitting is that an academic problem (say, delayed reading decoding) could arise from weaknesses in many different functions or combinations of functions. Therefore, those conducting assessments need to consider the relative contributions of a range of factors rather than looking for just one cause to name.

Splitting requires the capacity for task-analysis to break things down, including assessment tasks, academic skills, classroom lessons, courses, occupations, hobbies, sports, and other activities that may be important to a student. Splitting can become a mind-set, a way of thinking about the world, not just about assessment work. For example, if you're a splitter and buying a car, you might wonder about the neurodevelopmental prerequisites to being successful at selling cars or how your own profile might match up with car styles or features. Such task-analyzing out of curiosity helps to sharpen clinical acumen.

Splitting has implications not only for how findings are analyzed but also for how assessment sessions are planned and conducted. The splitting approach lends itself more to multi-method assessment than to fixed batteries; first calling on available history to determine the constructs and functions to examine firsthand, and then selecting tests to use. Building a battery is akin to assembling a sports team; it is useful to have some versatile players who can play several positions, but it is also important to have specialists who have narrower skill sets, but who really excel in those skills. Similarly, a battery should include some tasks that are intended to tap several neurodevelopmental areas. This is good for efficiency (because solid performance usually indicates intact functioning on several areas) and for seeing how constructs and functions interface for the student. But poor performance on a task that taps several functions can mean many different things, which is why it is also important to include specialized tasks with narrower assessment focus. The clinical contrasts that emerge can be used to identify recurring themes.

Framing the Work

Assessing to understand requires an underlying theory. I keep returning to the importance of a conceptual framework because its value is impossible to overstate. A conceptual framework is a blueprint that helps you organize information about a student, identify recurring themes, confront discrepancies in the findings (the clinical contrasts), and, ultimately, communicate effectively through demystification. The neurodevelopmental framework emphasized in this book is just one of several potential theoretical structures that can be used when assessing learning problems. But whatever framework you choose, you need to know it intimately, including assessment tactics that use multiple angles and linkages between its components and academic skills.

While it is possible to be eclectic (that is, to draw from more than one theory), it is important to be clear about multiple influences and be able to identify specific ingredients from various frameworks. It is just as important to avoid being bound by your theoretical underpinnings; no theory is all-encompassing, and factors outside the parameters of a given framework may be in play for a particular student. Also, some students show unique findings and patterns; a combination of factors may underlie a problem, with the individual factors operating appropriately in isolation but not when interfacing with each other. It is always best to be open to new possibilities about student learning.

Preparing the Mind

Observation is vital for assessing to understand, and, as Pasteur commented, prepared minds are in a better position to observe phenomena. The most important assessment tool you have is your mind, and the better insight you have into your own mind (that is, the better you are at metacognition), the better position you will be in to make insights into students' learning. Understanding your own neurodevelopmental profile helps you to appreciate the challenges facing students with learning issues. Identifying with struggling students facilitates demystification.

For example, I have trouble writing and listening at the same time (an interface between attention processing controls, graphomotor function, and short-term memory). I usually share this insight with students I am assessing, and to illustrate its effect, I relate an experience I had several years ago in a meeting. Someone told the group about an interesting Web site and provided the address orally. I managed to jot down the first few letters, so I asked her to repeat it. She did, and I got a few more letters. I asked again if she could state the address, by now feeling self-conscious about my inability to write down this relatively small piece of information. She went through it again, slowly, but I again failed to get it all on paper. Defeated, I acted as if I had been successful and was never able to visit the recommended Web site. Telling that kind of story to students—and we can all find similar stories in our own past—can really help you forge an alliance because it demonstrates to the students that you understand, at least a little bit, what it must be like for them as they struggle with learning.

It is also useful to think about your own level of assessment competence. I would describe three stages of competence in assessment through which people progress, albeit with some overlap and movement back and forth between stages at times. In the first stage, the focus is on the administration of tasks, test materials, and procedures. People in training are obviously working in this stage since all the assessment tasks are new to them. More experienced assessors may temporarily regress to this stage, however, when they are incorporating a new technique into their repertoire. In the second stage, you can start to focus more on the student; administration of tasks is automatic enough to enable looking more carefully at nuances in the student's behavior, subtle patterns of work, strategies, outcomes of limit-testing, and responses to interview questions. In the third stage, both administration and observation are second nature. Now, however, it is possible to keep an eye on your own work, to have a "camera over the shoulder" and consider your behavior and thinking in relation to the student. For example, at stage three you can think about how your interaction style (your tone of voice, use of redirection) affects the student's behavior and productivity, and even conduct experiments during the assessment (altering your tone of voice, employing different redirection tactics) to see which approaches might be useful to others who work with the student.

A prepared mind also knows its own limitations and biases. Even established professionals need to acknowledge weaknesses in their thinking. For instance, it might be hard to distinguish attention dysfunction from receptive language problems. You may be very adept at reviewing student work samples but less so with interviewing parents (while someone else may have the opposite skill set). Always ask, "Are there any interpretations or patterns that I seem biased toward or against?" Being open about such limitations is the first step to overcoming them. Teamwork can be a very effective remedy, as colleagues can complement their own abilities and support each other's weaknesses.

Passionate Curiosity

I have no special talents. I am only passionately curious.

—Albert Einstein

Earlier I differentiated an affinity from an asset. The former is a topic of passionate interest, whereas the latter is something at which one excels. For those responsible for students, assessing to understand has to be both an affinity and an asset. You need to be passionately curious about the root causes of a struggling student's learning problems. Put simply, you have to love asking why. Why is reading a challenge for this student? Why is writing such an onerous task? Why is getting organized such a frustrating experience? Why can't Jim learn his math facts? Why does Belle have such a hard time understanding history lectures?

Assessing to understand is about refusing easy answers such as "He has ADHD" or "She has a writing disability" or "He has dyslexia." Recent changes in federal law will push us to understand tests more completely than ever, to dig deeper into data, to integrate information from multiple sources, and to use the resulting insights to carefully select strategies; we will need to think more about the students we are serving instead of mechanically applying a methodology (Holdnack & Weiss, 2006). Everyone in the field needs to love digging deep, to take pride in unveiling mysteries and making that light bulb go on for students and their parents about why school is such a struggle. It is a powerful feeling to see a student realize that you finally understand, and to see parents finally get answers to their questions. By the way, apples rarely fall far from the tree; as an extra bonus of demystification, you will sometimes see parents getting demystified about their own school experience.

Talking the Talk and Walking the Walk

It is only when we forget all our learning that we begin to know.

—Henry David Thoreau

So how can we begin to incorporate this assessment approach when and where it may be challenging to do so? Our society can be very label-driven and category-oriented. Education and mental health care tend to follow suit. Hence, it may be an uphill climb to implement a model that is based on understanding and describing profiles, including assets and affinities, and that makes use of a broad range of findings, not just test scores. It will be necessary to confront the national tendency to lump things together (in red states and blue states, soccer moms and NASCAR dads, Baby Boomers and generation-Xers) with the equally characteristic love of getting to the bottom of things, of finding answers, of solving mysteries.

Clinicians often find themselves in settings that require the use of labels and categories to serve students. Insurance reimbursement entails documenting a diagnosis. In many school districts a label such as "LD" is needed for special education eligibility, even though it may have no more practical use for a child than for a dishwasher. But even when you're working in such circumstances, you can still assess to understand by doing what is absolutely needed to play the game but then layering on this approach to provide demystification and consultation on learning plans.

For example, a speech-language pathologist working in a hospital clinic needs to assign diagnoses to students, but the diagnoses could be confined to the paperwork documentation. When discussing findings with students and families, the pathologist can emphasize profiles instead of diagnoses. A school psychologist working in a school system may be expected to administer a standard IQ-achievement battery and look for an ability-achievement split in students' scores so as to determine eligibility for special education. However, the psychologist can open up the assessment to include other techniques besides the standard battery (for example, select a few additional tasks, interview, review history) and interpret findings from the battery using a conceptual framework, then look for clinical contrasts and search for recurring themes. Both of these clinicians can choose to provide demystification and to think of new and expressive ways to communicate findings.

In Chapter Four I pointed out that assessing to understand complements the emerging trend of response to intervention as a mechanism for identifying students for special education and determining level of service. Revealing a student's profile and clarifying linkages with academic work facilitates instructional decision making. In other words, better choices about teaching strategies can be made when student learning is understood. Assessment really should be viewed as consultation, anyway. The rationale for assessment is to get expertise on how to improve a student's academic performance and life success.

Assessing to understand is a model for thinking. The more this model is demonstrated to others, the more momentum it will gain. At every opportunity, professionals should display the tenets of this approach. For instance, school-based professionals are in a position to collaborate with teachers in observing phenomena and interpreting data. Such collaborations are opportunities to talk about students using a conceptual framework, to show the importance of multiple angles (instead of overrelying on testing), to display the utility of recurring themes and clinical contrasts, and to employ demystification.

> ☞ The Schools Attuned program for educators is offered by All Kinds of Minds (www.allkindsofminds.org). Schools Attuned is a professional development and service delivery program for educators that employs a neurodevelopmental framework to understand profiles. Demystification is one of the cornerstones of the program.

Professionals can also use this approach in a consultation mode, such as reviewing results from past evaluations or from testing conducted outside the school, helping others to make sense of the findings. It can also help the cause to give nonclinicians more insight into the work of assessment. Awareness workshops (for example, for parent groups) are one way to spread the word.

"Walking the walk," though, really comes back to the individual, who needs to make a commitment to conducting assessments with the goal of developing a deeper understanding of the student. This may mean swimming against the tide, depending on where you work and what expectations you have to meet. It may mean letting go of habits developed over years of professional experience. And that may mean opening yourself to a new kind of criticism, such as what you're apt to hear from those who think the only findings of value are those that are quantifiable and normed. All these struggles are worth it, though, to come to the place where students, particularly the struggling learners, are understood.

References

Aaron, P. G. (1995). Differential diagnosis of reading disabilities. *School Psychology Review, 24*, 345–360.

Anderson, V. (1998). Assessing executive functions in children: Biological, psychological, and developmental considerations. *Neuropsychological Rehabilitation, 8*, 319–349.

Apling, R. N., & Jones, N. L. (2005). *Individuals with Disabilities Education Act (IDEA): Analysis of changes made by P.L. 108–446.* (Congressional Research Service Report for Congress Order Code RL32716). Washington, DC: Library of Congress.

Ashbaker, M. H., & Swanson, H. L. (1996). Short-term memory and working memory operations and their contributions to reading in adolescents with and without learning disabilities. *Learning Disabilities Research and Practice, 11*, 206–213.

Badian, N. (2005). Does a visual-orthographic deficit contribute to reading disability? *Annals of Dyslexia, 55*, 28–52.

Banaschewski, T., Brandeis, D., Heinrich, H., Albrecht, B., Brunner, E., & Rothenberger, A. (2003). Association of ADHD and conduct disorder: Brain electrical evidence for the existence of a distinct subtype. *Journal of Child Psychology and Psychiatry, 44*, 356–376.

Barkley, R. A. (1996). Linkages between attention and executive functions. In G. R. Lyon & N. A. Krasnegor (Eds.), *Attention, memory, and executive function* (pp. 307–325). Baltimore: Brookes.

Barkley, R. A. (2000). *Taking charge of ADHD: The complete, authoritative guide for parents.* New York: Guilford Press.

Bauminger, N., Edelsztein, H. S., & Morash, J. (2005). Social information processing and emotional understanding in children with LD. *Journal of Learning Disabilities, 38*, 45–61.

Beal, C. R. (1993). Contributions of developmental psychology to understanding revision: Implications for consultation with classroom teachers. *School Psychology Review, 22*, 643–655.

Beery, K. E., & Beery, N. A. (2004). *The Beery-Buktenica Developmental Test of Visual-Motor Integration* (5th ed.). Minneapolis: NCS Pearson.

Bender, B. G. (1999). Learning disorders associated with asthma and allergies. *School Psychology Review, 28*, 204–214.

Berninger, V. W., Rutberg, J. E., Abbott, R. D., Garcia, N., Anderson-Youngstrom, M., Brooks, A., & Fulton, C. (2006). Tier 1 and Tier 2 early intervention for handwriting and composing. *Journal of School Psychology, 44*, 3–30.

Boden, C., & Brodeur, D. A. (1999). Visual processing of verbal and nonverbal stimuli in adolescents with reading disabilities. *Journal of Learning Disabilities, 32*, 58–71.

Bolles, R. C. (1993). *The story of psychology: A thematic history*. Pacific Grove, CA: Brooks/Cole.

Brandeis, D., Banaschewski, T., Baving, L., Georgiewa, P., Blanz, B., Schmidt, M. H., et al. (2002). Multicenter P300 brain mapping of impaired attention to cues in hyperkinetic children. *Journal of the American Academy of Child and Adolescent Psychiatry, 41*, 990–998.

Bronfenbrenner, U. (1977). Toward an experimental ecology of human development. *American Psychologist, 32*, 513–531.

Brooks, R., & Goldstein, S. (2001). *Raising resilient children: Fostering strength, hope, and optimism in your child*. New York: McGraw-Hill.

Brooks, R., & Goldstein, S. (2004). *The power of resilience: Achieving balance, confidence, and personal strength in your life*. New York: McGraw-Hill.

Brumback, C. R., Low, K. A., Gratton, G., & Fabiani, M. (2005). Putting things into perspective: Individual differences in working-memory span and the integration of information. *Experimental Psychology, 52*, 21–30.

Bull, R., & Johnson, R. (1997). Children's arithmetical difficulties: Contributions from processing speed, item identification, and short-term memory. *Journal of Experimental Child Psychology, 65*, 1–24.

Cacioppo, J. T., Semin, G. R., & Berntson, G. G. (2004). Realism, instrumentalism, and scientific symbiosis: Psychological theory as a search for truth and the discovery of solutions. *American Psychologist, 4*, 214–223.

Calhoun, S. L., & Dickerson Mayes, S. (2005). Processing speed in children with clinical disorders. *Psychology in the Schools, 42*, 333–343.

Carlisle, J. F. (1991). Planning an assessment of listening and reading comprehension. *Topics in Language Disorders, 12*, 17–31.

Carroll, J. B. (1993). *Human cognitive abilities: A survey of factor analytic studies*. New York: Cambridge University Press.

Case-Smith, J. (Ed.). (2005). *Occupational therapy for children* (5th ed.). St. Louis: Elsevier Mosby.

Cohen, J. (1994). On the differential diagnosis of reading, attentional and depressive disorders. *Annals of Dyslexia, 44*, 165–184.

Cohen, N. J. (2001). *Language impairment and psychopathology in infants, children, and adolescents*. Thousand Oaks, CA: Sage.

Cooper, J. D. (2000). *Literacy: Helping children construct meaning* (4th ed.). Boston: Houghton Mifflin.

Cornoldi, C., Vecchia, R. D., & Tressoldi, P. E. (1995). Visuo-spatial working memory limitations in low visuo-spatial high verbal intelligence children. *Journal of Child Psychology and Psychiatry, 36*, 1053–1064.

Coulter, D. L. (1999). Central nervous system disorders. In M. D. Levine, W. B. Carey, & A. C. Crocker (Eds.), *Developmental-behavioral pediatrics* (3rd ed.; pp. 276–288). Philadelphia: Saunders.

Crain, S., Shankweiler, D., Macaruso, P., & Bar Shalom, E. (1990). Working memory and comprehension of spoken sentences: Investigations of children with reading disorder. In G. Vallar & T. Shallice (Eds.), *Neuropsychological impairments of memory* (pp. 477–508). New York: Cambridge University Press.

Dale, H. (1994). Collaborative writing interactions in one ninth-grade classroom. *Journal of Educational Research, 87,* 334–344.

Daneman, M., & Green, I. (1986). Individual differences in comprehending and producing words in context. *Journal of Memory and Language, 25,* 1–18.

Darlington, R. B. (1990). *Regression and linear models.* New York: McGraw-Hill.

Das, J. P., Naglieri, J. A., & Kirby, J. R. (1994). *Assessment of cognitive processes: The PASS theory of intelligence.* Needham Heights, MA: Allyn & Bacon.

Denckla, M. B. (1996a). Biological correlates of learning and attention: What is relevant to learning disability and Attention-Deficit Hyperactivity Disorder? *Developmental and Behavioral Pediatrics, 17,* 114–119.

Denckla, M. B. (1996b). Research on executive function in a neurodevelopmental context: Application of clinical measures. *Developmental Neuropsychology, 12,* 5–15.

Dornbusch, S. M. (2002). Sleep and adolescence: A social psychologist's perspective. In M. A. Carskadon (Ed.), *Adolescent sleep patterns: Biological, social, psychological influences* (pp. 1–3). New York: Cambridge University Press.

Dudley-Marling, C. (2004). The social construction of learning disabilities. *Journal of Learning Disabilities, 37,* 482–489.

Eden, G. F., Stein, J. F., Wood, H. M., & Wood, F. B. (1995). Temporal and spatial processing in reading disabled and normal children. *Cortex, 31,* 451–468.

Elias, M. J. (2004). The connection between social-emotional learning and learning disabilities: Implications for intervention. *Learning Disability Quarterly, 27,* 53–63.

Eslinger, P. J. (1996). Conceptualizing, describing, and measuring components of executive function: A summary. In G. R. Lyon & N. A. Krasnegor (Eds.), *Attention, memory, and executive function* (pp. 367–395). Baltimore: Brookes.

Espin, C., Shin, J., & Deno, S. L. (2000). Identifying indicators of written expression proficiency for middle school students. *Journal of Special Education, 34,* 140–153.

Evans, J. J., Floyd, R. G., McGrew, K. S., & Leforgee, M. H. (2001). The relations between measures of Cattell-Horn-Carroll (CHC) cognitive abilities and reading achievement during childhood and adolescence. *School Psychology Review, 31,* 246–262.

Fancher, R. E. (1990). *Pioneers of psychology* (2nd ed.). New York: Norton.

Faraone, S. V., Biederman, J., & Milberger, S. (1995). How reliable are maternal reports of their children's psychopathology? One-year recall of psychiatric diagnoses of ADHD children. *Journal of the American Academy of Child and Adolescent Psychiatry, 34,* 1001–1008.

Farmer, M. E., & Klein, R. M. (1995). The evidence for a temporal processing deficit linked to dyslexia: A review. *Psychonomic Bulletin and Review, 2,* 460–493.

Fiorello, C. A., Hale, J. B., & Snyder, L. E. (2006). Cognitive hypothesis testing and response to intervention for children with reading problems. *Psychology in the Schools, 43,* 835–853.

Flanagan, D. P., McGrew, K. S., & Ortiz, S. (2000). *The Wechsler Intelligence Scales and Gf—Gc Theory: A contemporary approach to interpretation.* Needham Heights, MA: Allyn & Bacon.

Flanagan, D. P., Ortiz, S. O., Alfonso, V. C., & Dynda, A. M. (2006). Integration of response to intervention and norm-referenced tests in learning disability identification: Learning from the Tower of Babel. *Psychology in the Schools, 43,* 807–825.

Fletcher, J. M., Francis, D. J., Shaywitz, S. E., Lyon, G. R., Foorman, B. R., Stuebing, K. K., & Shaywitz, B. A. (1998). Intelligent testing and the discrepancy model for children with learning disabilities. *Learning Disabilities Research and Practice, 13,* 186–203.

Foorman, B. R. (1995). Research on "the great debate": Code-oriented versus whole language approaches to reading instruction. *School Psychology Review, 24,* 376–392.

Gang, M., & Siegel, L. S. (2002). Sound-symbol learning in children with dyslexia. *Journal of Learning Disabilities, 35,* 137–157.

Gaub, M., & Carson, C. L. (1997). Gender differences in ADHD: A meta-analysis and critical review. *Journal of the American Academy of Child and Adolescent Psychiatry, 36,* 1036–1045.

Gibb, G. S., & Wilder, L. K. (2002). Using functional analysis to improve reading instruction for students with learning disabilities and emotional/behavioral disorders. *Preventing School Failure, 46,* 152–157.

Gresham, F. M., & MacMillan, D. L. (1997). Social competence and affective characteristics of students with mild disabilities. *Review of Educational Research, 67,* 377–415.

Gross-Tsur, V., Shalev, R. S., Manor, O., & Amir, N. (1995). Developmental right-hemisphere dysfunction: Clinical spectrum of the nonverbal learning disability. *Journal of Learning Disabilities, 28,* 80–86.

Guastello, E. F., Beasley, T. M., & Sinatra, R. C. (2000). Concept mapping effects in science content comprehension of low-achieving inner-city seventh graders. *Remedial and Special Education, 21,* 356–365.

Guilford, J. P. (1982). Cognitive psychology's ambiguities: Some suggested remedies. *Psychological Review, 89,* 48–59.

Haager, D. S., & Vaughn, S. (1995). Parent, teacher, peer, and self-reports of the social competence of students with learning disabilities. *Journal of Learning Disabilities, 28,* 205–215.

Haddad, F. A., Garcia, Y. E., Naglieri, J. A., Grimditch, M., McAndrews, A., & Eubanks, J. (2003). Planning facilitation and reading comprehension: Instructional relevance of the PASS theory. *Journal of Psychoeducational Assessment, 21,* 282–289.

Hale, J. B., & Fiorello, C. A. (2004). *School neuropsychology: A practitioner's handbook.* New York: Guilford Press.

Hale, J. B., Fiorello, C. A., Bertin, M., & Sherman, R. (2003). Predicting math achievement through neuropsychological interpretation of WISC-III variance components. *Journal of Psychoeducational Assessment, 21,* 358–380.

Hale, J. B., Kaufman, A., Naglieri, J. A., & Kavale, K. A. (2006). Implementation of IDEA: Integrating response to intervention and cognitive assessment methods. *Psychology in the Schools, 43,* 753–770.

Halford, G. S., Baker, R., McCredden, J. E., & Bain, J. D. (2005). How many variables can humans process? *Psychological Science, 16,* 70–76.

Hall, C. W., Peterson, A. D., Webster, R. E., Bolen, L. M., & Brown, M. B. (1999). Perception of nonverbal social cues by regular education, ADHD, and ADHD/LD students. *Psychology in the Schools, 36,* 505–514.

Harris-Schmidt, G., & Fast, D. (1998). Fragile X syndrome: Genetics, characteristics, and educational implications. *Advances in Special Education, 11,* 187–222.

Heiervang, E., & Hugdahl, K. (2003). Impaired visual attention in children with dyslexia. *Journal of Learning Disabilities, 36,* 68–73.

Holdnack, J. A., & Weiss, L. G. (2006). IDEA 2004: Anticipated implications for clinical practice—integrating assessment and intervention. *Psychology in the Schools, 43,* 871–882.

Holland, J., McIntosh, D., & Huffman, L. (2004). The role of phonological awareness, rapid automatized naming, and orthographic processing in word reading. *Journal of Psychoeducational Assessment, 22*, 233–260.

Hooper, S. R., Montgomery, J., Swartz, C., Reed, M. S., Sandler, A. D., Levine, M. D., Watson, T. E., & Wasileski, T. (1994). Measurement of written language expression. In G. R. Lyon (Ed.), *Frames of reference for the assessment of learning disabilities: New views on measurement issues* (pp. 375–417). Baltimore: Brookes.

Hopko, D. R., Ashcraft, M. H., Gute, J., Ruggiero, K. J., & Lewis, C. (1998). Mathematics anxiety and working memory: Support for the existence of a deficient inhibition mechanism. *Journal of Anxiety Disorders, 12*, 343–355.

Johnson, D. J. (1993). Relationships between oral and written language. *School Psychology Review, 22*, 595–609.

Johnson, J. A., Bardos, A. N., & Tayebi, K. A. (2003). Discriminant validity of the Cognitive Assessment System for students with written expression disabilities. *Journal of Psychoeducational Assessment, 21*, 180–195.

Joshi, R. M. (1995). Assessing reading and spelling skills. *School Psychology Review, 24*, 361–375.

Keene, E. O., & Zimmermann, S. (1997). *Mosaic of thought: Teaching comprehension in a reader's workshop.* Portsmouth, NH: Heinemann.

Kelso, J.A.S. (1995). *Dynamic patterns: The self-organization of brain and behavior.* Cambridge, MA: MIT Press.

Kirby, J. R. (1993). Collaborative and competitive effects of verbal and spatial processes. *Learning and Instruction, 3*, 201–214.

Kosc, L. (1974). Developmental dyscalculia. *Journal of Learning Disabilities, 7*, 165–177.

Kravetz, S., Faust, M., & Lipshitz, S. (1999). LD, interpersonal understanding, and social behavior in the classroom. *Journal of Learning Disabilities, 32*, 248–255.

Levine, M. D. (1998). *Developmental variation and learning disorders* (2nd ed.). Cambridge, MA: Educators Publishing Service.

Levine, M. D. (2002). *A mind at a time.* New York: Simon & Schuster.

Levine, M. D. (2003). *The myth of laziness.* New York: Simon & Schuster.

Lezak, M. D. (1995). *Neuropsychological assessment* (3rd ed.). Oxford, UK: Oxford University Press.

Lidz, C. S. (1991). *Practitioner's guide to dynamic assessment.* New York: Guilford Press.

Lidz, C. S. (1995). Dynamic assessment and the legacy of L. S. Vygotsky. *School Psychology International, 16*, 143–153.

Luria, A. R. (1973). *The working brain: An introduction to neuropsychology* (B. Haigh, Trans.). New York: Basic Books.

Lyon, G. R., Fletcher, J. M., Shaywitz, S. E., Shaywitz, B. A., Torgesen, J. K., Wood, F. B., Schulte, A. & Olson, R. (2001). Rethinking learning disabilities. In C. E. Finn, A. J. Rotherham, & C. R. Hokanson (Eds.), *Rethinking special education for a new century.* Washington, DC: Thomas B. Fordham Foundation and the Progressive Policy Institute.

Marcotte, A. C., & Stern, C. (1997). Qualitative analysis of graphomotor output in children with attentional disorders. *Child Neuropsychology, 3*, 147–153.

Marshall, R. M., Hynd, G. W., Handwerk, M. J., & Hall, J. (1997). Academic underachievement in ADHD subtypes. *Journal of Learning Disabilities, 30*, 635–642.

Martens, V.E.G., & de Jong, P. F. (2006). The effect of word length on lexical decision in dyslexic and normal reading children. *Brain and Language, 98*, 140–149.

Martinez, R. S., & Semrud-Clikeman, M. (2004). Emotional adjustment and school functioning of young adolescents with multiple versus single learning disabilities. *Journal of Learning Disabilities, 37*, 411–420.

Mather, N., & Kaufman, N. (2006). Introduction to the special issue, part one: It's about the what, the how well, and the why. *Psychology in the Schools, 43*, 747–752.

Mauer, D. M., & Kamhi, A. G. (1996). Factors that influence phoneme-grapheme correspondence learning. *Journal of Learning Disabilities, 29*, 259–270.

McAlexander, P. J. (1996). Ideas in practice: Audience awareness and developmental composition. *Journal of Developmental Education, 20*, 28–30.

McCabe, P. C. (2005). Social and behavioral correlates of preschoolers with specific language impairment. *Psychology in the Schools, 42*, 373–387.

McCallum, R. S., Bell, S. M., Wood, M. S., Below, J. L., Choate, S. M., & McCane, S. J. (2006). What is the role of working memory in reading relative to the big three processing variables (orthography, phonology, and rapid naming)? *Journal of Psychoeducational Assessment, 24*, 243–259.

McCoy, J. D., & Ketterlin-Geller, L. R. (2004). Rethinking instructional delivery for diverse student populations: Serving all learners with concept-based instruction. *Intervention in School and Clinic, 40*, 88–95.

Meyer, G. J., Finn, S. E., Eyde, L. D., Kay, G. G., Moreland, K. L., Dies, R. R., Eisman, E. J., Kubiszyn, T. W., & Reed, G. M. (2001). Psychological testing and psychological assessment: A review of evidence and issues. *American Psychologist, 56*, 128–165.

Meyers, J. E., & Meyers, K. R. (1996). *Rey Complex Figure and Recognition Trial.* Lutz, FL: Psychological Assessment Resources.

Moats, L. C. (1994a). Assessment of spelling in learning disabilities research. In G. R. Lyon (Ed.), *Frames of reference for the assessment of learning disabilities: New views on measurement issues* (pp. 333–349). Baltimore: Brookes.

Moats, L. C. (1994b). Honing the concepts of listening and speaking: A prerequisite to the valid measurement of language behavior in children. In G. R. Lyon (Ed.), *Frames of reference for the assessment of learning disabilities: New views on measurement issues* (pp. 229–241). Baltimore: Brookes.

Neuhaus, G. F., & Swank, P. R. (2002). Understanding the relations between RAN letter subtest components and word reading in first-grade students. *Journal of Learning Disabilities, 35*, 158–174.

Nowicki, E. A. (2003). A meta-analysis of the social competence of children with learning disabilities compared to classmates of low and average to high achievement. *Learning Disability Quarterly, 26*, 171–188.

Pak, A.K.H., Cheng-Lai, A., Tso, I. F., Shu, H., Li, W., & Anderson, R. C. (2005). Visual chunking skills of Hong Kong children. *Reading and Writing, 18*, 437–454.

Pavri, S., & Monda-Amaya, L. (2001). Social support in inclusive schools: Student and teacher perspectives. *Exceptional Children, 67*, 391–411.

Proctor, B. E., Floyd, R. G., & Shaver, R. B. (2005). Cattell-Horn-Carroll broad cognitive ability profiles of low math achievers. *Psychology in the Schools, 42*, 1–12.

Prutting, C. A., & Kirchner, D. M. (1987). A clinical appraisal of the pragmatic aspects of language. *Journal of Speech and Hearing Disorders, 52,* 105–119.

Raskind, M. H., Goldberg, R. J., Higgins, F. L., & Herman, K. L. (1999). Patterns of change and predictors of success in individuals with learning disabilities: Results from a twenty-year longitudinal study. *Learning Disabilities Research and Practice, 14,* 35–49.

Reader, M. J., Harris, E. L., Schuerholz, L. J., & Denckla, M. B. (1994). Attention Deficit Hyperactivity Disorder and executive function. *Developmental Neuropsychology, 10,* 493–512.

Riccio, C. A., & Hynd, G. W. (1995). Contributions of neuropsychology to our understanding of developmental reading problems. *School Psychology Review, 24,* 415–425.

Roberts, R. J., Jr., & Pennington, B. F. (1996). An interactive framework for examining prefrontal cognitive processes. *Developmental Neuropsychology, 12,* 105–126.

Rourke, B. P., & Conway, J. (1997). Disabilities of arithmetic and mathematics reasoning: Perspectives from neurology and neuropsychology. *Journal of Learning Disabilities, 30,* 34–46.

Royer, J. M., Greene, B. A., & Sinatra, G. A. (1987). The Sentence Verification Technique: A practical procedure for testing comprehension. *Journal of Reading, 30,* 414–422.

Sabornie, E. J. (1994). Social-affective characteristics in early adolescents identified as learning disabled and nondisabled. *Learning Disability Quarterly, 17,* 268–279.

Seligman, M.E.P., & Csikszentmihalyi, M. (2000). Positive psychology: An introduction. *American Psychologist, 55,* 5–14.

Sergeant, J. (1996). A theory of attention: An information processing perspective. In G. R. Lyon & N. A. Krasnegor (Eds.), *Attention, memory, and executive function* (pp. 57–69). Baltimore: Brookes.

Siegal, L. S., & Ryan, E. B. (1989). The development of working memory in normally achieving and subtypes of learning disabled children. *Child Development, 60,* 973–990.

Siegler, R. S. (1986). *Children's thinking.* Upper Saddle River, NJ: Prentice Hall.

Snider, V. E. (1995). A primer on phonemic awareness: What it is, why it's important, and how to teach it. *School Psychology Review, 24,* 443–455.

Stanford, M. S., & Barratt, E. S. (1996). Verbal skills, finger tapping, and cognitive tempo define a second-order factor of temporal information processing. *Brain and Cognition, 31,* 35–45.

Stecker, P. M., Fuchs, L. S., & Fuchs, D. (2005). Using curriculum-based measurement to improve student achievement: Review of research. *Psychology in the Schools, 42,* 795–819.

Storch, S. A., & Whitehurst, G. J. (2002). Oral language and code-related precursors to reading: Evidence from a longitudinal structural model. *Developmental Psychology, 38,* 934–947.

Swanson, H. L., Cochran, K. F., & Ewers, C. A. (1990). Can learning disabilities be determined from working memory performance? *Journal of Learning Disabilities, 23,* 59–67.

Swanson, H. L., & Malone, S. (1992). Social skills and learning disabilities: A meta-analysis of the literature. *School Psychology Review, 21,* 427–443.

Thomas, C. L. (Ed.). (1997). *Taber's cyclopedic medical dictionary* (18th ed.). Philadelphia: Davis.

Torgesen, J. K. (1996). A model of memory from an information processing perspective: The special case of phonological memory. In G. R. Lyon & N. A. Krasnegor (Eds.), *Attention, memory, and executive function* (pp. 157–184). Baltimore: Brookes.

Troia, G. A., Graham, S., & Harris, K. R. (1999). Teaching students with learning disabilities to mindfully plan when writing. *Exceptional Children, 65,* 235–252.

Vallance, D. D., Cummings, R. L., & Humphries, T. (1998). Mediators of the risk for problem behavior in children with language learning disabilities. *Journal of Learning Disabilities, 31,* 160–171.

Vallecorsa, A., & DeBettencourt, L. U. (1997). Using a mapping procedure to teach reading and writing skills to middle grade students with learning disabilities. *Education and Treatment of Children, 20,* 173–188.

Vaughn, S., & Wilson, C. (1994). Mathematics assessment for students with learning disabilities. In G. R. Lyon (Ed.), *Frames of reference for the assessment of learning disabilities: New views on measurement issues* (pp. 459–472). Baltimore: Brookes.

Waber, D. P., & Bernstein, J. H. (1994). Repetitive graphomotor output in learning-disabled and nonlearning-disabled children: The Repeated Patterns Test. *Developmental Neuropsychology, 10,* 51–65.

Wagner, R. K. (1996). From simple structure to complex function: Major trends in the development of theories, models, and measurements of memory. In G. R. Lyon & N. A. Krasnegor (Eds.), *Attention, memory, and executive function* (pp. 139–155). Baltimore: Brookes.

Wagner, R. K., Torgesen, J. K., & Rashotte, C. A. (1999). *Comprehensive Test of Phonological Processing.* Austin, TX: PRO-ED.

Wenz-Gross, M., & Siperstein, G. N. (1998). Students with learning problems at risk in middle school: Stress, social support, and adjustment. *Exceptional Children, 65,* 91–100.

Werner, E. E., & Smith, R. S. (1992). *Overcoming the odds: High risk children from birth to adulthood.* New York: Cornell University Press.

Werner, E. E., & Smith, R. S. (2001). *Journeys from childhood to the midlife: Risk, resilience, and recovery.* New York: Cornell University Press.

Whitehurst, G. J., & Lonigan, C. J. (1998). Child development and early literacy. *Child Development, 69,* 848–872.

Willis, J. O., & Dumont, R. (2006). And never the twain shall meet: Can response to intervention and cognitive assessment be reconciled? *Psychology in the Schools, 43,* 901–908.

Windfuhr, K. L., & Snowling, M. J. (2001). The relationship between paired associate learning and phonological skills in normally developing readers. *Journal of Experimental Child Psychology, 80,* 160–173.

Yasutake, D., & Bryan, T. (1995). The influence of affect on the achievement and behavior of students with learning disabilities. *Journal of Learning Disabilities, 28,* 329–334.

Zentall, S. S. (1993). Research on the educational implications of Attention Deficit Hyperactivity Disorder. *Exceptional Children, 60,* 143–153.

Zera, D. A. (2001). A reconceptualization of learning disabilities via a self-organizing systems paradigm. *Journal of Learning Disabilities, 34,* 79–94.

Glossary of Terms

Academic skills: Skills that have been developed by humans over the course of civilization that include reading, writing, and mathematics; composed of component *subskills* (see *neurodevelopmental construct* and *neurodevelopmental function*).

Academic subskills: Components of *academic skills*.

Academic task: Assessment task designed to appraise an *academic skill;* examples include reading word lists, writing a short passage, and solving math word problems (see *neurodevelopmental task*).

Accommodation: Instructional or learning strategy that is intended to bypass a weak *skill* or circumvent a weak *function;* examples include not penalizing for spelling mistakes in a written report and reducing the number of math problems a student is to solve (see *intervention*).

Active working memory: Memory component that mentally suspends information while using or manipulating it, such as when solving a mental math problem.

Affinity: Topic or activity that a student finds deeply interesting; engaging in affinities can be gratifying, especially for struggling learners; affinities can be leveraged in learning plans (for example, to pique a student's interest); the student does not need to excel in something for it to be an affinity (see *asset*).

Ambiguous sentences: Task used to assess *sentence comprehension;* student identifies and explains at least two of the multiple possible meanings of a sentence; can be in multiple-choice format.

Assessment: Process of collecting and interpreting a broad range of data for the purpose of understanding the student's learning profile (see *testing*).

Asset: *Skill* or *function* that is working well for a student; applied activity (such as using computers) at which a student is adept; may be only relatively strong when compared to the rest of the student's *profile* (see *affinity*).

Attention: Network of interactive controls over mental functioning, including mental energy, incoming information, and regulation of output.

Automaticity: General capacity to perform tasks rapidly with little effort, such as decoding words and retrieving information from memory; being automatic with certain tasks frees up mental resources for other, potentially more sophisticated, tasks.

Base word: Core component of a word that is the crux of the word's meaning; *morphemes* are added to modify meanings; comes from English and can stand alone without other *morphemes* (see *root word*).

Basic figure copy: Task used to assess *spatial ordering* and *graphomotor function;* student copies relatively small, simple, and abstract figures.

Blend: Aspect of *phonological processing* and *phonics* in which *phonemes* are combined to form word sounds, with individual sounds being retained; types include consonant blends and vowel blends (the latter are also referred to as *diphthongs*).

Blending: Task used to assess *phonological processing;* student blends word sounds by stating the words at normal pace after hearing segmented words (for example, played at slow speed on audiotape).

Block construction: Task used to assess *spatial ordering;* student replicates patterns (modeled or displayed in a booklet) with colored blocks; can be in multiple-choice format with pictures of blocks.

Branching logic: Clinical thought process that employs the *discrepancy concept* and *clinical contrasts.* As evidence is gathered, questions are asked about the student's performance on tasks, leading the data analysis through a series of if-then statements to determine the student's *profile* and *linkages* with *academic skills.*

Category naming: Task used to assess *word retrieval;* the student quickly names words belonging to a category that is either semantic (for example, vegetables) or phonemic (for example, words that start with "t").

Chunk size: Cross-construct phenomenon describing the amount of material taken in (while reading or listening) or generated (for example, in writing).

Clinical contrast: Discrepant performance on two tasks that can be used to reveal or isolate components of a student's *profile.*

Cloze task: Language and reading assessment task in which parts are removed from the whole (for example, letters from words, words from text) and the student needs to use only the remaining information (for example, to identify words with missing letters, to understand text with missing words).

Cognitive activation: Attention processing control involved with linking incoming information with prior knowledge and experience; dysfunction with this control can range from underactivation or passive processing (not forming enough relevant associations) to overactivation or excessive processing (forming connections that are too tangential to the topic at hand).

Commission: Error involving a marked target or incorrect response, often during a *visual vigilance* or continuous performance task; can indicate attention production control weaknesses; also referred to as *false positive* (see *omission*).

Competing language: Task used to assess *active working memory;* student answers basic questions in sets, then recalls the last word from each question in the set.

Complex figure copy: Task used to assess *spatial ordering, production control system* of attention, and *graphomotor function;* student copies a large, complex, and abstract figure.

Complex sentences: Task used to assess *sentence comprehension;* student answers questions that are challenging in terms of sentence structure or vocabulary, or both; response may be oral or multiple-choice.

Concept: Set of features that often go together to form a category of ideas or objects; can take many forms, including verbal (due process, foreshadowing), nonverbal (place value, equations, planetary movements, geometric shapes), and process (water cycle, photosynthesis).

Conceptualization: *Higher-order cognition* function involved with integrating a set of features that often go together to form a category of ideas or objects; spares memory because all members of a category do not need to be memorized, just the critical features.

Confound: A factor that complicates or interferes with a given test, task or *skill;* for example, weak reading can be a confound for solving math *word problems.*

Construct: See *neurodevelopmental construct.*

Contextualized: Information that is familiar (and often relatively concrete) to the student (see *decontextualized*).

Continuous performance task: Task used to assess *attention;* student pushes a button or clicks a trigger when a target is heard or seen (usually on computer screen); requires inhibiting the impulse to respond to non-targets; usually lasts several minutes.

Convergent: Type of memory and thinking that involves specific or singular correct responses or appropriate ideas (see *divergent*).

Cross-construct phenomena: *Phenomena* that interact with all the *neurodevelopmental constructs* and their component parts; include *rate of processing and production, chunk size, metacognition,* and *strategy use.*

CPT: See *continuous performance task.*

Current history: Student information from the current or most recent school year, including reports from parents and teachers.

Curriculum-based measurement: System used by some teachers and other school-based professionals to track students' progress toward instructional objectives using quantitative data, often displayed on a graph; data are collected regularly and frequently via brief probes, such as counting the number of words read accurately during a one-minute oral reading sample from the curriculum.

Decoding: See *reading decoding.*

Decontextualized: Information that is unfamiliar (and often relatively abstract) to the student (see *contextualized*).

Deductive reasoning: Thinking from the general to the specific (such as starting with neurodevelopmental dysfunctions and then predicting the symptoms that might be caused by those dysfunctions); used when generating learning plans and when learning a theoretical framework (see *inductive reasoning*).

Demystification: Ongoing dialogue about the student's learning with the student; parameters are put around weaknesses, assets are highlighted, and a positive message about the future delivered; usually initiated by a professional (such as clinician or educator), but should be continued by a parent or caregiver.

Digit span: Task used to assess *short-term* and *active working memory;* student repeats series of orally presented numbers in same order or in reverse order.

Digraph: Type of *grapheme* consisting of two letters that represent a single sound such as "ph" for /f/ in "telegraph"; can involve consonant or vowels; in some cases the sound cannot be represented by a single letter, such as "ch-" in "chin" (see *diphthong*).

Diphthong: Type of *phoneme* in which two vowel sounds are blended to create a new sound in which two sounds are heard, such as /oi/ in "boy" (see *digraph*).

Direction following: Task used to assess *sentence comprehension;* student follows orally presented directions (such as by pointing to objects on an easel); extended directions usually also require *active working memory.*

Discourse processing: Language function involved with interpreting language beyond the boundaries of a sentence (such as paragraphs, chapters, stories) (see *discourse production*).

Discourse production: Language function involved with communicating information in a cohesive chain of sentences (such as paragraphs, essays) (see *discourse processing*).

Discrepancy concept: Clinical thought process of comparing one aspect of a student's mind to another aspect; integral to making *clinical contrasts.*

Divergent: Type of memory and thinking that involves nonspecific or multiple correct responses or appropriate ideas (see *convergent*).

Drawing recall: Task used to assess *short-term* and *long-term memory;* student draws one or more figures after a brief or extended delay; may also have a *recognition* trial.

Dynamic assessment: Flexible techniques that focus on the learning process and strategies used during tasks (rather than the product or outcome); clinician acts as a guide, mediating the task and actively engaging with the student; yields *qualitative findings* (see *standardized assessment*).

Elision: Task used to assess *phonological processing;* student transforms words by deleting phonemes from orally presented words.

Executive functions: Mental abilities that include self-regulation, selective inhibition of responding, response preparation, cognitive flexibility, and organizing; similar in definition to the *production control system.*

Expository discourse: Discourse intended to convey information; it is often nonfiction and detail-laden, such as what might be found in a science textbook (see *narrative discourse*).

Expressive language: Producing and communicating ideas orally and in writing (see *receptive language*).

Expressive vocabulary: Task used to assess *semantic use;* student orally defines words.

Facilitation and inhibition: Attention production control involved with selecting the best option before acting or starting a task (facilitation) and suppressing inappropriate decisions and behaviors (inhibition); weakness with this function leads to impulsivity.

Factual recall: Task used to assess *long-term memory;* student answers general knowledge questions, either *free recall* or *recognition* and multiple choice.

False negative: See *omission.*

False positive: See *commission.*

Figure matching: Task used to assess *spatial ordering;* student selects from a set the figure or shape that matches a target.

Fine motor function: Neuromotor function involved with manual dexterity (effective control of hands and fingers).

Finger localization: Task used to assess *fine motor function;* student makes specific finger movements (often demonstrated by examiner) without visual support.

Finger tapping: Task used to assess *fine motor function;* student taps one or more fingers rapidly; can be a repetitive movement (such as index finger on table) or a more complex sequence.

Fixed battery: Consistent set of procedures used for every student (though often differentiated by age or grade level), regardless of the *referral question* (see *multi-method assessment*).

Focal maintenance: Attention processing control involved with sustaining concentration for the appropriate period (also referred to as attention span or sustained attention).

Free recall: See *recall.*

Function: See *neurodevelopmental function.*

Graphemes: Printed letters and letter combinations (or *orthographic patterns*); connected with speech sounds (or *phonemes*) through the learning of *phonics.*

Graphomotor function: Neuromotor function involved with coordinating motor actions to maneuver a utensil to produce handwriting; using feedback to feel where the writing utensil is during letter formation; recalling movements needed to form letters and numbers.

Gross motor function: Neuromotor function involved with using the body's large muscles in a coordinated, effective manner; mobilizing the right muscles in the best order to achieve a motor goal.

Hand movements: Task used to assess *short-term* and *active working memory;* student replicates series of hand movements (such as involving a prop) in same order or in manipulated order.

Higher-order cognition: Complex and sophisticated thinking, such as understanding concepts, reasoning, and using logic.

Inductive reasoning: Thinking from the specific to the general (for example, starting with symptoms and then hypothesizing about the dysfunctions that might be causing them); used during assessment (see *deductive reasoning*).

Intervention: Instructional or learning strategy that is intended to remediate a weak *skill* or improve a weak *function;* examples include flash card drills for math facts and studying word families to develop vocabulary (see *accommodation*).

Intrusion: Type of *commission* error (or *false positive*) in which the student responds with non-list words during a *list recall* task; can indicate attention control weaknesses.

Irregularly spelled words: Words that do not follow *phonics* rules and usually need to be memorized as *sight words*.

Language: Understanding (receptive) and using (expressive) linguistic sounds, words, sentences, and discourse.

Learning plan: Student's road map to improved school and life success that addresses weak areas but also describes how to nurture and leverage assets and affinities; *demystification* is an important aspect of a plan.

Letter or number reordering: Task used to assess *active working memory;* student re-orders orally presented numbers (in serial order) and letters (in alphabetical order).

Limit testing: Stretching the way a testing instrument or procedure is administered to learn as much as possible about a student's neurodevelopmental functions and academic skills.

Linkage: Connections between an *academic skill* and the *neurodevelopmental functions* that contribute to it; such connections can also be drawn between *functions* and other applied areas, such as riding a bike or planning a birthday party.

List recall: Task used to assess *short-term* and *long-term memory;* student recalls list of words (or pairs) after initial learning trials or extended delay; may include a delayed *recognition* trial.

Listening comprehension: Understanding the meaning of orally presented language; listening tasks are used to assess *receptive language* without the *confound* of *reading decoding* skill level and *phonics* (see *reading comprehension*).

Long-term memory access: Memory component that retrieves information (such as knowledge, skills, experiences) after extended delays (see *long-term memory storage*).

Long-term memory storage: Memory component that consolidates information (such as knowledge, skills, experiences) after extended delays (see *long-term memory access*).

Math operations: Use of procedures to perform basic math computations (such as subtraction, simplifying fractions, balancing equations); the term *math operations* usually refers to solving relatively abstract, that is, non-applied problems (see *math reasoning*).

Math reasoning: Solving math problems by applying procedures in different situations with changing information; the term *math reasoning* usually refers to solving applied problems such as *word problems* (see *math operations*).

Matrix reasoning: Task used to assess *higher-order cognition;* student completes an analogy with pictures or symbols displayed on an easel; multiple-choice format.

Matthew Effect: "The rich get richer and the poor get poorer" in terms of the interplay between *neurodevelopmental functions* and *academic skill* development; the quality and use of skills strengthen or weaken the neurodevelopmental functions that were used to acquire the skills.

Maze tracing: Task used to assess *graphomotor function;* student draws a line along a narrow winding path without touching the sides.

Memory: Storage and retrieval of information temporarily (*short-term*), over extended periods (*long-term*), or while using the information (*active working*).

Mental energy control system: Set of attention controls for initiating and maintaining the cognitive energy level needed for optimal learning and behavior.

Metacognition: Cross-construct phenomenon describing the level of understanding about one's own mind and learning abilities.

Mnemonic strategies: Tactics used to facilitate *long-term memory storage* for more effective and efficient *long-term memory access;* such strategies are wide-ranging, from converting lists to acronyms to visualization.

Morphemes: Components of words that convey some meaning (such as prefixes, suffixes, inflectional endings, and *root words*); may be free (able to stand alone as a word) or bound (must be attached to carry meaning).

Morphological sense: Interpreting parts of words that convey some meaning (see *morphemes* and *morphological use*).

Morphological use: Employing parts of words that convey some meaning (see *morphemes* and *morphological sense*).

Morphology: See *morphological sense* and *morphological use.*

Multi-method assessment: Incorporating elements (such as subtests) from various tests and batteries into a customized battery for a student (see *fixed battery*).

Narrative discourse: Discourse tells a story or relates events and characters; it is often fictional, but may relate nonfiction such as personal anecdotes or historical events (see *expository discourse*).

Neurodevelopmental construct: Collection of mental abilities or *functions* that enables the performing of learned skills (see *academic skills*).

Neurodevelopmental functions: Mental abilities that are intrinsic to the human mind but develop through experience with the environment; enable the learning and performing of *academic skills;* are organized into *constructs* (see *academic skills*).

Neurodevelopmental profile: Student's balance sheet of *functions* and *constructs;* includes components that are strong, operating appropriately, and weak.

Neurodevelopmental task: Assessment task designed to appraise a *neurodevelopmental construct* or *function,* usually with material that is relatively nonacademic; examples include orally generating sentences from word prompts, copying complex figures, and reasoning with visual analogies (see *academic task*).

Neuromotor function: Nervous system's control over movement of large muscles (*gross motor function*), hands and fingers (*fine motor function*), mouth muscles for speech (*oromotor function*), and handwriting (*graphomotor function*).

Nonsense words: Words manufactured for decoding and spelling assessment purposes only (such as "pliv"); also referred to as non-words or pseudowords.

Nonverbal pragmatics: Interpreting and employing nonverbal behaviors (such as eye contact, body language) for *socialization* (see *verbal pragmatics*).

Omission: Error involving a missed target or response, often during a *visual vigilance* or continuous performance task; can indicate attention processing control weaknesses; also referred to as *false negative* (see *commission*).

Onset-rime: A unit intermediate between the whole word and the *phoneme;* the onset is the initial consonant or consonant cluster and the rime is the vowel and the remainder of the syllable.

Oral expression: Communication of verbal ideas via speaking; oral communication tasks are used to isolate *expressive language* from other functions involved in writing, such as *graphomotor function* (see *written expression*).

Organization: Capacity to keep track of materials and schedules, and to approach tasks in systematic and efficient ways; can be undermined by several *constructs,* including attention.

Oromotor function: Using mouth muscles effectively, enunciating correctly and generating smooth, intelligible speech.

Orthographic memory: Capacity to store and recall common letter patterns found in a language (or *orthographic patterns*), particularly important with *irregularly spelled words;* orthographic recognition is used for *reading decoding.*

Orthographic patterns: Printed letter combinations typically found in a language, such as "tion" and "pre" and other elements.

Orthography: See *orthographic memory* and *orthographic patterns.*

Pacing: Attention production control involved with working at the most appropriate speed, without rushing.

Paired associate memory: Memory component that links and stores two related data bits, then retrieves one piece of information when presented with the other piece (such as a sound with a symbol).

Passage listening comprehension: Task used to assess *discourse comprehension;* student answers questions about orally presented passages; response may be oral or multiple-choice.

Passage recall: Task used to assess *short-term* and *long-term memory;* student recalls and summarizes information from an orally presented passage after a brief or extended delay; may include a delayed *recognition* trial.

Past history: Student information from earlier school years, including reports from parents and teachers.

Perseveration: Type of *commission* error (or *false positive*) in which the student repeats words during a *list recall* task; can indicate weak *self-monitoring* or *active working memory.*

Personal norms: Clinician's experience with assessment tasks and *academic skills;* important for developing expectations for typical student performance.

Phenomena: Bits of information that are gathered and interpreted to better understand a student's learning; can be academic or neurodevelopmental in nature; can be gathered via history reports or direct observation (for example, during testing).

Phenomenological: Emphasizing *phenomena* in assessment to describe a student's *profile,* in lieu of categorizing or labeling the student.

Phonemes: Individual sound in words (for example, the word *tag* contains three phonemes: /t/, /a/, /g/); English contains forty-four word sounds, which are linked with *graphemes* for *phonics.*

Phonics: Linking speech sounds (or *phonemes*) with printed letters and letter combinations (or *graphemes*) (see *phonological processing*).

Phonological processing: Language function involved with identifying, distinguishing, and manipulating the individual sounds in words (or *phonemes*); this is an oral process that gets applied to print through the learning of *phonics;* also referred to as phonology (see *phonics*).

Phonology: See *phonological processing.*

Picture recall: Task used to assess *short-term* and *long-term memory;* student names details or identifies altered elements in drawings of real-life scenarios.

Positivism: School of thought speculating that the universe has a structure and that science seeks to understand that structure (see *relativism*).

Previewing: Attention production control involved with anticipating and predicting likely outcomes of actions, events, and problems; planning how to solve a problem or complete a task before starting to work.

Procedural memory: Memory component that stores and retrieves skills and processes that involve steps or sequences (for example, for *math operations*).

Process observations: Category of *qualitative findings* that involves how the student arrived at a response or completed a task (see *product observations*).

Processing control system: Set of attention controls for handling information entering through the senses.

Processing depth: Attention processing control involved with focusing with sufficient intensity to capture details (such as instructions); weak (or shallow and superficial) processing is glossing over information and missing details (that is, "in one ear and out the other").

Product observations: Category of *qualitative findings* that appraise features of the student's response or output (see *process observations*).

Production control system: Set of attention controls for regulating thinking for academic and behavioral output.

Profile: See *neurodevelopmental profile*.

Qualitative findings: Findings that are typically derived from *dynamic assessment* techniques, such as *limit testing* and interviewing (as opposed to *standardized assessment*); include both *process observations* and *product observations* (see *quantitative findings*).

Quantitative findings: Findings that are typically derived from *standardized assessment* techniques (as opposed to *dynamic assessment*); usually includes a *standard score* of some kind (see *qualitative findings*).

Rapid automatic naming: Task used to assess *word retrieval;* student quickly names visually displayed letters, numbers, or objects.

Rate of processing and production: Cross-construct phenomenon describing the speed with which material is processed or generated.

Reading comprehension: Understanding the meaning of printed text (see *reading decoding* and *listening comprehension*).

Reading decoding: Reading individual printed words (for example, calling out what the word is though not necessarily having an understanding of it); decoding employs both *word attack* and *sight word recognition* (see *reading comprehension*).

Reasoning and logic: *Higher-order cognition* function involved with application of systematic and stepwise approaches to complex questions or challenges, such as when solving math problems or word analogies.

Re-blending: Putting word sounds together; involves *phonological processing;* used for *word attack* but can occur without letter knowledge (see *segmenting*).

Recall: Open-ended questions (such as what and how questions); used to tap both *long-term memory storage* and *long-term memory access* (see *recognition*).

Receptive language: Processing and understanding incoming oral and written information (see *expressive language*).

Receptive vocabulary: Task used to assess *semantic understanding;* student points to picture of orally presented word in a multiple-choice array or selects the correct definition of a word in a multiple-choice format.

Recognition: Forced-choice questions (such as multiple-choice and matching); used to isolate *long-term memory storage* (see *recall*).

Referral concern: Problem areas and issues leading to the *assessment.* Parents or teachers often pose the questions, and although more specific questions are generally better for planning an *assessment,* the clinician can usually clarify more general questions through interviewing.

Referral question: See *referral concern.*

Regularly spelled words: Words that follow *phonics* rules and can be decoded readily through *word attack.*

Relativism: School of thought positing that structures are merely imposed on the universe, to be used as long as they seem to describe it (see *positivism*).

Response to intervention: Approach to identifying students with learning problems and for determining what level and type of instruction they should receive in school, including special education; identification is usually based on curriculum-specific probes that measure using local norms (that is, comparing a student to peers in the same class or school); often referred to as "RTI."

Root word: Core component of a word that is the crux of the word's meaning; *morphemes* are added to modify meanings. The root generally comes from a non-English language and will not stand alone without other *morphemes* (see *base word*).

Rule use: *Higher-order cognition* function involved with understanding rules and principles. This function involves more than just remembering rules; rather, it involves comprehending them deeply enough to apply them under different circumstances.

Saliency determination: Attention processing control involved with discriminating between important and unimportant information; avoiding distractions (also known as selective attention).

Scientific instrumentalism: Notion that scientific theories produce intellectual structures that predict what is observed and that are frameworks that facilitate the answering of questions and the solving of problems (see *scientific realism*).

Scientific realism: Notion that scientific theories go beyond data to posit the existence of nonobservable entities that actually exist (see *scientific instrumentalism*).

Secondary attention deficits: Behaviors or signs that appear to be attention problems but are actually due to other neurodevelopmental dysfunctions; can arise from weaknesses in *receptive language, expressive language, active working memory, spatial ordering,* and *graphomotor function.*

Segmenting: Breaking apart word sounds; involves *phonological processing.* Used for *word attack* but can occur without letter knowledge (see *reblending*).

Self-monitoring: Attention production control involved with tracking one's output and making necessary modifications and revisions; finding and correcting mistakes in one's work.

Semantic understanding: Language function involved with knowing the meanings of words, although not necessarily using or defining the words (see *semantic use*).

Semantic use: Language function involved with properly applying word meanings, defining words, and using words in context (see *semantic understanding*).

Semantics: See *semantic understanding* and *semantic use.*

Sentence comprehension: Language function involved with understanding sentences and sentence structures when listening or reading (see *sentence formulation*).

Sentence construction: Task used to assess *sentence formulation;* student generates oral sentences that include provided sets of words.

Sentence formulation: Language function involved with expressing thoughts in complete, grammatically correct sentences when speaking and writing (see *sentence comprehension*).

Sentence repetition: Task used to assess *short-term memory;* student recalls orally presented sentences after a brief delay.

Sequence completion: Task used to assess *temporal-sequential ordering,* where the student completes sequences often involving pictures, symbols, and numbers. Response can be verbal, nonverbal (pointing), or written.

Sequential output: Aspect of *temporal-sequential ordering* involved with generating products in which the content is arranged in a linear way (see *sequential perception*).

Sequential perception: Aspect of *temporal-sequential ordering* involved with processing the order of incoming linear information (see *sequential output*).

Short-term memory: Memory component that briefly registers new information that is subsequently used (in *active working memory*), stored (in long-term memory), or discarded.

Sight word recognition: Decoding words through recognition of *sight words* (see *word attack*).

Sight words: Words that can be recognized visually (rather than having to be decoded through *word attack*); often short and high-use (such as "of" and "the").

Similarities: Task used to assess *higher-order cognition.* The student describes how two or three words are related or similar, and the format may be open-ended or multiple-choice.

Skill: See *academic skill.*

Social cognition: Set of abilities that guide interaction with others; includes verbal (such as maintaining a conversation) and nonverbal (such as using appropriate body language) aspects (see *socialization*).

Social vignettes: Task used to assess *social cognition;* student describes appropriate responses for social scenarios, presented orally or through a picture, or both.

Socialization: Interacting with others in a positive manner; requires the application of several *neurodevelopmental functions* (see *social cognition*).

Sound matching: Task used to assess *phonological processing.* The student matches pictures of objects with similar initial word sound or final word sound, and the response can be by speaking or pointing.

Sound-symbol recall: Task used to assess *short-term* and *long-term memory (paired associate memory).* The student recalls the name for a symbol or picture after initial learning trials or extended delay.

Spatial ordering: Processing or producing material that is visual or in a spatial array (see *temporal-sequential ordering*).

Spatial organization: Aspect of *spatial ordering* involved with keeping one's surrounding spaces and work resources systematically arranged (see *temporal organization*).

Spatial output: Aspect of *spatial ordering* involved with generation of material and products that have visual-spatial characteristics, such as drawings and models (see *spatial perception*).

Spatial perception: Aspect of *spatial ordering* involved with interpreting relationships within and between visual-spatial patterns, such as pictures and diagrams (see *spatial output*).

Standard score: Score that represents a comparison between a student's performance and that of relevant peer groups. Scores of this type are derived from tests with uniform stimuli and questions that serve as consistent criteria for measurement; designed to enable developmental judgments about performance levels.

Standardized assessment: Structured techniques that focus on consistent administration of tasks and comparisons with relevant peer groups. It yields *quantitative findings,* often a *standard score* (see *dynamic assessment*).

Strategy use: Cross-construct phenomenon describing the capacity to solve problems and complete tasks in systematic ways.

Stroop task: Task used to assess *facilitation and inhibition;* the student identifies the color in which displayed words are printed, resisting the urge to read the words themselves (even though the words spell names of various colors).

Subskill: See *academic subskill.*

Syntax: See *sentence comprehension* and *sentence formulation.*

Target tag: See *visual vigilance.*

Task-analysis: Identification of the component parts of a task or skill. The process usually involves a theoretical framework for scaffolding and organization, and it can be applied to *academic skills, academic tasks,* and *neurodevelopmental tasks.*

Temporal organization: Aspect of *temporal-sequential ordering* involved with keeping track of time, schedules, and the staging of extended work (see *spatial organization*).

Temporal-sequential ordering: Processing or producing material that is linear or in a serial order (see *spatial ordering*).

Testing: Use of an instrument (often standardized) for collecting data in a relatively structured way (see *assessment*).

Tower: Task used to assess *higher-order cognition* and the *production control system* of attention; the student shifts balls or disks from one peg to another in a set of three, attempting to use a specific number of moves to match a picture displayed on an easel. Multiple rules must be followed (for example, not to put ball or disk on table).

Use of feedback: Task used to assess *higher-order cognition;* student figures out a rule to guide subsequent responses (for example, sort cards, pick category members) using only feedback (from examiner or computer) about the accuracy of preceding responses.

Verbal elaboration: Language function involved with extending and developing ideas through speaking and writing.

Verbal pragmatics: Interpreting and employing language (such as conversational turn-taking) for *socialization* (see *nonverbal pragmatics*).

Visual concepts: Task used to assess *higher order cognition;* student selects the two or three pictures or symbols that are related or similar.

Visual vigilance: Task used to assess *attention;* student searches through an array of pictures, symbols, numbers, and letters and marks only those that are identical to the given target or targets. The task often has a time limit (such as one to three minutes).

Word attack: Decoding words through segments and sounds (see *sight word recognition*).

Word problem: Type of *math reasoning* problem in which the premise and information needed for calculation is presented via text (usually written). Students with weak *reading comprehension* usually have difficulty solving this type of math problem.

Word retrieval: Language function involved with efficiently finding the right words when speaking or writing.

Working memory: See *active working memory.*

Written expression: Communication of verbal ideas on paper, via hand-writing or word processing software (see *oral expression*).

Appendix A: Supporting Research for a Neurodevelopmental Framework

THE NEURODEVELOPMENTAL FRAMEWORK emphasized in this book draws heavily from the model developed by Levine (1998). It was developed via a review of theory and research on brain functioning that is significantly connected to academic skill development and performance. A vast amount of evidence supports the constructs and functions included in this framework, especially regarding such established entities as attention, memory, and language. The following tables present a sampling of the relevant literature, including theory and research.

Attention
Mental Energy Control System
Initiates and maintains the cognitive fuel needed for optimal learning, productivity, and behavior

Supporting Literature	Comments
Luria, A. R. (1973). The working brain: An introduction to neuropsychology. *New York: Basic Books.*	• *Unit 1 of brain function regulates levels of cortical activity and alertness*
Banaschewski, T., Brandeis, D., Heinrich, H., Albrecht, B., Brunner, E., & Rothenberger, A. (2003). Association of ADHD and conduct disorder: Brain electrical evidence for the existence of a distinct subtype. Journal of Child Psychology and Psychiatry, 44, *356–376.*	• *Students with attention deficits show suboptimal arousal*

Supporting Literature	Comments
Brandeis, D., Banaschewski, T., Baving, L., Georgiewa, P., Blanz, B., Schmidt, M. H., et al. (2002). Multicenter P300 brain mapping of impaired attention to cues in hyperkinetic children. Journal of the American Academy of Child and Adolescent Psychiatry, 41, 990–998.	• Students with attention deficits show suboptimal arousal
Calhoun, S. L., & Dickerson Mayes, S. (2005). Processing speed in children with clinical disorders. Psychology in the Schools, 42, 333–343.	• There may be a subtype of inattention characterized not just by inattention but by sluggish cognitive tempo, underarousal, and lethargy

Processing Control System
Handles information entering through the senses

Supporting Literature	Comments
Luria, A. R. (1973). The working brain: An introduction to neuropsychology. New York: Basic Books.	• Unit 2 of brain function analyzes and stores newly received information (input)
Sergeant, J. (1996). A theory of attention: An information processing perspective. In G. R. Lyon & N. A. Krasnegor (Eds.), Attention, memory, and executive function (pp. 57–69). Baltimore: Brookes.	• A focused attention deficit is when resources are allocated to irrelevant stimuli (with knowledge of what is relevant); a sustained attention deficit refers to a decline in controlled processing over time
Das, J. P., Naglieri, J. A., & Kirby, J. R. (1994). Assessment of cognitive processes: The PASS theory of intelligence. Boston: Allyn & Bacon.	• PASS model includes the attention factor, which handles input of information

Production Control System
Regulates thinking for academic and behavioral output

Supporting Literature	Comments
Luria, A. R. (1973). The working brain: An introduction to neuropsychology. New York: Basic Books.	• Unit 3 of brain function programs and regulates activity (output)

Supporting Literature	Comments
Denckla, M. B. (1996a). Biological correlates of learning and attention: What is relevant to learning disability and Attention-Deficit Hyperactivity Disorder? Developmental and Behavioral Pediatrics, 17, 114–119.	• Self-monitoring (as an aspect of executive functioning)
Anderson, V. (1998). Assessing executive functions in children: Biological, psychological, and developmental considerations. Neuropsychological Rehabilitation, 8, 319–349.	• Inhibition, planning, and self-monitoring (as aspects of executive functioning)
Das, J. P., Naglieri, J. A., & Kirby, J. R. (1994). Assessment of cognitive processes: The PASS theory of intelligence. Boston: Allyn & Bacon.	• PASS model includes the planning factor, which controls output

Memory

Short-Term Memory

Registers information for a brief time

Supporting Literature	Comments
Wagner, R. K. (1996). From simple structure to complex function: Major trends in the development of theories, models, and measurements of memory. In G. R. Lyon & N. A. Krasnegor (Eds.), Attention, memory, and executive function (pp. 139–155). Baltimore: Brookes.	• Short-term memory can be conceptualized as a component of long-term memory that is temporarily at a heightened state of activation at a particular moment (the focus of attention); information in short-term memory begins to decay unless it undergoes processing or rehearsal
Ashbaker, M. H., & Swanson, H. L. (1996). Short-term memory and working memory operations and their contributions to reading in adolescents with and without learning disabilities. Learning Disabilities Research and Practice, 11, 206–213.	• Short-term memory is more responsible for passive recall than active, effortful processing

Active Working Memory

Mentally suspends information while using or manipulating it

Supporting Literature	Comments
Denckla, M. B. (1996a). Biological correlates of learning and attention: What is relevant to learning disability and Attention-Deficit Hyperactivity Disorder? Developmental and Behavioral Pediatrics, 17, 114–119.	• Working memory can be divided into phonological and spatial
Cornoldi, C., Vecchia, R. D., & Tressoldi, P. E. (1995). Visuo-spatial working memory limitations in low visuo-spatial high verbal intelligence children. Journal of Child Psychology and Psychiatry, 36, 1053–1064.	• Specific visual-spatial working memory limitations can be found in children with normal language and low spatial intelligence; spatial active working memory limitations are likely to affect spatial intelligence, though a more general spatial deficit may be reflected both in spatial working memory tasks and in a variety of other tasks
Ashbaker, M. H., & Swanson, H. L. (1996). Short-term memory and working memory operations and their contributions to reading in adolescents with and without learning disabilities. Learning Disabilities Research and Practice, 11, 206–213.	• The working memory system conducts active, effortful processing and is more closely related to higher cognitive tasks

Long-Term Memory

Places information in memory that can be retrieved after a delay

Supporting Literature	Comments
Evans, J. J., Floyd, R. G., McGrew, K. S., & Leforgee, M. H. (2001). The relations between measures of Cattell-Horn-Carroll (CHC) cognitive abilities and reading achievement during childhood and adolescence. School Psychology Review, 31, 246–262.	• Long-term retrieval (Glr), defined as storing and retrieving information in long-term memory, is one of the broad cognitive (stratum II) abilities in the Cattell-Horn-Carroll (CHC) framework

Supporting Literature	Comments
Windfuhr, K. L., & Snowling, M. J. (2001). The relationship between paired associate learning and phonological skills in normally developing readers. Journal of Experimental Child Psychology, 80, 160–173.	• Paired associate memory (visual-verbal) accounts for independent variance in reading even when phonology is controlled
Mauer, D. M., & Kamhi, A. G. (1996). Factors that influence phoneme-grapheme correspondence learning. Journal of Learning Disabilities, 29, 259–270.	• Students (ages five through nine years) with reading problems required significantly more trials to learn novel phoneme-grapheme correspondences
Berninger, V. W., Rutberg, J. E., Abbott, R. D., Garcia, N., Anderson-Youngstrom, M., Brooks, A., & Fulton, C. (2006). Tier 1 and Tier 2 early intervention for handwriting and composing. Journal of School Psychology, 44, 3–30.	• Orthographic coding refers to drawing on letter forms stored in memory while handwriting and may contribute more to handwriting development than motor ability, which may be mediated through orthographic coding

Language

Receptive Language

Processing and understanding incoming oral and written information

Supporting Literature	Comments
Johnson, D. J. (1993). Relationships between oral and written language. School Psychology Review, 22, 595–609.	• Auditory receptive language begins at about nine months, followed by expressive language, which emerges at about one year; assessment should consider single words, sentences, and connected discourse
Cohen, N. J. (2001). Language impairment and psychopathology in infants, children, and adolescents. Thousand Oaks, CA: Sage.	• Language is about understanding words, sounds, sentences, sentences linked into coherent narratives, gestures, and social and cultural rules for communication

Expressive Language
Communicating and producing ideas orally or in writing

Supporting Literature	Comments
Johnson, D. J. (1993). Relationships between oral and written language. School Psychology Review, 22, 595–609.	• Auditory receptive language begins at about nine months, followed by expressive language, which emerges at about one year; assessment should consider single words, sentences, and connected discourse
Cohen, N. J. (2001). Language impairment and psychopathology in infants, children, and adolescents. Thousand Oaks, CA: Sage.	• Language is about producing and using words, sounds, sentences, sentences linked into coherent narratives, gestures, and social and cultural rules for communication

Spatial Ordering
Processing and production of material that is visual or spatial

Supporting Literature	Comments
Kirby, J. R. (1993). Collaborative and competitive effects of verbal and spatial processes. Learning and Instruction, 3, 201–214.	• Spatial processing (in the form of mental imagery) can enhance recall of verbal information (and vice versa)
Guilford, J. P. (1982). Cognitive psychology's ambiguities: Some suggested remedies. Psychological Review, 89, 48–59.	• "Visual" is one of five content dimensions in Guilford's Structure of Intellect (SOI) model
Evans, J. J., Floyd, R. G., McGrew, K. S., & Leforgee, M. H. (2001). The relations between measures of Cattell-Horn-Carroll (CHC) cognitive abilities and reading achievement during childhood and adolescence. School Psychology Review, 31, 246–262.	• Visual processing (Gv) is one of the broad cognitive (stratum II) abilities in the Cattell-Horn-Carroll (CHC) framework
Das, J. P., Naglieri, J. A., & Kirby, J. R. (1994). Assessment of cognitive processes: The PASS theory of intelligence. Boston: Allyn & Bacon.	• PASS model includes the simultaneous factor, relating to material that is perceived, interpreted, and remembered as a gestalt (for example, visual-spatial)

Temporal-Sequential Ordering

Processing and production of material that is serial (including the understanding and management of time)

Supporting Literature	Comments
Johnson, D. J. (1993). Relationships between oral and written language. School Psychology Review, 22, 595–609.	• Sequential memory is necessary for developing oral language
Boden, C., & Brodeur, D. A. (1999). Visual processing of verbal and nonverbal stimuli in adolescents with reading disabilities. Journal of Learning Disabilities, 32, 58–71.	• Processing and remembering rapidly sequenced bits of information is important in learning to read
Farmer, M. E., & Klein, R. M. (1995). The evidence for a temporal processing deficit linked to dyslexia: A review. Psychonomic Bulletin and Review, 2, 460–493.	• Some individuals with reading problems have a general temporal processing deficit, though phonological difficulties may not always be attributable to temporal processing difficulties; visual temporal processing deficit might affect the acquisitions of orthographic representations or might make reading difficult and unpleasant
Stanford, M. S., & Barratt, E. S. (1996). Verbal skills, finger tapping, and cognitive tempo define a second-order factor of temporal information processing. Brain and Cognition, 31, 35–45.	• Study found evidence of a temporal information processing factor with 155 male adolescents

Neuromotor Function

Gross Motor Function

Controlling the body's large muscles

Supporting Literature	Comments
Levine, M. D. (1998). Developmental variation and learning disorders (2nd ed.). Cambridge, MA: Educators Publishing Service.	• Gross motor function involves large muscles and movement of the body as a whole

Supporting Literature	Comments
Case-Smith, J. (Ed.). (2005). Occupational therapy for children (5th ed.). St. Louis: Elsevier Mosby.	• Gross motor refers to large muscle and whole-body movement
Thomas, C. L. (Ed.). (1997). Taber's cyclopedic medical dictionary (18th ed.). Philadelphia: Davis.	• Gross motor functioning relates to large muscle groups and movement of the body as a whole

Fine Motor Function

Controlling hands and fingers (that is, manual dexterity)

Supporting Literature	Comments
Levine, M. D. (1998). Developmental variation and learning disorders (2nd ed.). Cambridge, MA: Educators Publishing Service.	• Fine motor function refers to actions of the hands and fingers
Case-Smith, J. (Ed.). (2005). Occupational therapy for children (5th ed.). St. Louis: Elsevier Mosby.	• Fine motor refers to hand and finger muscles
Thomas, C. L. (Ed.). (1997). Taber's cyclopedic medical dictionary (18th ed.). Philadelphia: Davis.	• Fine motor functioning relates to hand and finger movement

Graphomotor Function

Controlling hands and fingers for the purpose of handwriting

Supporting Literature	Comments
Marcotte, A. C., & Stern, C. (1997). Qualitative analysis of graphomotor output in children with attentional disorders. Child Neuropsychology, 3, 147–153.	• Demonstrated the effect of graphomotor function (in conjunction with attention) on writing skill
Waber, D. P., & Bernstein, J. H. (1994). Repetitive graphomotor output in learning-disabled and nonlearning-disabled children: The Repeated Patterns Test. Developmental Neuropsychology, 10, 51–65.	• Different features of graphomotor function include establishment of rhythmicity, generation of a smooth flow of movement, and directional change

Higher Order Cognition
Complex and sophisticated thinking

Supporting Literature	Comments
Evans, J. J., Floyd, R. G., McGrew, K. S., & Leforgee, M. H. (2001). The relations between measures of Cattell-Horn-Carroll (CHC) cognitive abilities and reading achievement during childhood and adolescence. School Psychology Review, 31, 246–262.	• Fluid reasoning (Gf), which includes forming and recognizing logical relationships among patterns and making deductive and inductive inferences, is one of the broad cognitive (stratum II) abilities in the Cattell-Horn-Carroll (CHC) framework
Siegler, R. S. (1986). Children's thinking. Upper Saddle River, NJ: Prentice Hall.	• Concepts are objects, qualities, and ideas that are grouped together as similar and that have in common one or more defining features; concepts allow for drawing inferences beyond experience with specific objects and events, to go beyond given information

Social Cognition
Verbal Pragmatics
Use and understanding of language within social contexts and for the purpose of fostering optimal relationships with others

Supporting Literature	Comments
Prutting, C. A., & Kirchner, D. M. (1987). A clinical appraisal of the pragmatic aspects of language. Journal of Speech and Hearing Disorders, 52, 105–119.	• Verbal pragmatics include selecting a topic for conversation, maintaining or changing the topic, and turn-taking
Cohen, N. J. (2001). Language impairment and psychopathology in infants, children, and adolescents. Thousand Oaks, CA: Sage.	• Pragmatics are rules that regulate language use, including information flow, conversational turn-taking, and addressing miscommunications

Nonverbal Pragmatics

Behaviors and nonverbal tactics that foster optimal relationships with others

Supporting Literature	Comments
Prutting, C. A., & Kirchner, D. M. (1987). A clinical appraisal of the pragmatic aspects of language. Journal of Speech and Hearing Disorders, 52, *105–119.*	• *Nonverbal pragmatics include vocal intensity, physical proximity, body posture, gestures, and facial expression*
Bauminger, N., Edelsztein, H. S., & Morash, J. (2005). Social information processing and emotional understanding in children with LD. Journal of Learning Disabilities, 38, *45–61.*	• *Social information processing includes understanding how complex emotions operate*
Elias, M. J. (2004). The connection between social-emotional learning and learning disabilities: Implications for intervention. Learning Disability Quarterly, 27, *53–63.*	• *Social information processing includes regulating strong emotions and recognizing emotions in self and others*

Cross-Construct Phenomena
Rate of Processing and Production

The *speed* with which material is processed or generated

Supporting Literature	Comments
Bull, R., & Johnson, R. (1997). Children's arithmetical difficulties: Contributions from processing speed, item identification, and short-term memory. Journal of Experimental Child Psychology, 65, *1–24.*	• *A fundamental speed-of-processing deficit could underlie math difficulties*
Evans, J. J., Floyd, R. G., McGrew, K. S., & Leforgee, M. H. (2001). The relations between measures of Cattell-Horn-Carroll (CHC) cognitive abilities and reading achievement during childhood and adolescence. School Psychology Review, 31, *246–262.*	• *Processing speed (Gs) is one of the broad cognitive (stratum II) abilities in the Cattell-Horn-Carroll (CHC) framework*

Chunk Size

The *amount* of material processed or generated

Supporting Literature	Comments
Brumback, C. R., Low, K. A., Gratton, G., & Fabiani, M. (2005). Putting things into perspective: Individual differences in working-memory span and the integration of information. Experimental Psychology, 52, 21–30.	• Found individual variability in working memory span
Halford, G. S., Baker, R., McCredden, J. E., & Bain, J. D. (2005). How many variables can humans process? Psychological Science, 16, 70–76.	• Four variables (tasks involving complex computations) were found to be the limit of processing capacity (for example, for reasoning and decision making)
Martens, V.E.G., & de Jong, P. F. (2006). The effect of word length on lexical decision in dyslexic and normal reading children. Brain and Language, 98, 140–149.	• Word length effects were found to be much more severe in weak readers than in controls
Pak, A.K.H., Cheng-Lai, A., Tso, I. F., Shu, H., Li, W., & Anderson, R. C. (2005). Visual chunking skills of Hong Kong children. Reading and Writing, 18, 437–454.	• Developmental differences found in visual chunking of Chinese characters in Hong Kong students

Metacognition

The level of understanding about one's mind and learning abilities

Supporting Literature	Comments
Joshi, R. M. (1995). Assessing reading and spelling skills. School Psychology Review, 24, 361–375.	• Metacognition is a component of reading comprehension
Siegler, R. S. (1986). Children's thinking. Upper Saddle River, NJ: Prentice Hall.	• Metacognition has several facets; metalinguistic awareness refers to what one knows and does not know about language; metamemory is knowledge about memory, including strategies for boosting recall

Supporting Literature	Comments
Keene, E. O., & Zimmermann, S. (1997). Mosaic of thought: Teaching comprehension in a reader's workshop. Portsmouth, NH: Heinemann.	• Metacognition refers to thinking about thinking

Strategy Use

The capacity to solve problems and complete tasks in systematic ways for rate of processing and production

Supporting Literature	Comments
Hooper, S. R., Montgomery, J., Swartz, C., Reed, M. S., Sandler, A. D., Levine, M. D., Watson, T. E., & Wasileski, T. (1994). Measurement of written language expression. In G. R. Lyon (Ed.), Frames of reference for the assessment of learning disabilities: New views on measurement issues (pp. 375–417). Baltimore: Brookes.	• Strategy use is a component of written comprehension
Das, J. P., Naglieri, J. A., & Kirby, J. R. (1994). Assessment of cognitive processes: The PASS theory of intelligence. Boston: Allyn & Bacon.	• PASS model includes the planning factor, which controls output
Siegler, R. S. (1986). Children's thinking. Upper Saddle River, NJ: Prentice Hall.	• Strategy construction involves identifying consistent patterns in task environments adapting to demands

Appendix B: Assessment Task-Analysis Guide

- ☐ Task name (which could be a subtest from a battery)

- ☐ Task description (which should include such features as time limits)

- ☐ Neurodevelopmental factors (focusing on the major ingredients underlying components)

- ☐ Other considerations (such as age range or complexity of instructions)

- ☐ Qualitative observations that could be made

- ☐ Potential limit-testing techniques

Appendix C: Index of Potential Findings

THE TABLE IN THIS APPENDIX summarizes findings that typically inform components of the neurodevelopmental framework. The general findings category (column 2) includes qualitative information (for example, history, observations, work pattern analysis, responses to interview questions). Clinical contrasts are discrepancies in a student's performance on different tasks (see Chapter Six for more discussion), and are included in column 3 whenever applicable. Column 4 includes tasks that were discussed in Chapters Eight through Eleven and are described in the glossary. For each construct or function, asset indicators (that is, signs of intact functioning) are listed along with signs of dysfunction. This table does not represent an exhaustive list of potential findings of learning problems, but rather of sampling of possible signs to guide the assessment process.

Construct or Function	General Findings	Clinical Contrasts	Tasks
Attention: mental energy control system	Asset Indicators • *Appears to have ample energy when working* • *Easily starts and completes tasks* • *Appropriate and consistent working speed*	Asset Indicators • *Written expression stronger than oral expression*	*Not applicable*
	Signs of Dysfunction • *Cognitive effort and academic work seems excessively draining*	Signs of Dysfunction • *Better performance on recognition tasks than free-recall tasks*	

Construct or Function	General Findings	Clinical Contrasts	Tasks
	• Irregular sleep/wake cycles (trouble falling or staying asleep, or waking in morning) • Inconsistent levels of alertness and mental fuel • Student describes feeling overwhelmed and drained by work		
Attention: cognitive activation	Asset Indicators • Making innovative connections from the topic at hand to other information • Extensive elaboration • Citing prior knowledge in connection to reading passage	Asset Indicators	• List recall (commissions, intrusions within category)
	Signs of Dysfunction • Comments tangential to the discussion topic • Student describes thoughts that race from topic to topic • Forming few relevant associations, passive thinking, trouble seeing the big picture • Being excessively reminded of prior knowledge when working with decontextualized material • Disorganized train of thought in written expression or oral expression	Signs of Dysfunction • Better performance on free-recall tasks than recognition tasks • Listening comprehension for expository discourse stronger than for narrative discourse • Comprehension of decontextualized information stronger than of contextualized information	
Attention: focal maintenance	Asset Indicators • Maintaining concentration for extended periods	Asset Indicators	• Visual vigilance or target tag (omissions, false negatives)
	Signs of Dysfunction • Concentration fading during lessons and academic work • Excessive daydreaming	Signs of Dysfunction	• Continuous performance task (omissions, false negatives)

Construct or Function	General Findings	Clinical Contrasts	Tasks
	• Inconsistent accuracy pattern (for example, missing easy items or words, getting harder items or words) • Student describes focus often drifting (for example, "zoning in and out")		
Attention: processing depth	Asset Indicators • Detecting small details in a copy of a complex figure or picture • Picking up subtle pieces of information when reading or listening	Asset Indicators	• Visual vigilance or target tag (omissions, false negatives) • Continuous performance task (omissions, false negatives) • Sentence verification technique
	Signs of Dysfunction • Asking for repetitions of oral instructions • Errors in listening comprehension that are readily corrected after repetition • Inconsistent accuracy pattern (for example, missing easy items or words and getting harder items or words) • Getting stuck on little details encountered in reading and other assignments • Student describes tendency to skim over material • Decoding errors that are visually close with some phonics (inside for insist) • Math errors stemming from misread signs and details in problems	Signs of Dysfunction • Complex form copying weaker than basic form copying • Listening comprehension for narrative discourse stronger than for expository discourse • Comprehension of contextualized information stronger than decontextualized information • Reading comprehension stronger than listening comprehension	

Construct or Function	General Findings	Clinical Contrasts	Tasks
Attention: saliency determination	**Asset Indicators** • *Identifying main points in reading text* • *Selecting the most important information to study for a test*	**Asset Indicators** • *Math reasoning stronger than math operations*	• *Visual vigilance or target tag (omissions, false negatives)* • *Continuous performance task (omissions, false negatives)*
	Signs of Dysfunction • *Distractibility* • *Focusing on irrelevant details in math word problems* • *Student describes tendency for focus to be lured away from the topic or material at hand* • *Disorganization with materials, trouble filtering and prioritizing what to keep and what to discard*	**Signs of Dysfunction** • *Better performance on free-recall tasks than recognition tasks* • *Listening comprehension for narrative discourse stronger than for expository discourse* • *Comprehension of decontextualized information stronger than contextualized information*	
Attention: facilitation and inhibition	**Asset Indicators** • *Well-controlled behavior (not giving in to urges)* • *Pausing before starting a task to survey it* • *Taking a moment to think before answering a question*	**Asset Indicators**	• *Visual vigilance or target tag (commissions, false positives)* • *Continuous performance task (commissions, false positives)* • *Complex figure copy* • *Stroop task* • *Tower* • *Navigating mazes* • *Strategic tracing* • *List recall (commissions, intrusions outside category)*
	Signs of Dysfunction • *Jumping too quickly into work or tasks* • *Impulsive behaviors in the classroom or in social situations*	**Signs of Dysfunction** • *Listening comprehension stronger than reading comprehension*	

Construct or Function	General Findings	Clinical Contrasts	Tasks
	• *Student describes urge to act too quickly* • *Decoding errors that are visually close with some phonics (*inside *for* insist*)*		
Attention: pacing	Asset Indicators • *Copying a complex figure at an appropriate pace* • *Spatially organized math work (for example, aligned columns)*	Asset Indicators	• *Visual vigilance or target tag (commissions, false positives)* • *Complex figure copy*
	Signs of Dysfunction • *Rushing through homework or other assignments* • *Student describes tendency to work too quickly*	Signs of Dysfunction • *Listening comprehension stronger than reading comprehension*	
Attention: previewing	Asset Indicators • *Planning and outlining an essay, report, or term paper* • *Forming a good plan for copying a complex figure* • *Estimating what the solution to a math problem will be prior to solving it*	Asset Indicators	• *Complex figure copy* • *Tower* • *Navigating mazes* • *Strategic tracing*
	Signs of Dysfunction • *Starting to solve a math problem without first thinking through the best approach* • *Student describes a tendency to work on assignments without initially planning them*	Signs of Dysfunction • *Math operations stronger than math reasoning* • *Complex form copying weaker than basic form copying* • *Oral expression stronger than written expression*	
Attention: self-monitoring	Asset Indicators • *Editing and revising written work* • *Catching errors in math problems* • *Checking comprehension when reading*	Asset Indicators	• *Complex figure copy* • *Scribe procedure for reading comprehension* • *Error detection for writing mechanics or spelling*

Construct or Function	General Findings	Clinical Contrasts	Tasks
	• Comparing the copy of a complex figure with the model • Detecting personal effect on peers in social situations		• Error detection for math • List recall (perseverations) • Category naming (perseverations)
	Signs of Dysfunction • Making errors that the student can readily correct when they are pointed out • Inconsistent accuracy pattern (for example, missing easy items or words and getting harder items or words) • Student describes trouble with detecting errors in own work or with sensing work quality	Signs of Dysfunction • Decoding better in isolation than in context • Spelling better in isolation than in context • Math operations stronger than math reasoning • Sentence formulation with word cards better than sentence formulation with easel • Oral expression stronger than written expression	
Memory: short-term	Asset Indicators • Minimal recall that significantly improves after repetition	Asset Indicators	• Digit span (forward) • Hand movements (forward) • Drawing recall • Picture recall • List recall • Sentence repetition • Passage recall • Sound-symbol recall
	Signs of Dysfunction • Student describes trouble remembering recently heard or seen material • Recalling information predominantly from the end of an orally presented passage	Signs of Dysfunction	

Construct or Function	General Findings	Clinical Contrasts	Tasks
Memory: active working	Asset Indicators • *Mentally juggling various task components when writing (such as punctuation, ideation, grammar, spelling)* • *Segmenting and re-blending long and unfamiliar words* • *Making connections within extended text* • *Accurate mental math calculations*	Asset Indicators	• *List recall (perseverations)* • *Category naming (perseverations)* • *Sequence manipulation (for example, reversing the months of the year)* • *Complex counting (for example, alternating letters and numbers)* • *Digit span (backward)* • *Hand movements (backward)* • *Letter or number reordering* • *Competing language*
	Signs of Dysfunction • *Errors within multistep math procedures* • *Minimal recall that does not improve much after repetition* • *Difficulty following multistep instructions, especially when steps are given in different order from how they should be executed* • *Needing to refer back to text to answer comprehension questions* • *Student describes trouble manipulating information mentally*	Signs of Dysfunction • *Decoding better in isolation than in context* • *Reading decoding stronger than reading comprehension* • *Spelling better in isolation than in context* • *Math operations stronger than math reasoning* • *Sentence formulation with word cards better than sentence formulation with easel* • *Oral expression stronger than written expression*	

Construct or Function	General Findings	Clinical Contrasts	Tasks
Memory: long-term storage	Asset Indicators • *Identifying sight words and irregularly spelled words*	Asset Indicators • *Decoding better than spelling* • *Better performance on recognition tasks than free recall tasks*	• *Factual recall (recognition items)* • *Drawing recall (recognition items)* • *Picture recall* • *List recall (recognition items)* • *Passage recall (recognition items)*
	Signs of Dysfunction • *Student describes weak recognition (for example, on true/false tests)* • *Decoding errors that are visually close but with poor phonics (siege for sieve or fat for first)* • *Weak sight word recognition and laborious sounding out of basic words*	Signs of Dysfunction • *Decoding nonsense words better than decoding real words*	
Memory: long-term access	Asset Indicators • *Recalling math procedures (such as long division, finding least common denominator, factoring an equation)* • *Recalling math facts* • *Recalling factual information for quizzes and exams* • *Retrieving phonemes that are matched with certain graphemes* • *Citing prior knowledge in connection to reading passage*	Asset Indicators • *Decoding better in isolation than in context* • *Spelling better in isolation than in context*	• *Factual recall (recall items)* • *Drawing recall* • *List recall* • *Passage recall* • *Sound-symbol recall*
	Signs of Dysfunction • *Student describes trouble recalling information on tests, quizzes, and during class discussions*	Signs of Dysfunction • *Decoding better than spelling* • *Math reasoning stronger than math operations*	

Construct or Function	General Findings	Clinical Contrasts	Tasks
	• Trouble recalling academic rules (for example, for spelling, punctuation, math) • Hesitancy when called on in class • Misspellings that are phonetically logical, but err in terms of letter patterns (for example, enuf for enough)	• Better performance on recognition tasks than free-recall tasks • Listening comprehension stronger than reading comprehension • Oral expression stronger than written expression	
Language (receptive): phonological processing	Asset Indicators • Decoding words (including nonsense words) through phonics-based word attack strategies such as segmenting and re-blending (as opposed to recognizing sight words) • Rhyming words and syllables • Misspellings that are phonetically logical (for example, enuf for enough)	Asset Indicators • Decoding better in isolation than in context • Spelling better in isolation than in context • Decoding better than spelling • Decoding nonsense words better than decoding real words	• Elision • Sound matching • Blending • Cloze tasks omitting letters from real and nonsense words
	Signs of Dysfunction • Reading dysfluently and with little rhythm • Misspellings that are not phonetically logical (for example, alpel for apple) • Decoding errors that are visually close but with poor phonics (siege for sieve or fat for first)	Signs of Dysfunction • Reading comprehension stronger than reading decoding • Listening comprehension stronger than reading comprehension • Oral expression stronger than written expression	
Language (receptive): morphological sense	Asset Indicators • Identifying words that are related via root or base	Asset Indicators	• Cloze tasks omitting morphemes from words

Construct or Function	General Findings	Clinical Contrasts	Tasks
	Signs of Dysfunction • *Trouble determining meaning of a word by looking at its component parts* • *Decoding errors involving omissions of prefixes and suffixes (for example,* distribute *for* distributed*)*	Signs of Dysfunction	
Language (receptive): semantic understanding	Asset Indicators • *Understanding words encountered in reading* • *Grasping math and science terminology* • *Correctly spelling homophones (for example,* piece *and* peace*) based on context*	Asset Indicators • *Spelling better in context than in isolation*	• *Receptive vocabulary* • *Cloze tasks omitting words from sentences and passages*
	Signs of Dysfunction • *Student describes trouble understanding words teachers use* • *Trouble understanding social lingo* • *Decoding errors involving stress on wrong syllable (*dom-IN-ate *for* dominate*)*	Signs of Dysfunction • *Reading decoding stronger than reading comprehension* • *Listening comprehension for narrative discourse stronger than for expository discourse*	
Language (receptive): sentence comprehension	Asset Indicators • *Understanding task instructions* • *Reading math word problems and identifying the procedure needed to solve the problem* • *Self-correcting decoding errors based on context*	Asset Indicators • *Decoding better in context than in isolation*	• *Sentence verification technique* • *Direction following* • *Complex sentences* • *Ambiguous sentences* • *Cloze tasks omitting words from sentences*

Construct or Function	General Findings	Clinical Contrasts	Tasks
	Signs of Dysfunction • *Errors in listening comprehension that are not readily corrected after repetition* • *Trouble answering comprehension questions about reading* • *Difficulty determining word meanings based on sentence context*	Signs of Dysfunction • *Reading decoding stronger than reading comprehension* • *Math operations stronger than math reasoning*	
Language (receptive): discourse processing	Asset Indicators • *Comprehending lectures and class discussions* • *Reading math word problems and identifying the procedure needed to solve the problem* • *Self-correcting decoding errors based on context*	Asset Indicators • *Decoding better in context than in isolation*	• *Sentence verification technique* • *Passage listening comprehension* • *Cloze tasks omitting words from passages*
	Signs of Dysfunction • *Errors in listening comprehension that are not readily corrected after repetition* • *Trouble answering comprehension questions about reading (such as drawing inferences)* • *Difficulty determining word meanings based on passage context*	Signs of Dysfunction • *Reading decoding stronger than reading comprehension*	
Language (expressive): morphological use	Asset Indicators • *Figuring out how to spell words based on morphemes (for example, "idio-syn-crat-ic")*	Asset Indicators • *Spelling better in context than in isolation*	• *Word manipulation (for example, using prefixes and suffixes, changing tense, converting singular to plural)*

Construct or Function	General Findings	Clinical Contrasts	Tasks
	Signs of Dysfunction • *Spelling errors that reveal limited understanding of morphemes (for example, carsik for carsick)*	Signs of Dysfunction	
Language (expressive): word retrieval	Asset Indicators • *Good automaticity and fluency with decoding*	Asset Indicators • *Decoding better in isolation than in context* • *Decoding better than spelling* • *Decoding nonsense words better than decoding real words*	• *Category naming* • *Rapid automatic naming*
	Signs of Dysfunction • *Overrelying on nondescript words such as* stuff *and* things, *in speech and writing*	Signs of Dysfunction	
Language (expressive): semantic use	Asset Indicators • *Accurately defining terms on tests and quizzes* • *Explaining meanings of words encountered when reading* • *Forming clear answers to comprehension questions*	Asset Indicators	• *Expressive vocabulary*
	Signs of Dysfunction • *Erroneous, vague, or limited word use in speech and writing* • *Difficulty using social lingo*	Signs of Dysfunction	
Language (expressive): sentence formulation	Asset Indicators • *Adroitly rephrasing ambiguous sentences into other versions that convey multiple meanings* • *Forming clear answers to comprehension questions*	Asset Indicators • *Sentence formulation with word cards better than sentence formulation with easel*	• *Sentence construction*

Construct or Function	General Findings	Clinical Contrasts	Tasks
	Signs of Dysfunction • Repetitive or frequent use of simplistic sentence structures in written work • Trouble with grammar (for example, unclear pronouns, noun-verb disagreements)	Signs of Dysfunction	
Language (expressive): discourse production	Asset Indicators • Providing good summaries of listening or reading passages • Forming clear answers to comprehension questions	Asset Indicators	• Response to written or picture prompt, orally or in writing
	Signs of Dysfunction • Disorganized ideas in written work, sentences not connected cohesively • Trouble describing personal experiences in a clear fashion	Signs of Dysfunction	
Language (expressive): verbal elaboration	Asset Indicators • Sharing developed thinking during class discussions • Ideas extended through oral and written expression	Asset Indicators	Not applicable
	Signs of Dysfunction • Frequent use of very brief responses to questions • Having a hard time explaining how problems were solved or tasks approached • Minimal written and oral output	Signs of Dysfunction	
Spatial ordering	Asset Indicators • Creating drawings • Constructing models • Fixing devices • Spatially organized math work (for example, aligned columns) • Using graphic organizers for note-taking and outlining • Understanding fractions and geometry concepts	Asset Indicators • Complex form copying weaker than basic form copying • Basic form copying weaker than matching or identifying forms • Stronger performance with matrix analogies than with verbal analogies	• Figure matching • Basic figure copy • Complex figure copy • Perceiving the elements of a complex figure (for example, proportions, part-to-whole relationships, intersections) • Block construction

Construct or Function	General Findings	Clinical Contrasts	Tasks
	Signs of Dysfunction • Trouble discerning visual patterns (such as geometric shapes, diagrams, charts, graphs) • Disheveled work and storage spaces (such as locker and notebook) • Not benefiting from visual strategies for math problems (for example, diagrams) • Spatially disorganized written output (for example, skewed margins, inconsistent word spacing)	Signs of Dysfunction • Weaker performance in ball sports than those requiring minimal eye-hand coordination (such as wrestling or swimming)	
Temporal-sequential ordering	Asset Indicators • Understanding and recalling historical time lines • Summarizing elements of a story or passage in proper order • Executing multistep math procedures (such as long division) in proper order • Good stepwisdom for extended work projects	Asset Indicators	• Sequence completion • Sequence manipulation (for example, reversing the months of the year) • Complex counting (for example, alternating letters and numbers) • Digit span • Hand movements • Passage recall (sequence of story elements)
	Signs of Dysfunction • Difficulty re-ordering pieces of information (for example, alphabetically) • Writing that is not organized sequentially • Trouble with solving geometric proofs • Confusion about elapsed time math problems	Signs of Dysfunction • Weaker athletic skills involving sequences (such as swimming strokes or tennis serve) than nonsequential skills (such as running or catching)	

Construct or Function	General Findings	Clinical Contrasts	Tasks
Neuromotor function: gross motor	Asset Indicators • Good overall body coordination	Asset Indicators	• Maintaining balance (for example, on one foot) for several seconds • Replicating a hopping sequence • Catching a ball in a cup
	Signs of Dysfunction • Physical awkwardness during sports and activities such as dance	Signs of Dysfunction	
Neuromotor function: fine motor	Asset Indicators • Playing musical instruments requiring manual dexterity, such as the piano, strings, and woodwinds	Asset Indicators	• Finger localization • Finger tapping
	Signs of Dysfunction • Trouble learning to keyboard • Difficulty handling small tools such as scissors	Signs of Dysfunction	
Neuromotor function: graphomotor	Asset Indicators • Legible handwriting—letters and numbers • Good pencil control when drawing	Asset Indicators	• Basic figure copy • Complex figure copy • Maze tracing
	Signs of Dysfunction • Tight pencil or pen grip • Excessive pressure applied against paper when handwriting • Close proximity of eyes to tip of pencil or pen • Slow overall handwriting speed • Hesitations on certain letters (slow recall of letter formation)	Signs of Dysfunction • Reading comprehension stronger than written expression • Basic form copying weaker than matching or identifying forms • Oral expression stronger than written expression	

Construct or Function	General Findings	Clinical Contrasts	Tasks
Higher order cognition	Asset Indicators • *Understanding math concepts (such as the inverse relationship between multiplication and division, regrouping, and factoring)* • *Setting up a science experiment to test a hypothesis* • *Forming a logical argument that includes critical thinking* • *Generating innovative ideas, brainstorming (for example, when writing)*	Asset Indicators • *Reading comprehension stronger than reading decoding* • *Math reasoning stronger than math operations* • *Listening comprehension for expository discourse stronger than for narrative discourse* • *Comprehension of decontextualized information stronger than contextualized information*	• *List recall (use of categorical clustering)* • *Category naming (use of categorical clustering)* • *Similarities* • *Visual concepts* • *Matrix reasoning* • *Tower* • *Use of feedback*
	Signs of Dysfunction • *Trouble using logic and reasoning to solve math problems* • *Difficulty solving a social dilemma* • *Tenuous understanding of rules (for example, grammar, math algorithms)*	Signs of Dysfunction	
Social cognition: verbal pragmatics	Asset Indicators • *Resiliency in social situations (that is, readily bounces back from interpersonal setbacks)* • *Being adept with the give-and-take of conversation* • *Leadership ability* • *Political acumen* • *Collaboration and conflict resolution skills*	Asset Indicators	• *Social vignettes (interpreting dialogue, suggesting verbal responses)* • *Social skills rating scales* • *Writing sample about a social topic (for example, resolving a conflict)*
	Signs of Dysfunction • *Peer rejection* • *Preference for playing or being alone* • *Inappropriate comments to others* • *Limited awareness of audience in written work*	Signs of Dysfunction • *Listening comprehension for expository discourse stronger than for narrative discourse* • *More trouble performing in team sports than individual sports*	

Construct or Function	General Findings	Clinical Contrasts	Tasks
Social cognition: nonverbal pragmatics	Asset Indicators • Good understanding, regulation, and identification of emotions (for example, showing empathy) Signs of Dysfunction • Peer rejection • Preference for playing or being alone • Taking inappropriate actions when relating to others • Limited eye contact • Miscues with body language (such as personal space)	Asset Indicators Signs of Dysfunction • More trouble performing in team sports than individual sports	• Social vignettes (interpreting nonverbal cues in pictures, suggesting behavioral responses) • Social skills rating scales • Writing sample about a social topic (such as resolving a conflict)
Cross-construct: rate of processing and production	Asset Indicators • Overall work efficiency • Not feeling overwhelmed by homework Signs of Dysfunction • Slow work rate across a variety of skills and tasks (that is, not just with language-based material)	Asset Indicators Signs of Dysfunction • Reading comprehension stronger than listening comprehension • Written expression stronger than oral expression	• Any task that has a time component
Cross-construct: chunk size	Asset Indicators • Capacity to recall items across all portions of an extended list • Handling a large amount of visual input, such as a complex figure Signs of Dysfunction • Breakdowns in performance as amount of material increases (for example, extended math problems, writing assignments, information to memorize)	Asset Indicators Signs of Dysfunction • Decoding better in isolation than in context • Reading decoding stronger than reading comprehension • Spelling better in isolation than in context	Not applicable

Construct or Function	General Findings	Clinical Contrasts	Tasks
Cross-construct: metacognition	Asset Indicators • Making insightful comments about own learning	Asset Indicators	Not applicable
	Signs of Dysfunction • Difficulty engaging in meaningful dialogue about profile and learning	Signs of Dysfunction • Student's description of skills and abilities discrepant from other history or performance on assessment tasks	
Cross-construct: strategy use	Asset Indicators • Student describes a good approach to studying Signs of Dysfunction • Haphazardly approaching math reasoning problems (that is, trial and error)	Asset Indicators • Math reasoning stronger than math operations Signs of Dysfunction • Complex form copying weaker than basic form copying	• List recall (use of categorical clustering) • Category naming (use of categorical clustering) • Complex figure copy (approach, such as thinking about what the figure looks like)

Appendix D: Tests and Batteries for Neurodevelopmental Assessment

Acronym or Brief Title	Full Title	Publisher
Bender	Bender Visual-Motor Gestalt Test	American Orthopsychiatric Association, Inc.
CAS	Cognitive Assessment System	Riverside
CASL	Comprehensive Assessment of Spoken Language	American Guidance Service
CCPT	Conners' Continuous Performance Test	Multi-Health Systems
CCT	Children's Category Test	PsychCorp
CELF-IV	Clinical Evaluation of Language Fundamentals—Fourth Edition	PsychCorp
CMS	Children's Memory Scale	PsychCorp
CTONI	Comprehensive Test of Nonverbal Intelligence	PRO-ED
CTOPP	Comprehensive Test of Phonological Processing	PRO-ED
CVLT-C	California Verbal Learning Test—Children's Version	PsychCorp
DAS	Differential Ability Scales	PsychCorp
D-KEFS	Delis-Kaplan Executive Function System	PsychCorp
K-BIT-2	Kaufman Brief Intelligence Test—Second Edition	American Guidance Service

Acronym or Brief Title	Full Title	Publisher
NEPSY	NEPSY: A Developmental Neuropsychological Assessment	PsychCorp
PAL	Process Assessment of the Learner	PsychCorp
PEERAMID-2	Pediatric Examination of Educational Readiness at Middle Childhood 2	Educators Publishing Service
PEEX-2	Pediatric Early Elementary Examination 2	Educators Publishing Service
PPVT-III	Peabody Picture Vocabulary Test—Third Edition	American Guidance Service
RCFT	Rey Complex Figure Test and Recognition Trial	Psychological Assessment Resources
Roberts-2	Roberts Apperception Test for Children—Second Edition	Western Psychological Services
SB5	Stanford-Binet Intelligence Scales—Fifth Edition	Riverside
TEMAS	Tell-Me-A-Story	Western Psychological Services
TLC	Test of Language Competence—Expanded Edition	PsychCorp
TOPA	Test of Phonological Awareness	PRO-ED
TOVA	Test of Variables of Attention	Universal Attention Disorders
VMI	Beery-Buktenica Developmental Test of Visual-Motor Integration—Fifth Edition	Modern Curriculum Press
WAIS-III	Wechsler Adult Intelligence Scale—Third Edition	PsychCorp
WISC-IV Integrated	Wechsler Intelligence Scale for Children—Fourth Edition Integrated	PsychCorp
WCST	Wisconsin Card Sorting Test	Psychological Assessment Resources
WJ-III Cognitive	Woodcock-Johnson III Tests of Cognitive Abilities	Riverside
WRAML 2	Wide Range Assessment of Memory and Learning—Second Edition	Wide Range Incorporated

Appendix E: Learning Plan Resources

AN *INTERVENTION* IS AN instructional or learning strategy that is intended to remediate a weak academic skill or improve a weak neurodevelopmental function. Numerous interventions have been designed to address a wide range of learning problems.

An *accommodation* is an instructional or learning strategy that is intended to bypass a weak academic skill or circumvent a weak neurodevelopmental function. As is the case with interventions, there are many possibilities when it comes to bypassing learning problems.

After outlining a variety of types of interventions and accommodations, this appendix provides a list of online resources that provide additional information you can use as you develop your own approach to assessment for understanding.

Interventions

This section describes common categories (not mutually exclusive) of interventions, including examples. These categories make it easier to develop individualized interventions for students based on each one's unique learning needs. In other words, these categories can serve as catalysts for the generation of learning plans.

Reformat for Understanding

Students using this type of intervention learn to convert information to another format, usually one better matched to their profiles. This transformation deepens engagement with the material, and the new format provides an alternative for studying.

For example, students might create a graphic or diagram to depict ideas from a book chapter, develop a pair of lists to compare and contrast the two World Wars, or talk through the factoring of an algebraic equation. Areas that can be addressed include

- Receptive language
- Higher-order cognition
- Spatial ordering
- Temporal-sequential ordering

Skill and Drill

This category involves isolating a weak area for work, then providing focused and repetitive exercises to automatize essential skills and functions.

For example, students could work with flash cards for vocabulary words, software for phonology, guided handwriting practice, or math fact games. Areas that can be addressed include

- Language
- Long-term memory storage and access
- Graphomotor function

Leveraging

When students learn to apply their assets and affinities to address weak functions and skills, they tend to develop more interest in their schoolwork.

For example, a student with good spatial ordering might construct a diagram to represent elements of a math word problem. For a student passionate about mountaineering, teaching math procedures (for example, calculating averages) with problems based on an alpine expedition might transform bland manipulation of numbers into matters of great interest. Areas that can be addressed include

- Attention
- Memory
- Language

- Temporal-sequential ordering
- Spatial ordering
- Higher-order cognition

Scaffolding

Students benefit from a cognitive structure that they can use to stimulate and organize their thinking. It may be tangible or spoken, and can be gradually removed as the student becomes more independent.

For example, hand out blank or partially completed outlines for a lecture or reading assignment, model solutions for math problems, and provide mnemonic devices for studying. Areas that can be addressed include

- Attention
- Memory
- Language
- Temporal-sequential ordering
- Spatial ordering
- Higher-order cognition

Student Databases

Many students need to have critical academic information at their fingertips. Students also benefit from the process of creating (perhaps with support) and maintaining a personalized database.

For example, the student could keep a journal with challenging spelling words, definitions, and sentence starters. Other options include an atlas of solved word problems highlighting procedural steps, or a list of problematic punctuation and grammar rules. Areas that can be addressed include

- Long-term memory storage and access
- Expressive language

Accommodations

Accommodations also come in various categories. Here is a list, including examples. (Note that a given strategy may combine elements of multiple categories of interventions and accommodations. Also, a given strategy may both intervene and accommodate simultaneously.)

Reformat to Bypass Difficult Areas

It can help students to convert information from the usual format to one better suited to their assets, so as to circumvent weak functions or skills.

For example, a student might give an oral presentation instead of turning in a written report, listen to a book on tape in lieu of reading an assignment, or get written instructions rather than orally presented directions. Areas that can be addressed include

- Language
- Long-term memory storage and access
- Higher-order cognition
- Spatial ordering
- Graphomotor function

Inventive Downsizing

A "divide and conquer" approach can make a big difference for some students. By reducing work expectations in terms of amount, time, or complexity, they can begin to cope and to build skills for longer or more difficult assignments.

For example, have a student complete only the odd-numbered math homework problems or a detailed outline instead of a written essay. Present a floating spelling list with several repeated words. Areas that can be addressed include

- Language
- Rate of processing and production
- Chunk size
- Graphomotor function
- Higher-order cognition

Instruments and Technology

Many tools, devices, and software applications can ease the time demands or the complexity of work, or both.

Students often find it helpful to use word processing software, including features such as a spelling checker. Away from the computer, such things as handwriting grips for pencils, math fact reference grids, and calculators can bring assignments within reach. Areas that can be addressed include

- Attention production control system
- Active working memory
- Long-term memory storage and access
- Graphomotor function

Web Sites with Resources for Learning Plans

The three sites listed here all provide a variety of useful resources.

All Kinds of Minds

Slogan: "Understanding Differences in Learning"
URL: www.allkindsofminds.org

General Comments

- Features for educators, parents, and clinicians
- Espouses a nonlabeling, descriptive philosophy about learning difficulties
- Extensive content from Dr. Mel Levine

Features and Resources of Note

1. "Library" section includes links to extensive content sources, including the "LearningBase," which provides "Helpful Tips" on several academic topics:
   a. "Thinking with Numbers"
   b. "Mastering the Challenges of Reading"
   c. "Getting Thoughts on Paper"
   d. "Developing Control Over Attention"
   e. "Understanding Ideas"
   f. "Producing & Communicating Ideas"
   g. "Getting Organized & Good Work Habits"

2. "Parent Toolkit" includes numerous online activities that simulate the experience of having learning problems (helpful for demystification), such as:
   a. "Auditory Distraction"
   b. "Problems with Basic Facts"
   c. "Decoding Difficulty"
   d. "Graphomotor Difficulty"

SchwabLearning.org

Slogan: "A Parent's Guide to Helping Kids with Learning Difficulties"
URL: www.SchwabLearning.org

General Comments

- Articles on topics such as "Supporting Your Struggling Learner" and "What the Science Says: Effective Reading Instruction for Kids with Learning Disabilities"
- Uses labels such as "LD" and "ADHD"

Features and Resources of Note

1. "Managing Your Child: Support Your Child's Social and Emotional Needs"
2. "Managing School and Learning," with links to:
   a. "Technology That Supports Learning"
   b. "Reading, Writing, and Math"
   c. "Homework"
3. "Managing School and Learning: Work with the School to Help Your Child"
4. "Resources," with links to searchable databases:
   a. "Books, Videos, and Web Sites"
   b. "Technology to Help Kids"
   c. "LD and ADHD Organizations"
   d. "Summer Camps"

LD Online

Slogan: "The world's leading Web site on learning disabilities and ADHD"
URL: www.ldonline.org

General Comments

- Articles on various topics such as "Components of Effective Reading Instruction" and "Tool Kit for Parents: Being an Efficient Homework Helper"
- Uses labels such as "LD" and "ADHD"

Features and Resources of Note

1. "Especially for. . ." links to resources for "Educators," "Parents," and "Students." The "Students" section includes an art gallery of submitted student work, student stories, and recommended books on learning problems written for students.
2. "Finding Help" links to "LD online yellow pages" for finding professionals, products, schools, camps, and learning centers.

Index